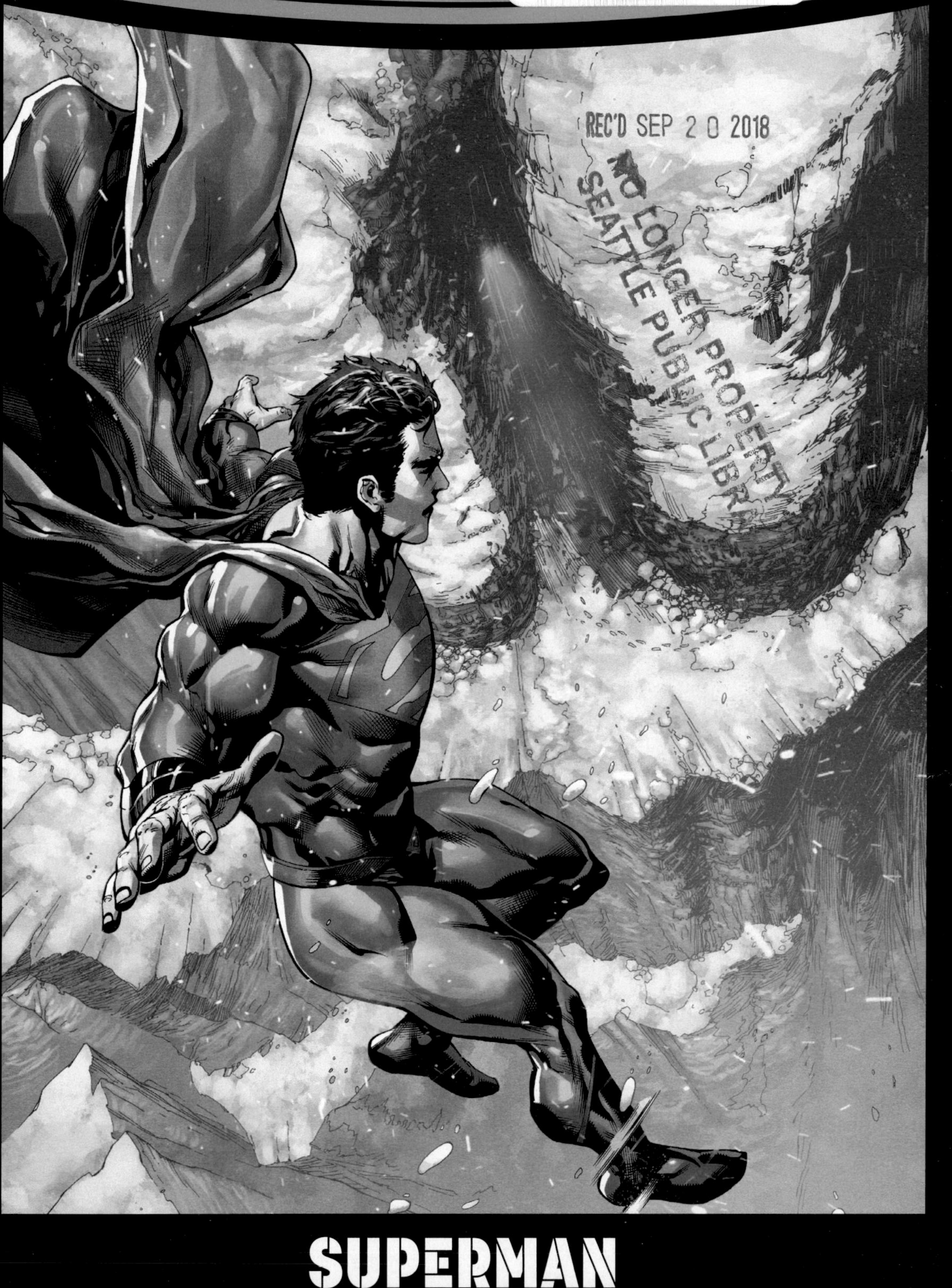

SUPERMAN
REBORN

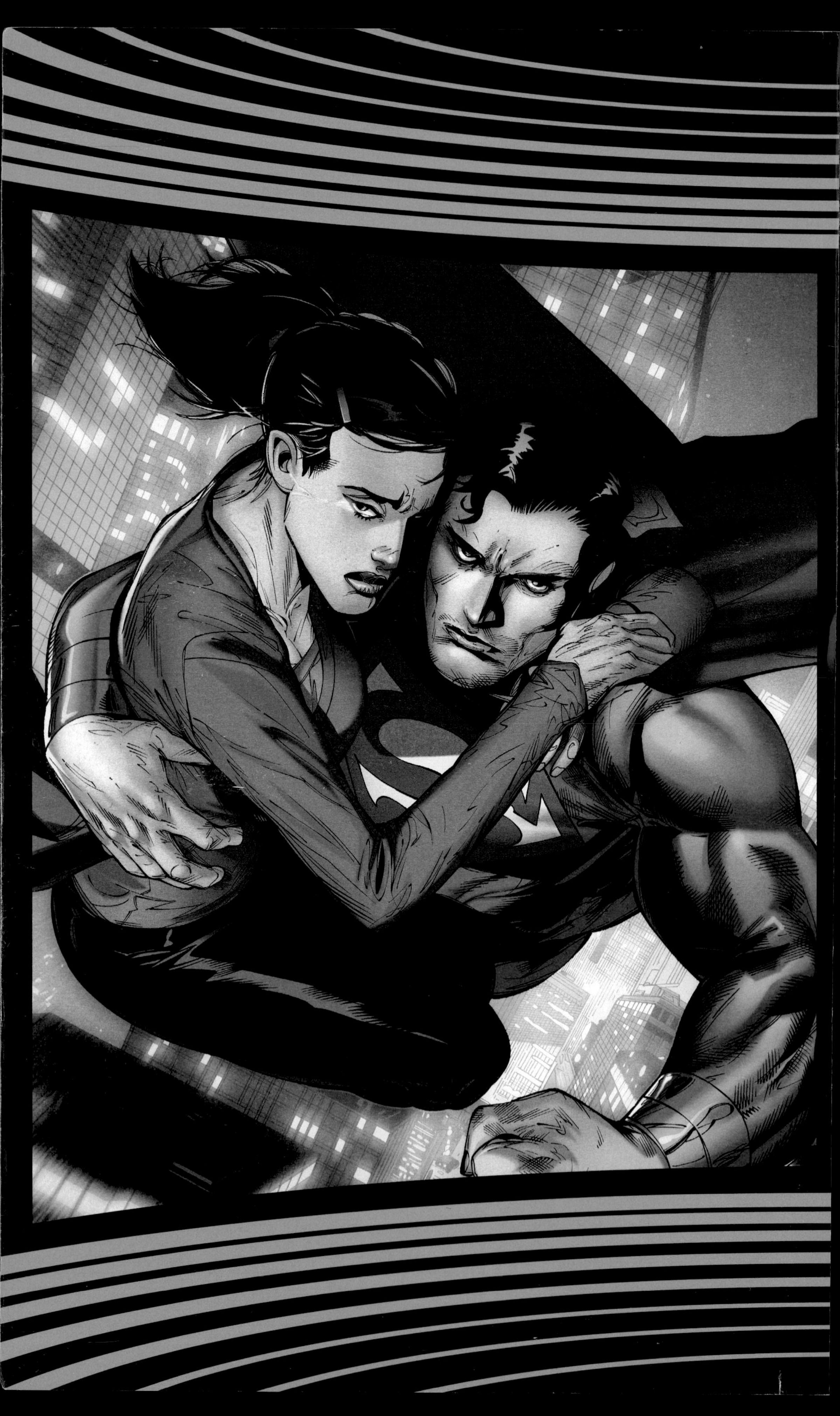

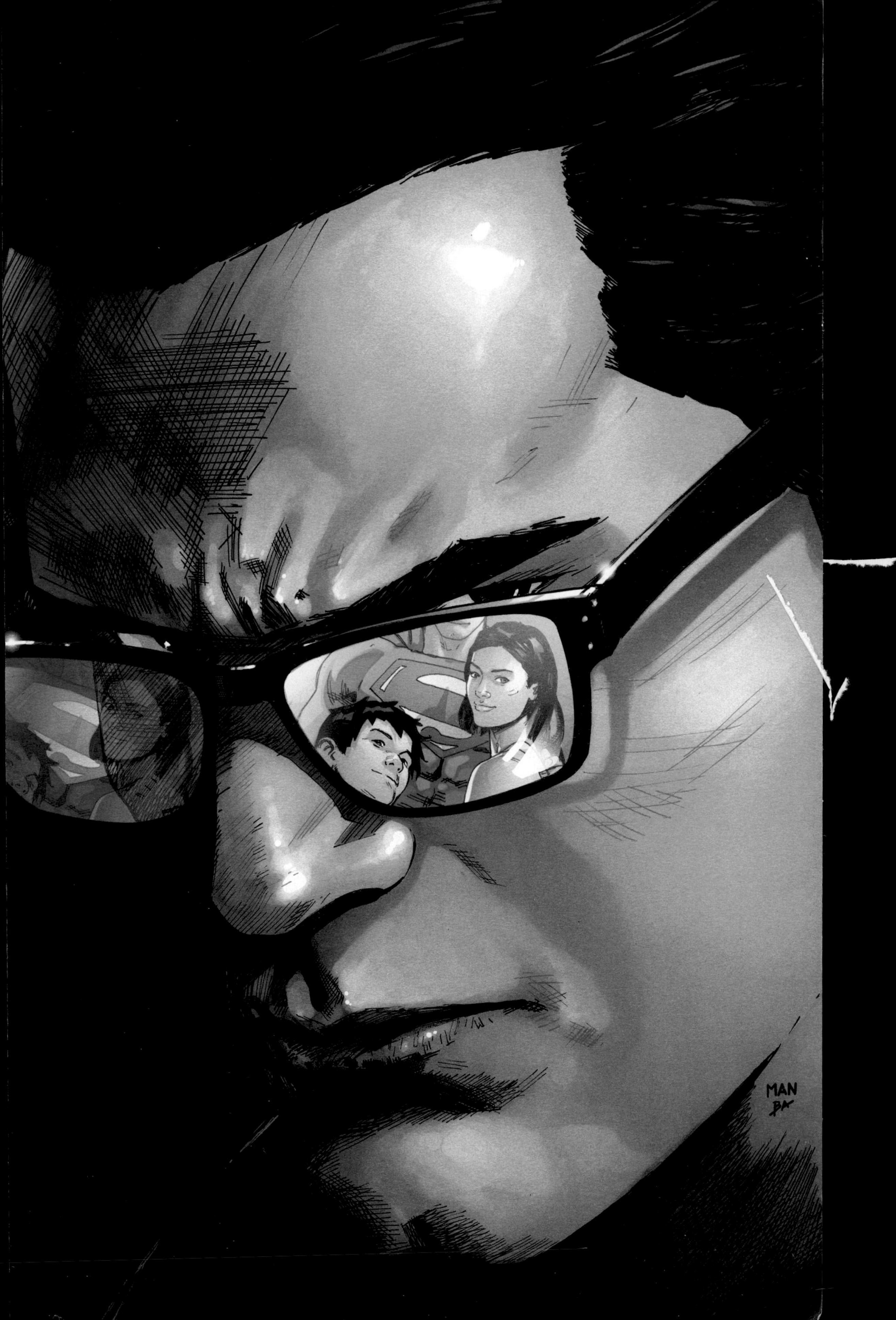

MILD MANNERED part one

DAN JURGENS writer * PATCH ZIRCHER & STEPHEN SEGOVIA pencillers
PATCH ZIRCHER & ART THIBERT inkers * ARIF PRIANTO colorist
CLAY MANN & BRAD ANDERSON cover art

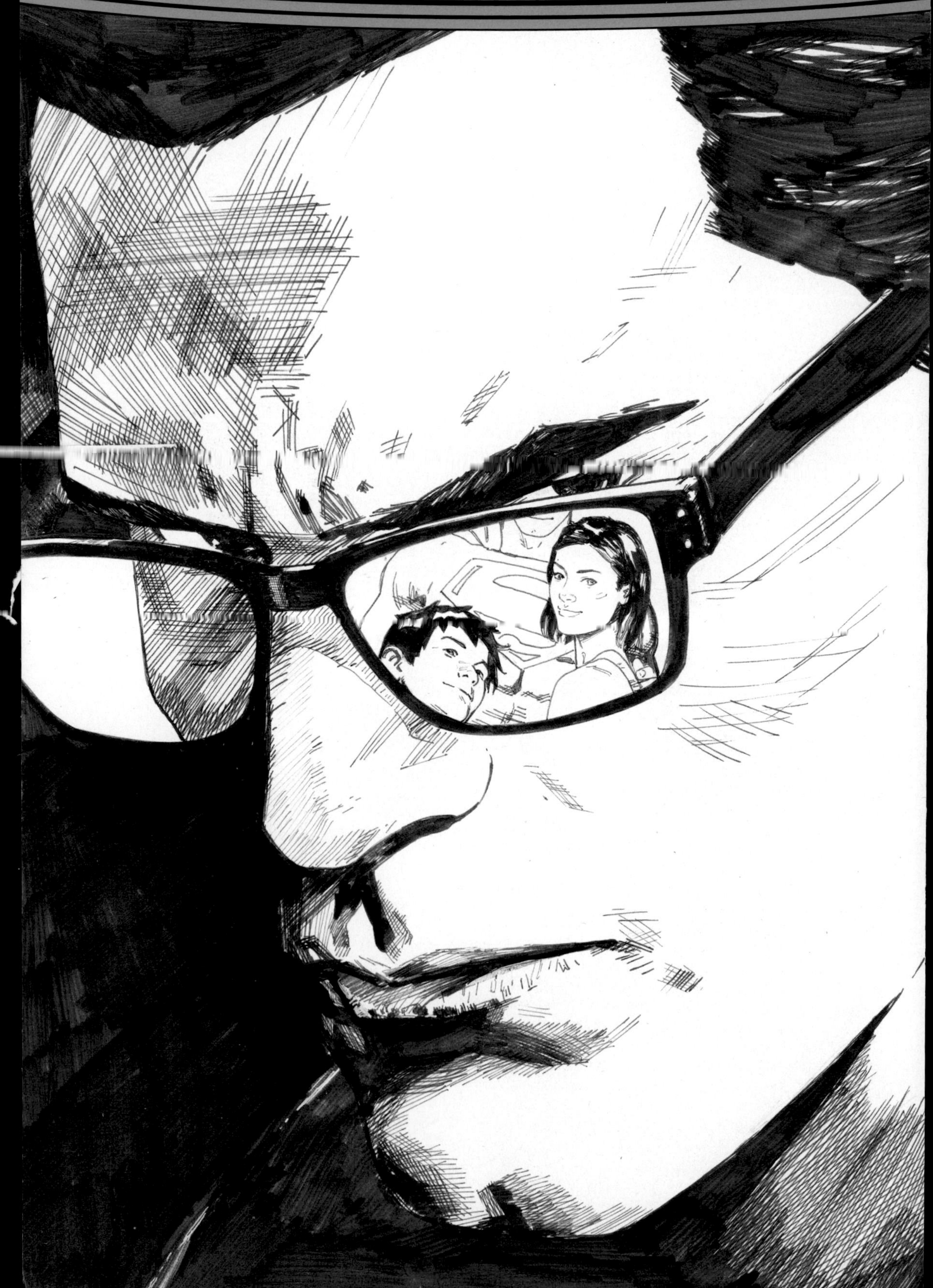

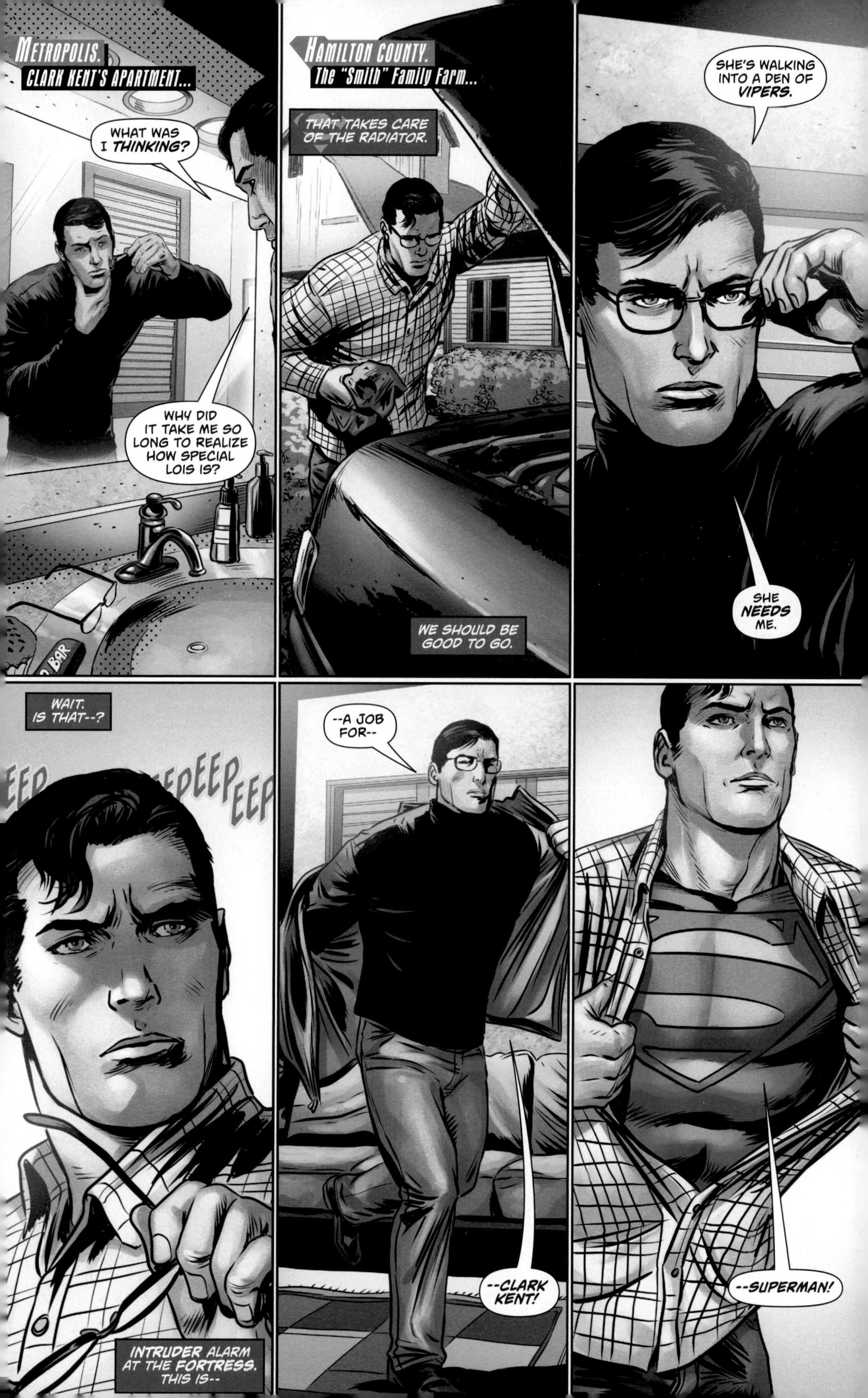

METROPOLIS.
CLARK KENT'S APARTMENT...
WHAT WAS I THINKING?
WHY DID IT TAKE ME SO LONG TO REALIZE HOW SPECIAL LOIS IS?
HAMILTON COUNTY.
The "Smith" Family Farm...
THAT TAKES CARE OF THE RADIATOR.
WE SHOULD BE GOOD TO GO.
SHE'S WALKING INTO A DEN OF VIPERS.
SHE NEEDS ME.
WAIT. IS THAT--?
EEPEEPEEPEEP
INTRUDER ALARM AT THE FORTRESS. THIS IS--
--A JOB FOR--
--CLARK KENT!
--SUPERMAN!

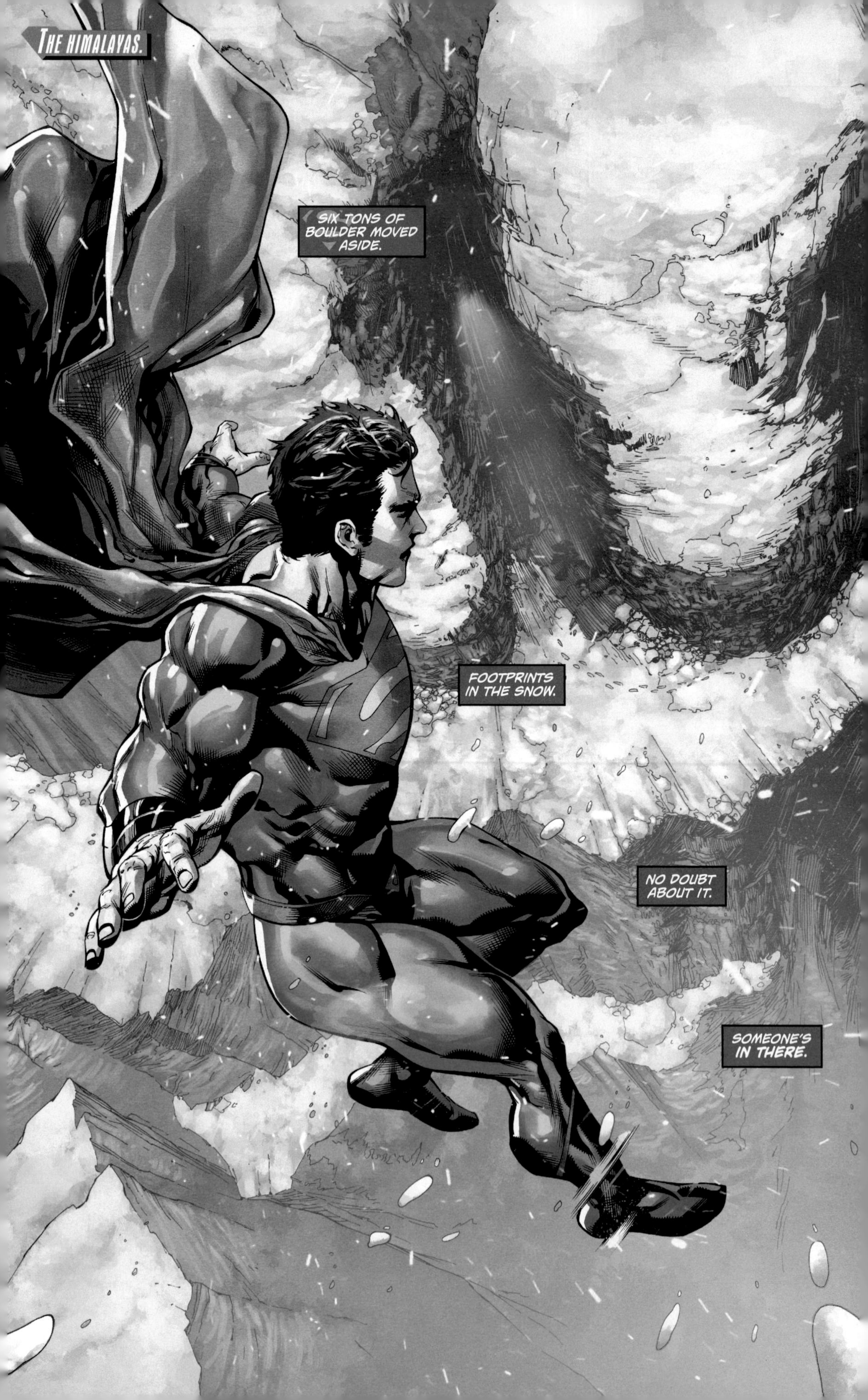
THE HIMALAYAS.
SIX TONS OF BOULDER MOVED ASIDE.
FOOTPRINTS IN THE SNOW.
NO DOUBT ABOUT IT.
SOMEONE'S IN THERE.

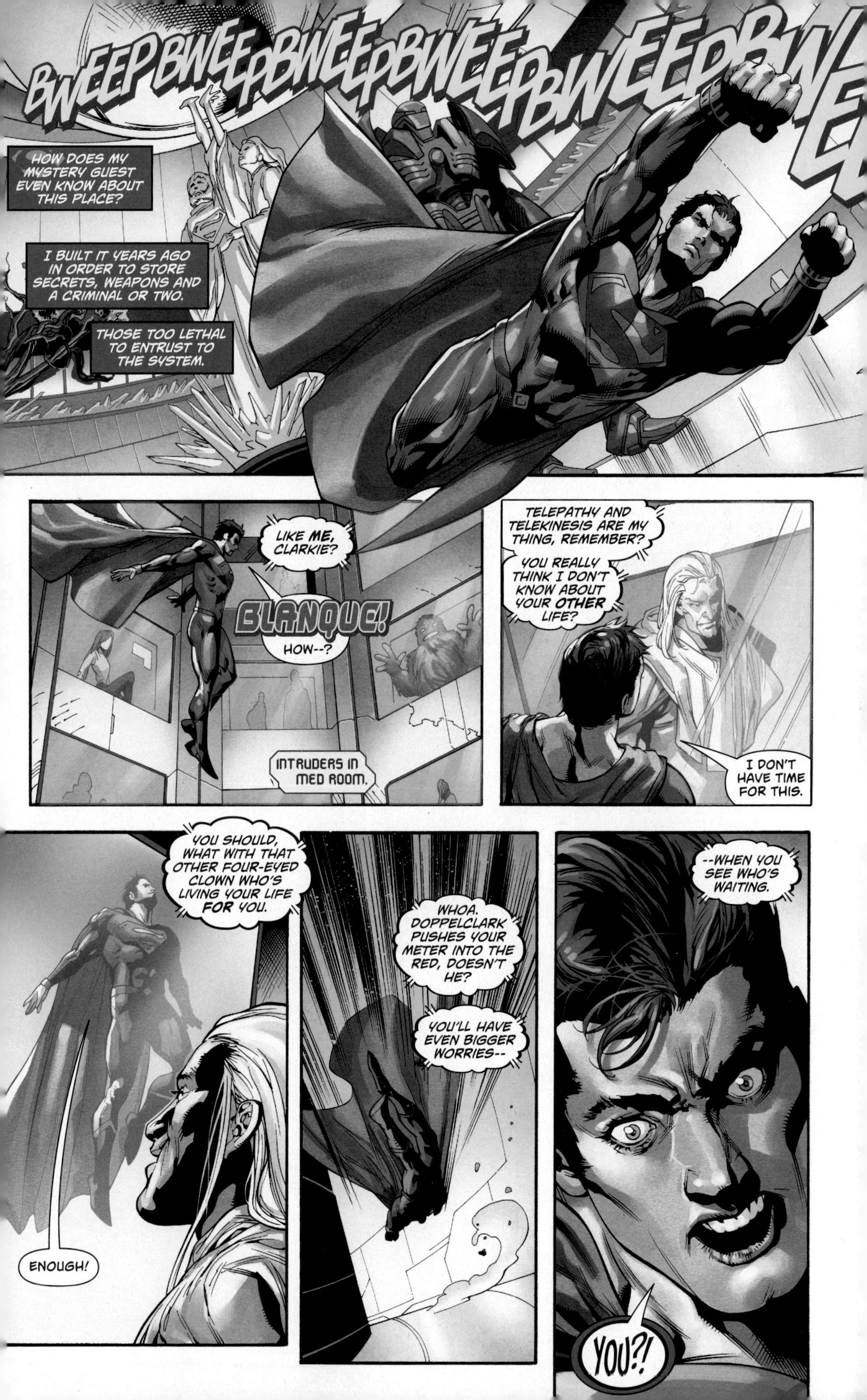
BWEEPBWEEPBWEEPBWEEPBWEEPBWEE
HOW DOES MY MYSTERY GUEST EVEN KNOW ABOUT THIS PLACE?
I BUILT IT YEARS AGO IN ORDER TO STORE SECRETS, WEAPONS AND A CRIMINAL OR TWO.
THOSE TOO LETHAL TO ENTRUST TO THE SYSTEM.
LIKE ME, CLARKIE?
BLANQUE!
HOW--?
INTRUDERS IN MED ROOM.
TELEPATHY AND TELEKINESIS ARE MY THING, REMEMBER?
YOU REALLY THINK I DON'T KNOW ABOUT YOUR OTHER LIFE?
I DON'T HAVE TIME FOR THIS.
YOU SHOULD, WHAT WITH THAT OTHER FOUR-EYED CLOWN WHO'S LIVING YOUR LIFE FOR YOU.
ENOUGH!
WHOA. DOPPELCLARK PUSHES YOUR METER INTO THE RED, DOESN'T HE?
YOU'LL HAVE EVEN BIGGER WORRIES--
--WHEN YOU SEE WHO'S WAITING.
YOU?!

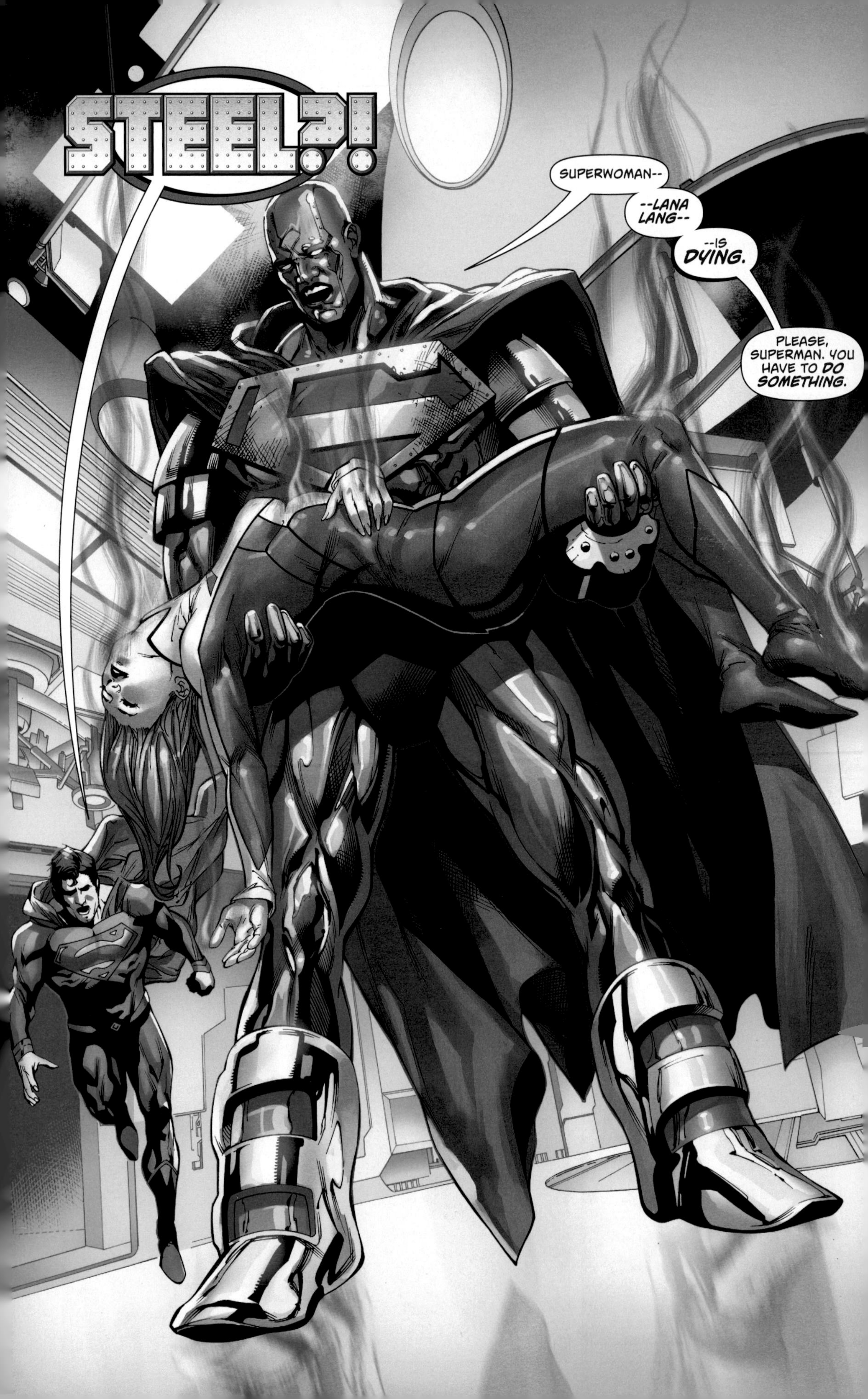
STEEL?!
SUPERWOMAN--
--LANA LANG--
--IS DYING.
PLEASE, SUPERMAN. YOU HAVE TO DO SOMETHING.

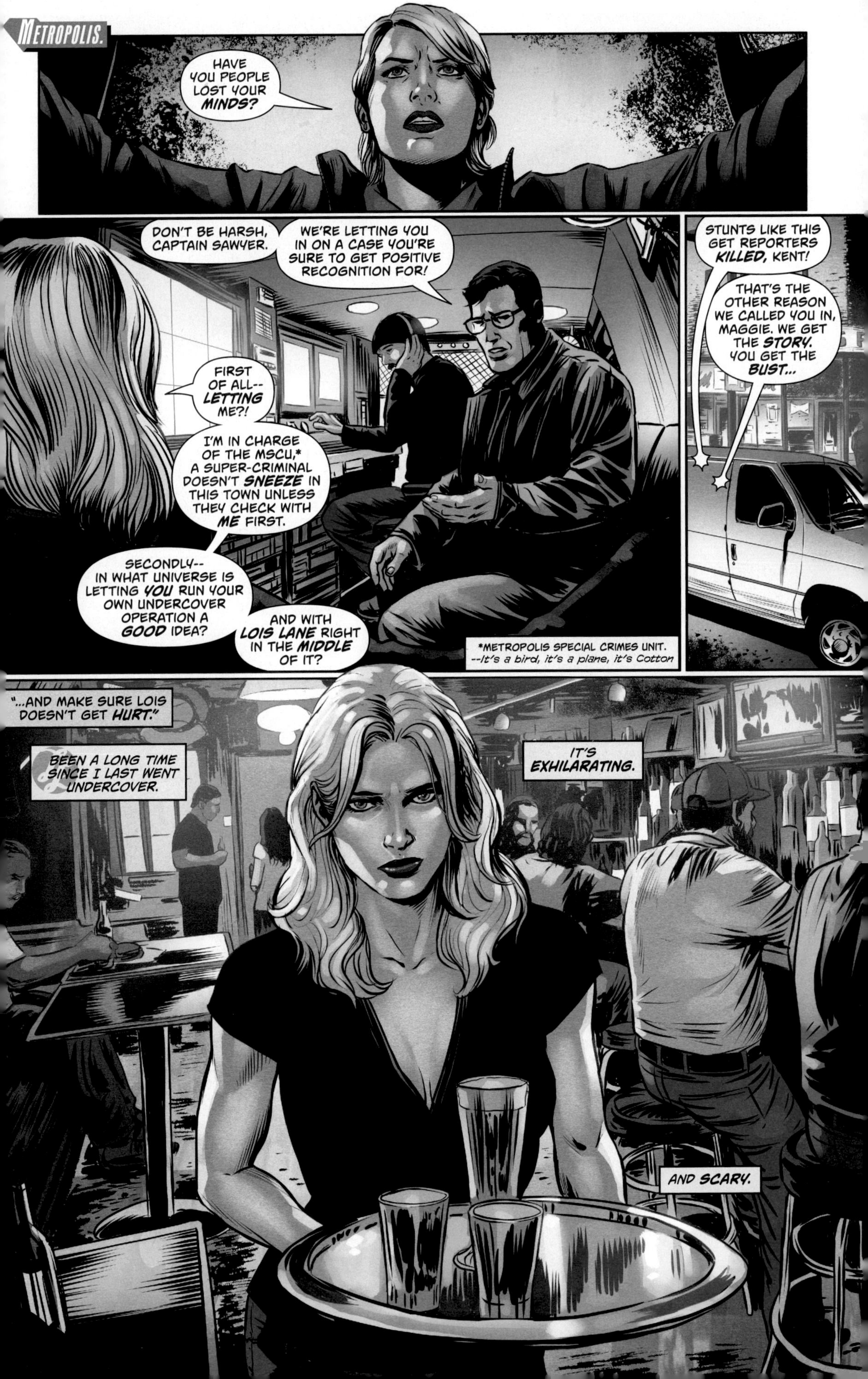
METROPOLIS.
HAVE YOU PEOPLE LOST YOUR MINDS?
DON'T BE HARSH, CAPTAIN SAWYER.
WE'RE LETTING YOU IN ON A CASE YOU'RE SURE TO GET POSITIVE RECOGNITION FOR!
FIRST OF ALL-- LETTING ME?!
I'M IN CHARGE OF THE MSCU,* A SUPER-CRIMINAL DOESN'T SNEEZE IN THIS TOWN UNLESS THEY CHECK WITH ME FIRST.
SECONDLY-- IN WHAT UNIVERSE IS LETTING YOU RUN YOUR OWN UNDERCOVER OPERATION A GOOD IDEA?
AND WITH LOIS LANE RIGHT IN THE MIDDLE OF IT?
*METROPOLIS SPECIAL CRIMES UNIT. --It's a bird, it's a plane, it's Cotton
STUNTS LIKE THIS GET REPORTERS KILLED, KENT!
THAT'S THE OTHER REASON WE CALLED YOU IN, MAGGIE. WE GET THE STORY. YOU GET THE BUST...
"...AND MAKE SURE LOIS DOESN'T GET HURT."
BEEN A LONG TIME SINCE I LAST WENT UNDERCOVER.
IT'S EXHILARATING.
AND SCARY.

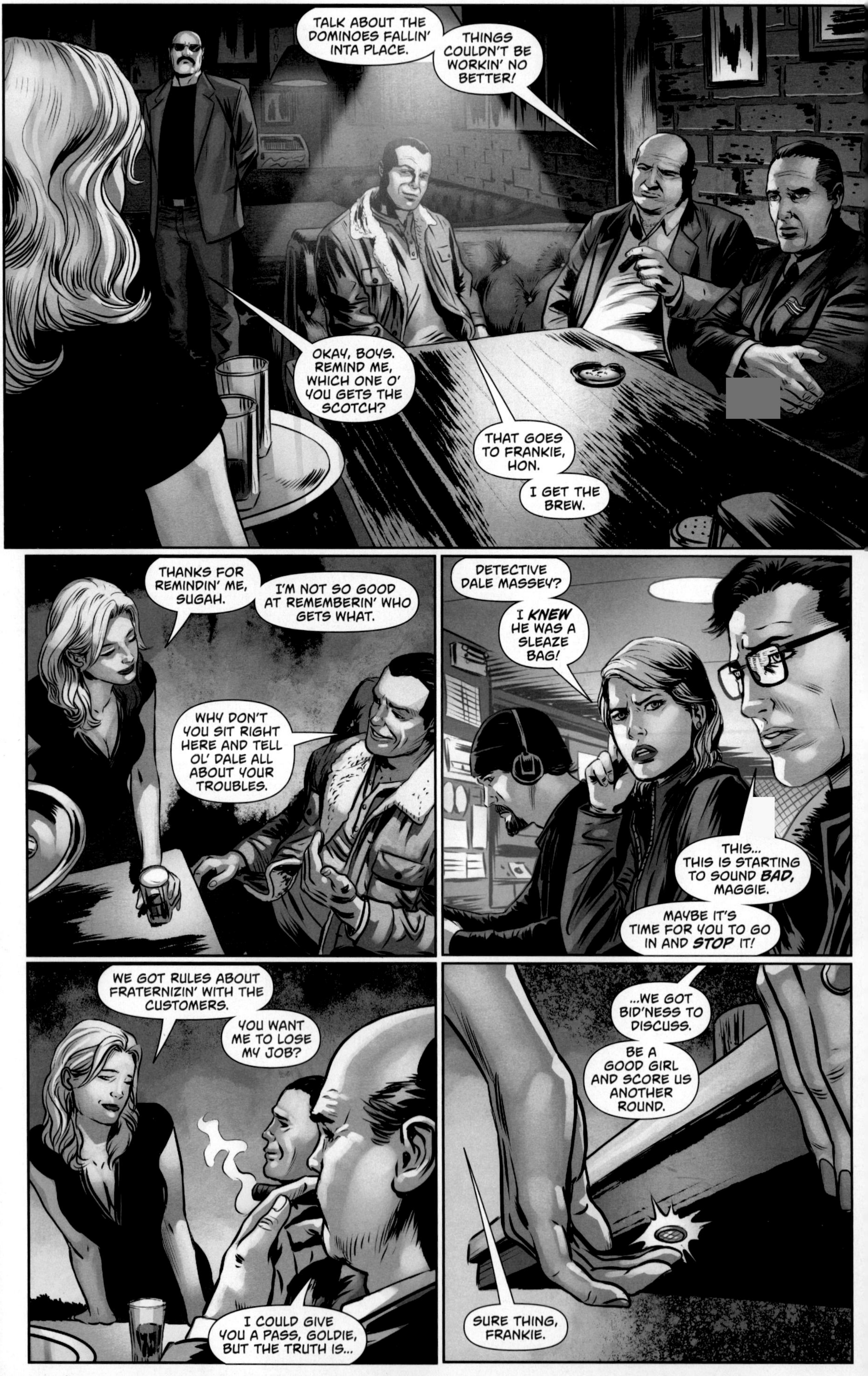
TALK ABOUT THE DOMINOES FALLIN' INTA PLACE.
THINGS COULDN'T BE WORKIN' NO BETTER!
OKAY, BOYS. REMIND ME, WHICH ONE O' YOU GETS THE SCOTCH?
THAT GOES TO FRANKIE, HON.
I GET THE BREW.
THANKS FOR REMINDIN' ME, SUGAH.
I'M NOT SO GOOD AT REMEMBERIN' WHO GETS WHAT.
WHY DON'T YOU SIT RIGHT HERE AND TELL OL' DALE ALL ABOUT YOUR TROUBLES.
DETECTIVE DALE MASSEY?
I KNEW HE WAS A SLEAZE BAG!
THIS... THIS IS STARTING TO SOUND BAD, MAGGIE.
MAYBE IT'S TIME FOR YOU TO GO IN AND STOP IT!
WE GOT RULES ABOUT FRATERNIZIN' WITH THE CUSTOMERS.
YOU WANT ME TO LOSE MY JOB?
I COULD GIVE YOU A PASS, GOLDIE, BUT THE TRUTH IS...
...WE GOT BID'NESS TO DISCUSS.
BE A GOOD GIRL AND SCORE US ANOTHER ROUND.
SURE THING, FRANKIE.

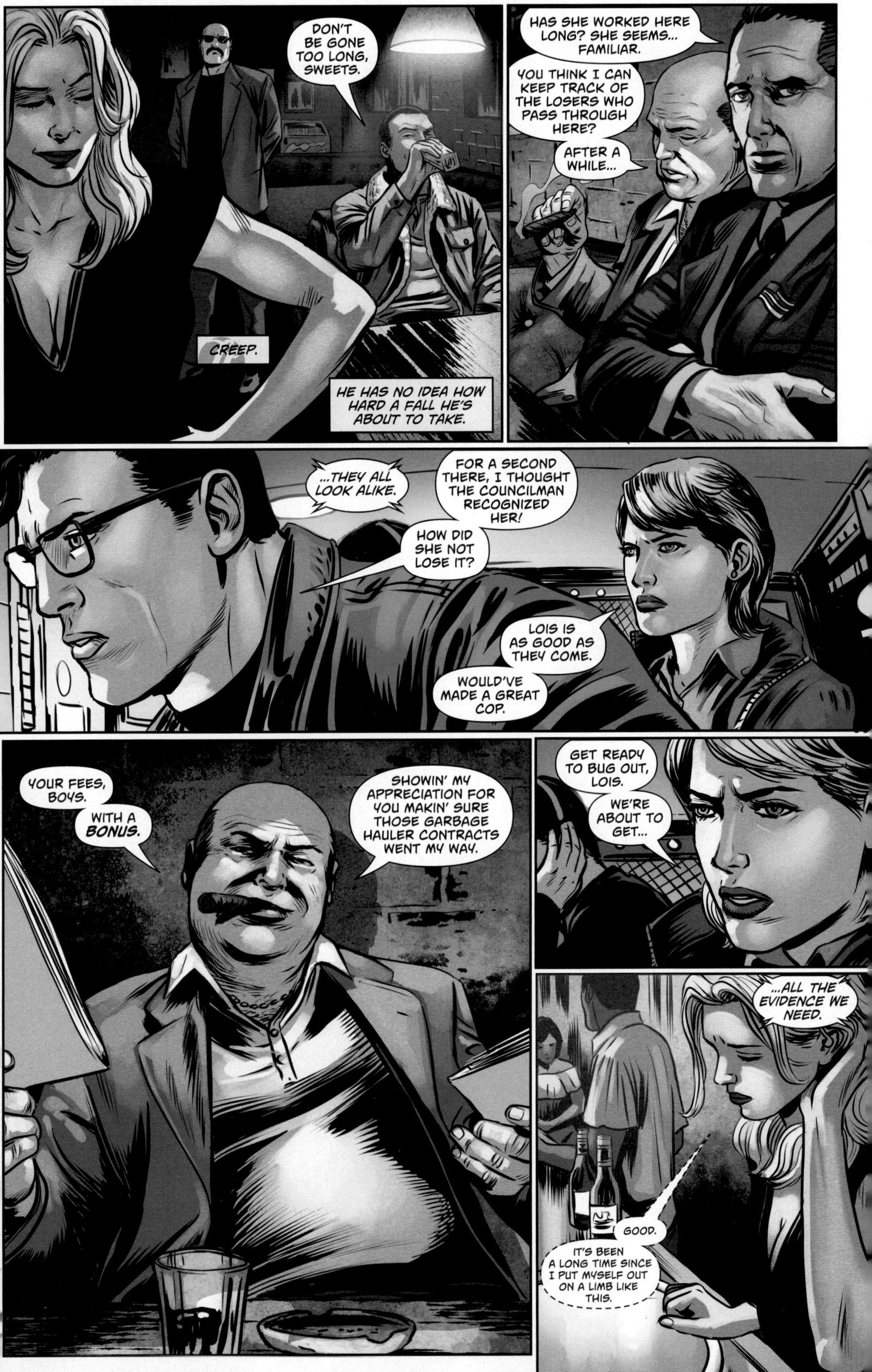
DON'T BE GONE TOO LONG, SWEETS.
CREEP.
HE HAS NO IDEA HOW HARD A FALL HE'S ABOUT TO TAKE.
HAS SHE WORKED HERE LONG? SHE SEEMS... FAMILIAR.
YOU THINK I CAN KEEP TRACK OF THE LOSERS WHO PASS THROUGH HERE?
AFTER A WHILE...
...THEY ALL LOOK ALIKE.
FOR A SECOND THERE, I THOUGHT THE COUNCILMAN RECOGNIZED HER!
HOW DID SHE NOT LOSE IT?
LOIS IS AS GOOD AS THEY COME.
WOULD'VE MADE A GREAT COP.
YOUR FEES, BOYS.
WITH A **BONUS**.
SHOWIN' MY APPRECIATION FOR YOU MAKIN' SURE THOSE GARBAGE HAULER CONTRACTS WENT MY WAY.
GET READY TO BUG OUT, LOIS.
WE'RE ABOUT TO GET...
...ALL THE EVIDENCE WE NEED.
GOOD.
IT'S BEEN A LONG TIME SINCE I PUT MYSELF OUT ON A LIMB LIKE THIS.

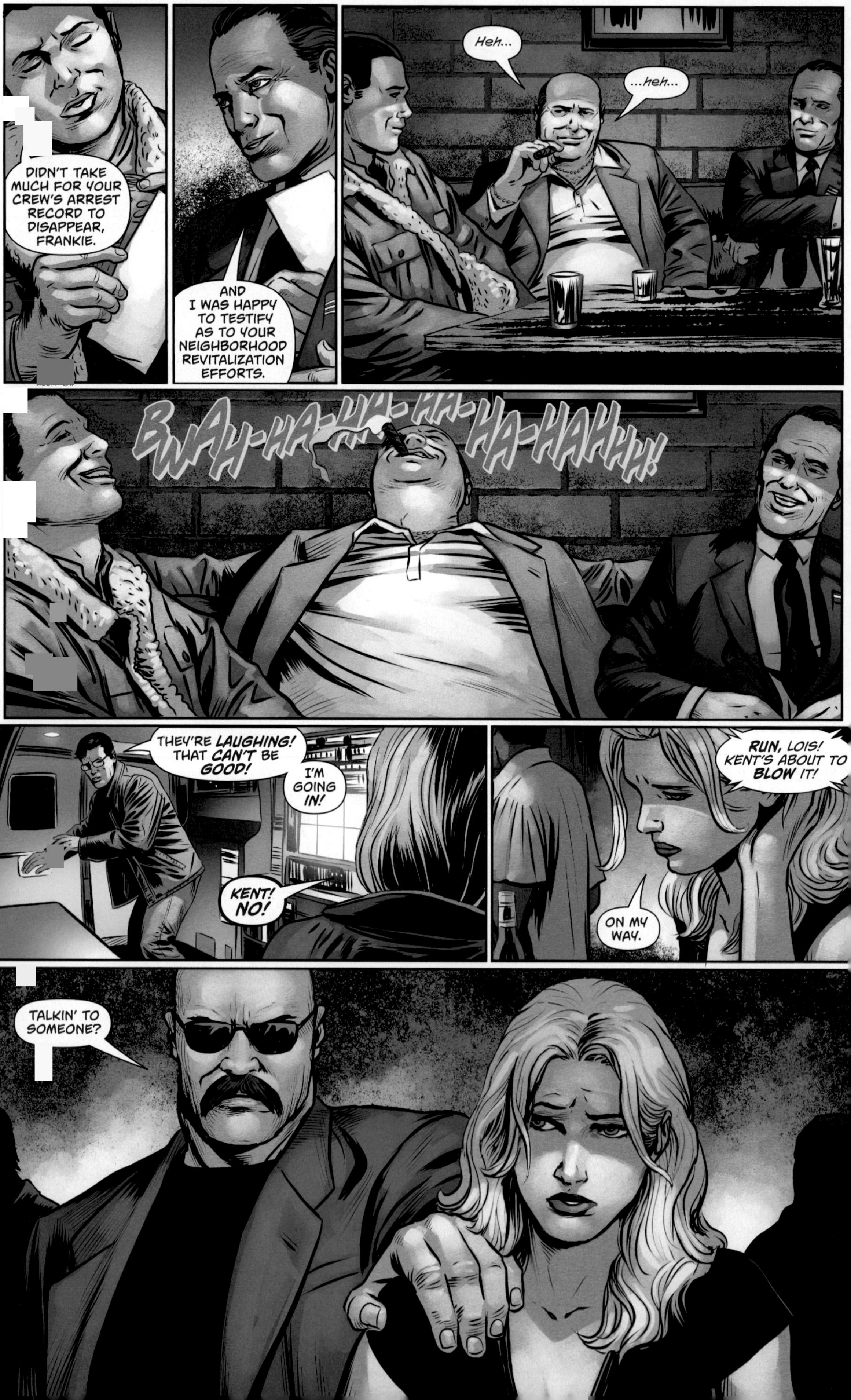
DIDN'T TAKE MUCH FOR YOUR CREW'S ARREST RECORD TO DISAPPEAR, FRANKIE.
AND I WAS HAPPY TO TESTIFY AS TO YOUR NEIGHBORHOOD REVITALIZATION EFFORTS.
Heh...
...heh...
BWAH-HA-HA-HA-HA-HAHHH!
THEY'RE LAUGHING! THAT CAN'T BE GOOD!
I'M GOING IN!
KENT! NO!
RUN, LOIS! KENT'S ABOUT TO BLOW IT!
ON MY WAY.
TALKIN' TO SOMEONE?

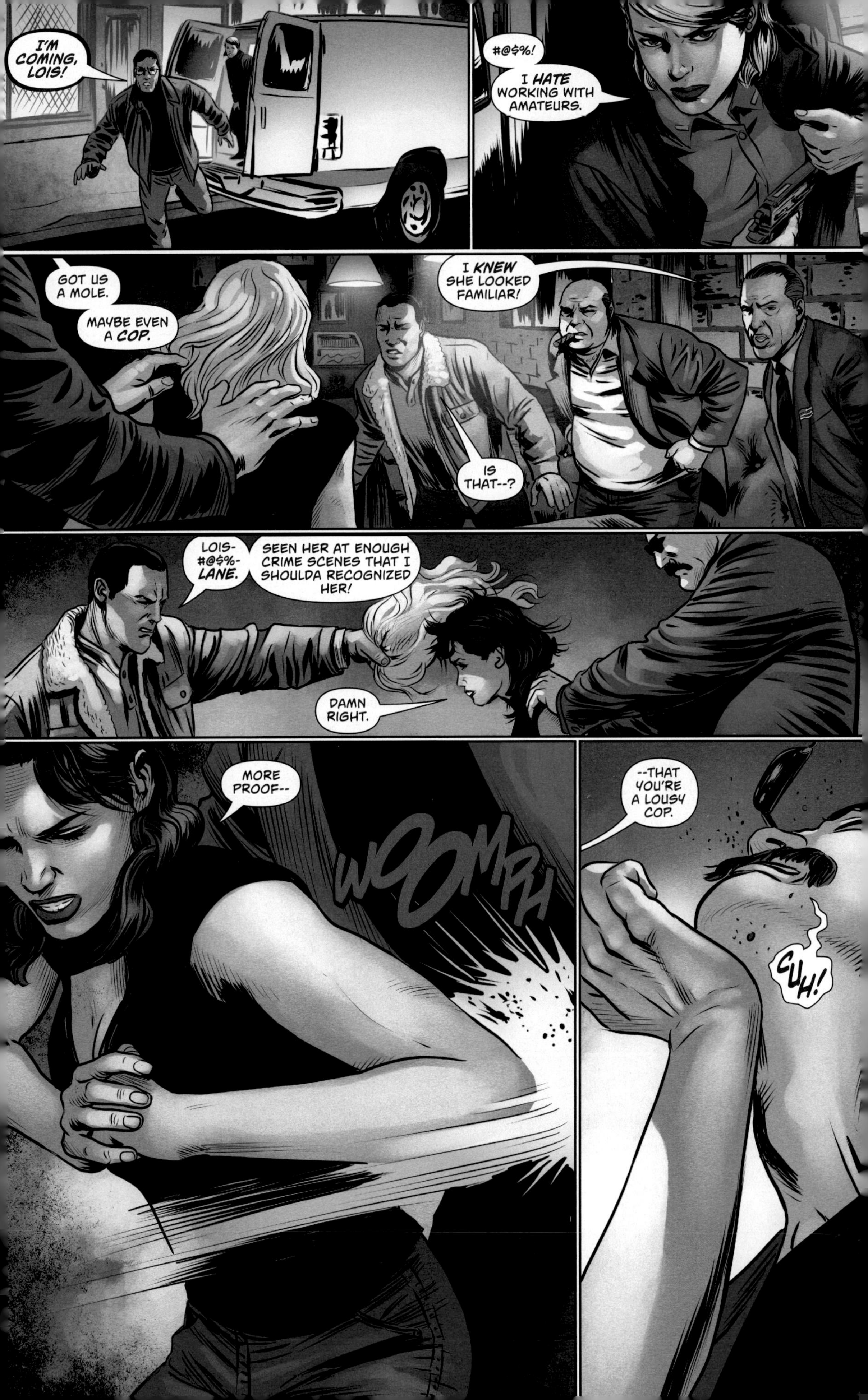
I'M COMING, LOIS!
#@$%!
I HATE WORKING WITH AMATEURS.
GOT US A MOLE.
MAYBE EVEN A COP.
I KNEW SHE LOOKED FAMILIAR!
IS THAT--?
LOIS-#@$%-LANE.
SEEN HER AT ENOUGH CRIME SCENES THAT I SHOULDA RECOGNIZED HER!
DAMN RIGHT.
MORE PROOF--
WOOMPH
--THAT YOU'RE A LOUSY COP.
CUH!

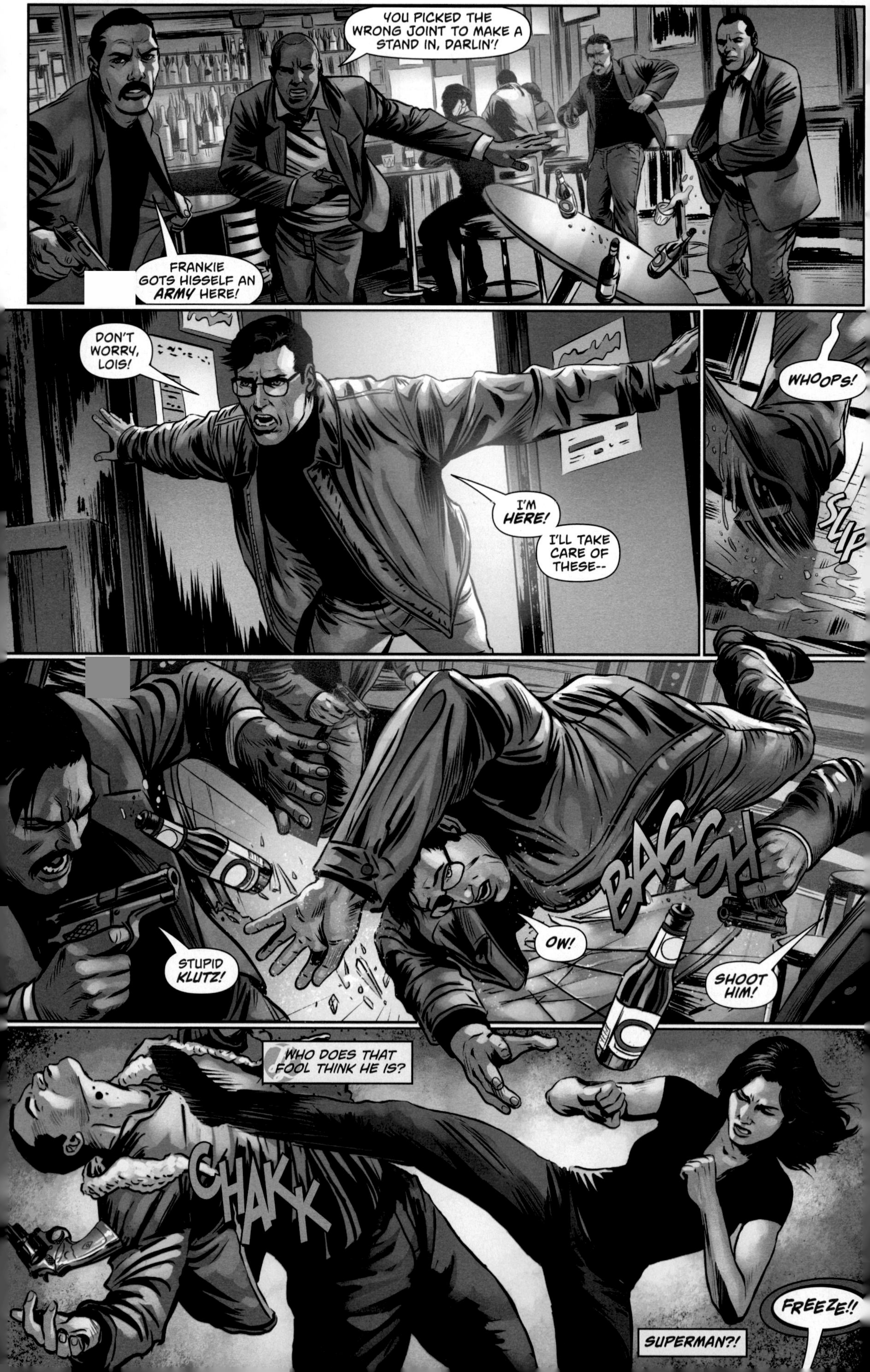
YOU PICKED THE WRONG JOINT TO MAKE A STAND IN, DARLIN'!
FRANKIE GOTS HISSELF AN ARMY HERE!
DON'T WORRY, LOIS!
I'M HERE!
I'LL TAKE CARE OF THESE--
WHOOPS!
SLIP
BASGH
STUPID KLUTZ!
OW!
SHOOT HIM!
WHO DOES THAT FOOL THINK HE IS?
CHAKK
SUPERMAN?!
FREEZE!!

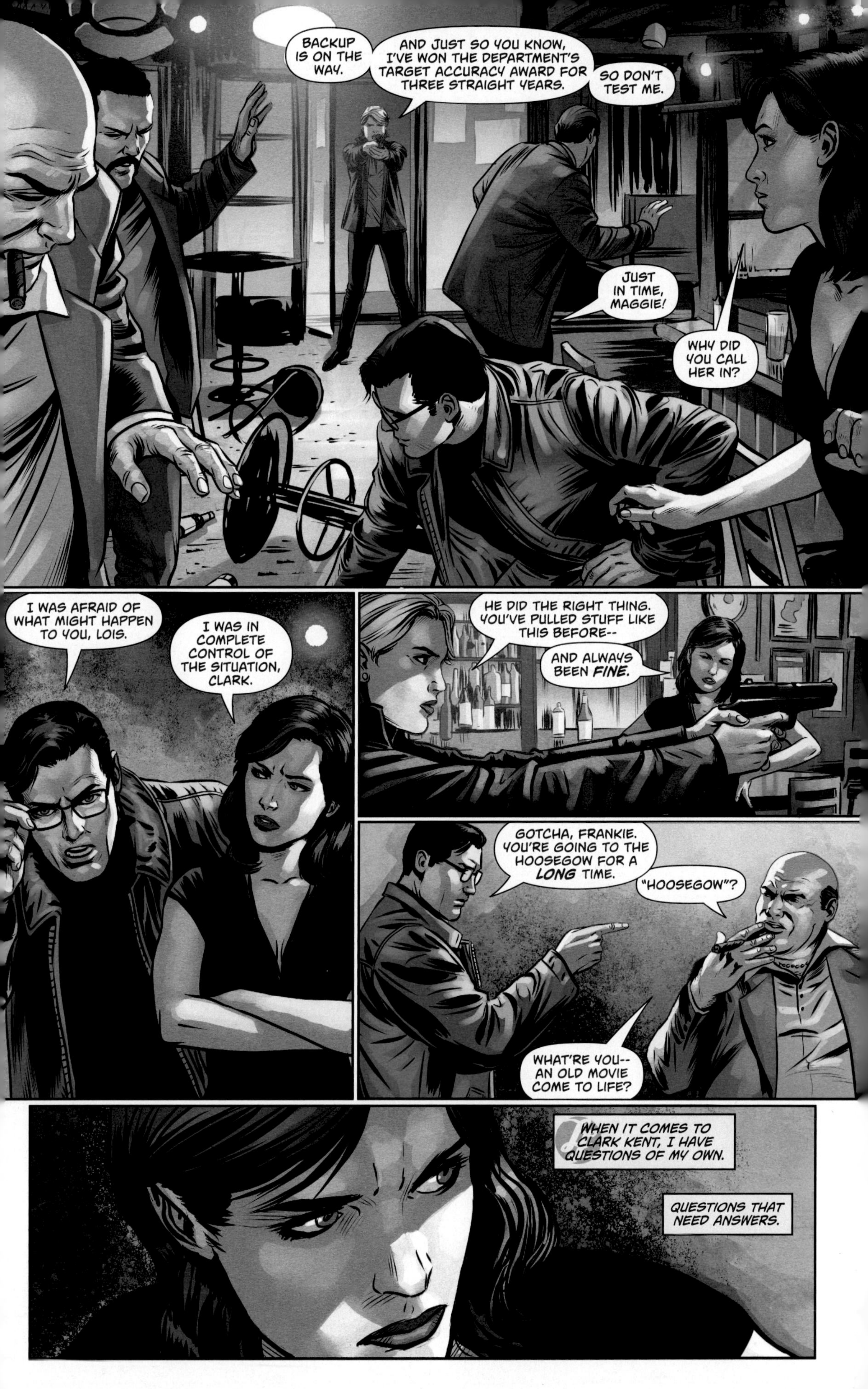
BACKUP IS ON THE WAY.
AND JUST SO YOU KNOW, I'VE WON THE DEPARTMENT'S TARGET ACCURACY AWARD FOR THREE STRAIGHT YEARS.
SO DON'T TEST ME.
JUST IN TIME, MAGGIE!
WHY DID YOU CALL HER IN?
I WAS AFRAID OF WHAT MIGHT HAPPEN TO YOU, LOIS.
I WAS IN COMPLETE CONTROL OF THE SITUATION, CLARK.
HE DID THE RIGHT THING. YOU'VE PULLED STUFF LIKE THIS BEFORE--
AND ALWAYS BEEN *FINE*.
GOTCHA, FRANKIE. YOU'RE GOING TO THE HOOSEGOW FOR A *LONG* TIME.
"HOOSEGOW"?
WHAT'RE YOU-- AN OLD MOVIE COME TO LIFE?
WHEN IT COMES TO CLARK KENT, I HAVE QUESTIONS OF MY OWN.
QUESTIONS THAT NEED ANSWERS.

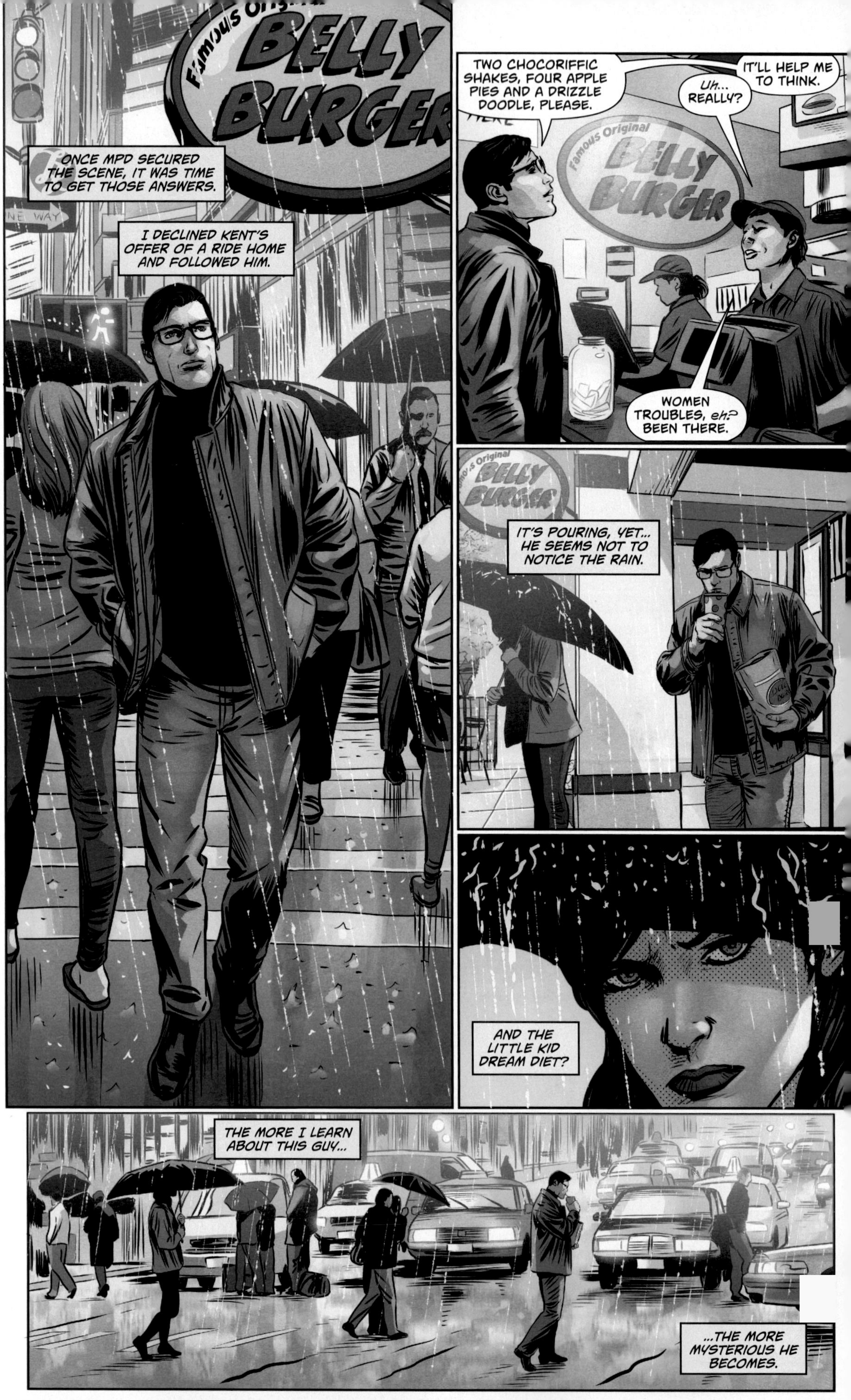
Famous Original
BELLY BURGER
ONCE MPD SECURED THE SCENE, IT WAS TIME TO GET THOSE ANSWERS.
I DECLINED KENT'S OFFER OF A RIDE HOME AND FOLLOWED HIM.
ONE WAY
TWO CHOCORIFFIC SHAKES, FOUR APPLE PIES AND A DRIZZLE DOODLE, PLEASE.
Uh... REALLY?
IT'LL HELP ME TO THINK.
Famous Original
BELLY BURGER
WOMEN TROUBLES, eh? BEEN THERE.
BELLY BURGER
IT'S POURING, YET... HE SEEMS NOT TO NOTICE THE RAIN.
AND THE LITTLE KID DREAM DIET?
THE MORE I LEARN ABOUT THIS GUY...
...THE MORE MYSTERIOUS HE BECOMES.

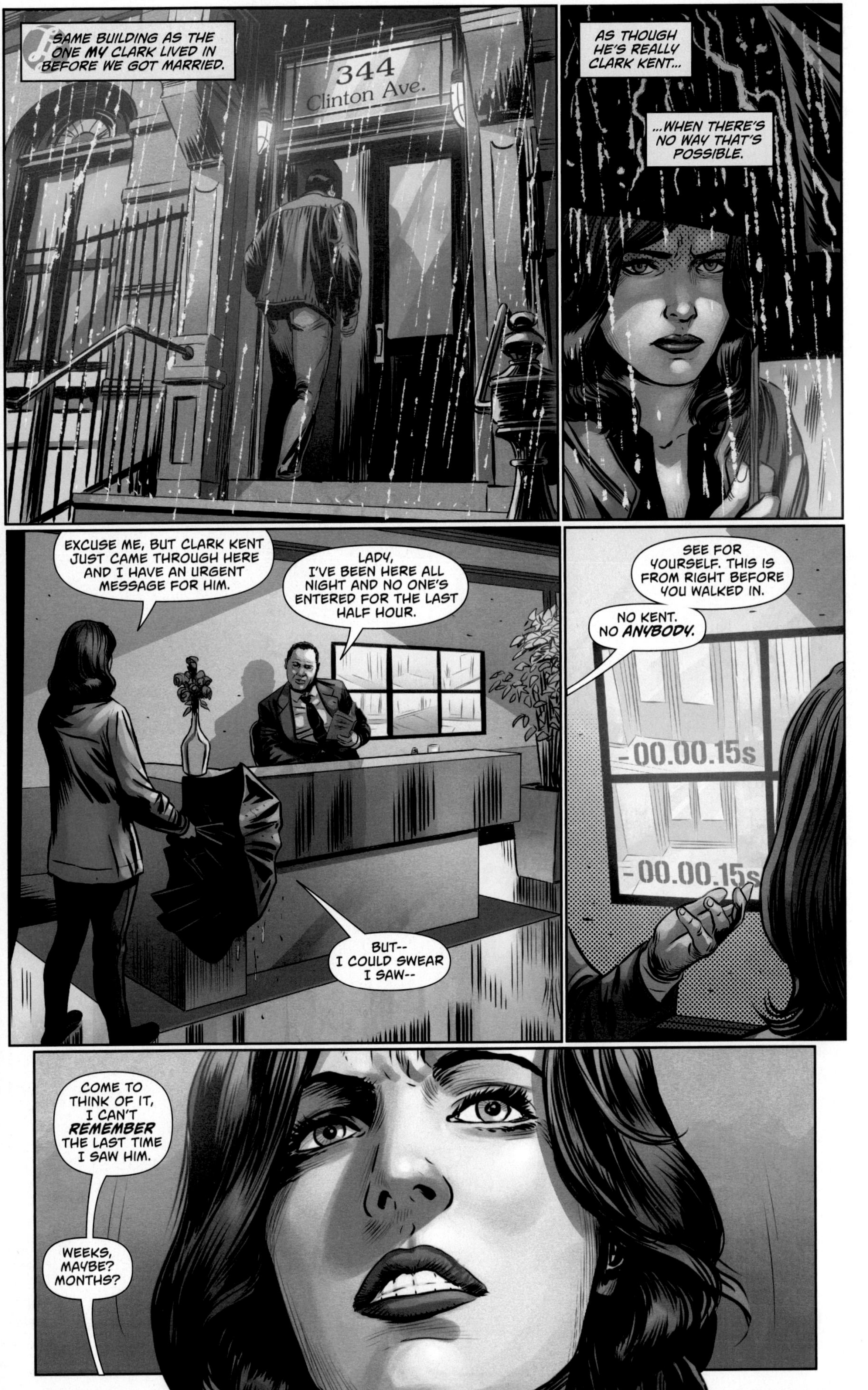
SAME BUILDING AS THE ONE MY CLARK LIVED IN BEFORE WE GOT MARRIED.
344 Clinton Ave.
AS THOUGH HE'S REALLY CLARK KENT...
...WHEN THERE'S NO WAY THAT'S POSSIBLE.
EXCUSE ME, BUT CLARK KENT JUST CAME THROUGH HERE AND I HAVE AN URGENT MESSAGE FOR HIM.
LADY, I'VE BEEN HERE ALL NIGHT AND NO ONE'S ENTERED FOR THE LAST HALF HOUR.
BUT-- I COULD SWEAR I SAW--
SEE FOR YOURSELF. THIS IS FROM RIGHT BEFORE YOU WALKED IN.
NO KENT. NO ANYBODY.
-00.00.15s
-00.00.15s
COME TO THINK OF IT, I CAN'T REMEMBER THE LAST TIME I SAW HIM.
WEEKS, MAYBE? MONTHS?

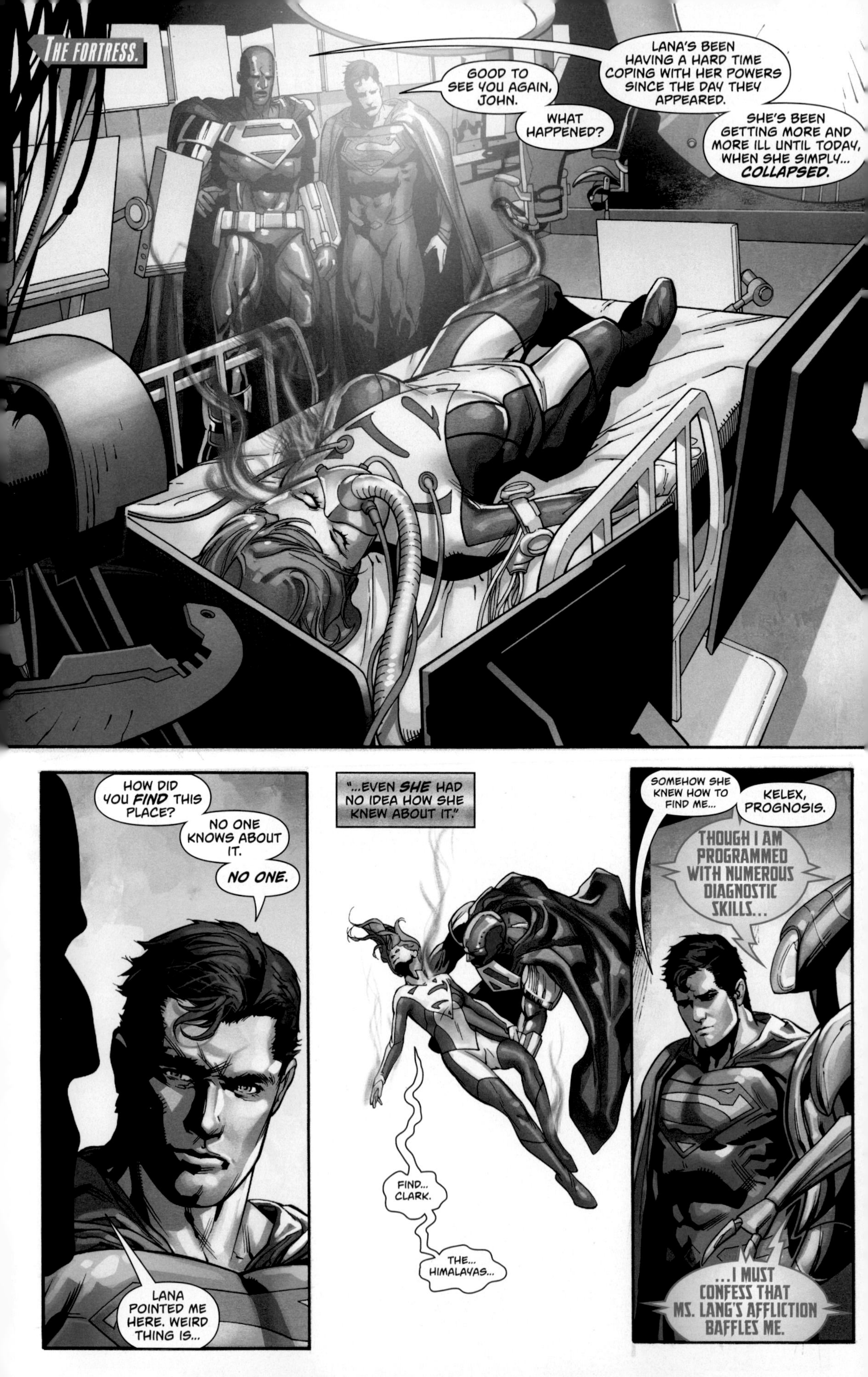
THE FORTRESS.
GOOD TO SEE YOU AGAIN, JOHN.
WHAT HAPPENED?
LANA'S BEEN HAVING A HARD TIME COPING WITH HER POWERS SINCE THE DAY THEY APPEARED.
SHE'S BEEN GETTING MORE AND MORE ILL UNTIL TODAY, WHEN SHE SIMPLY... COLLAPSED.
HOW DID YOU FIND THIS PLACE?
NO ONE KNOWS ABOUT IT.
NO ONE.
LANA POINTED ME HERE. WEIRD THING IS...
"...EVEN SHE HAD NO IDEA HOW SHE KNEW ABOUT IT."
FIND... CLARK.
THE... HIMALAYAS...
SOMEHOW SHE KNEW HOW TO FIND ME...
KELEX, PROGNOSIS.
THOUGH I AM PROGRAMMED WITH NUMEROUS DIAGNOSTIC SKILLS...
...I MUST CONFESS THAT MS. LANG'S AFFLICTION BAFFLES ME.

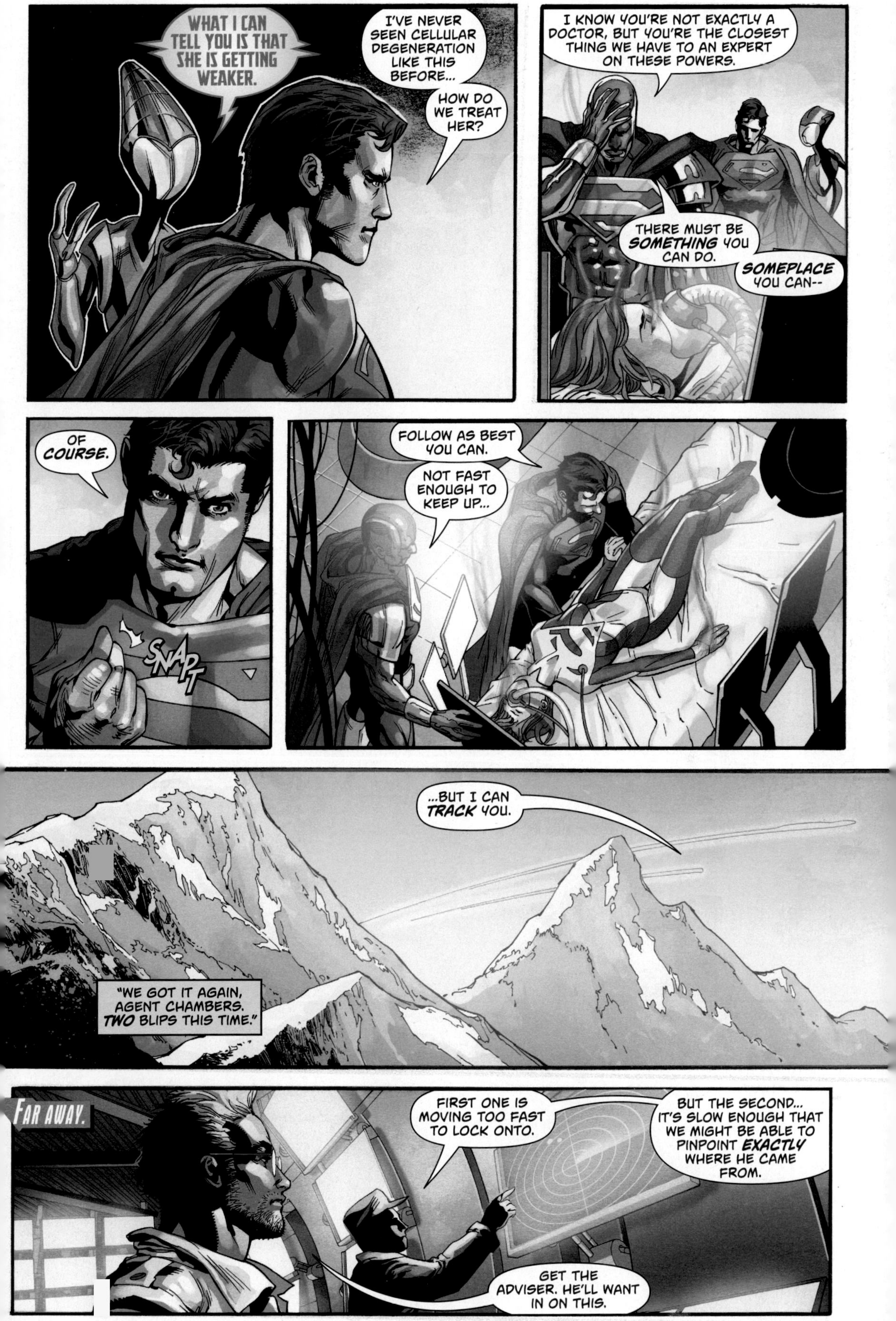
WHAT I CAN TELL YOU IS THAT SHE IS GETTING WEAKER.
I'VE NEVER SEEN CELLULAR DEGENERATION LIKE THIS BEFORE...
HOW DO WE TREAT HER?
I KNOW YOU'RE NOT EXACTLY A DOCTOR, BUT YOU'RE THE CLOSEST THING WE HAVE TO AN EXPERT ON THESE POWERS.
THERE MUST BE *SOMETHING* YOU CAN DO.
SOMEPLACE YOU CAN--
OF *COURSE*.
SNAP!
FOLLOW AS BEST YOU CAN.
NOT FAST ENOUGH TO KEEP UP...
...BUT I CAN *TRACK* YOU.
"WE GOT IT AGAIN, AGENT CHAMBERS. *TWO* BLIPS THIS TIME."
FAR AWAY.
FIRST ONE IS MOVING TOO FAST TO LOCK ONTO.
BUT THE SECOND... IT'S SLOW ENOUGH THAT WE MIGHT BE ABLE TO PINPOINT *EXACTLY* WHERE HE CAME FROM.
GET THE ADVISER. HE'LL WANT IN ON THIS.

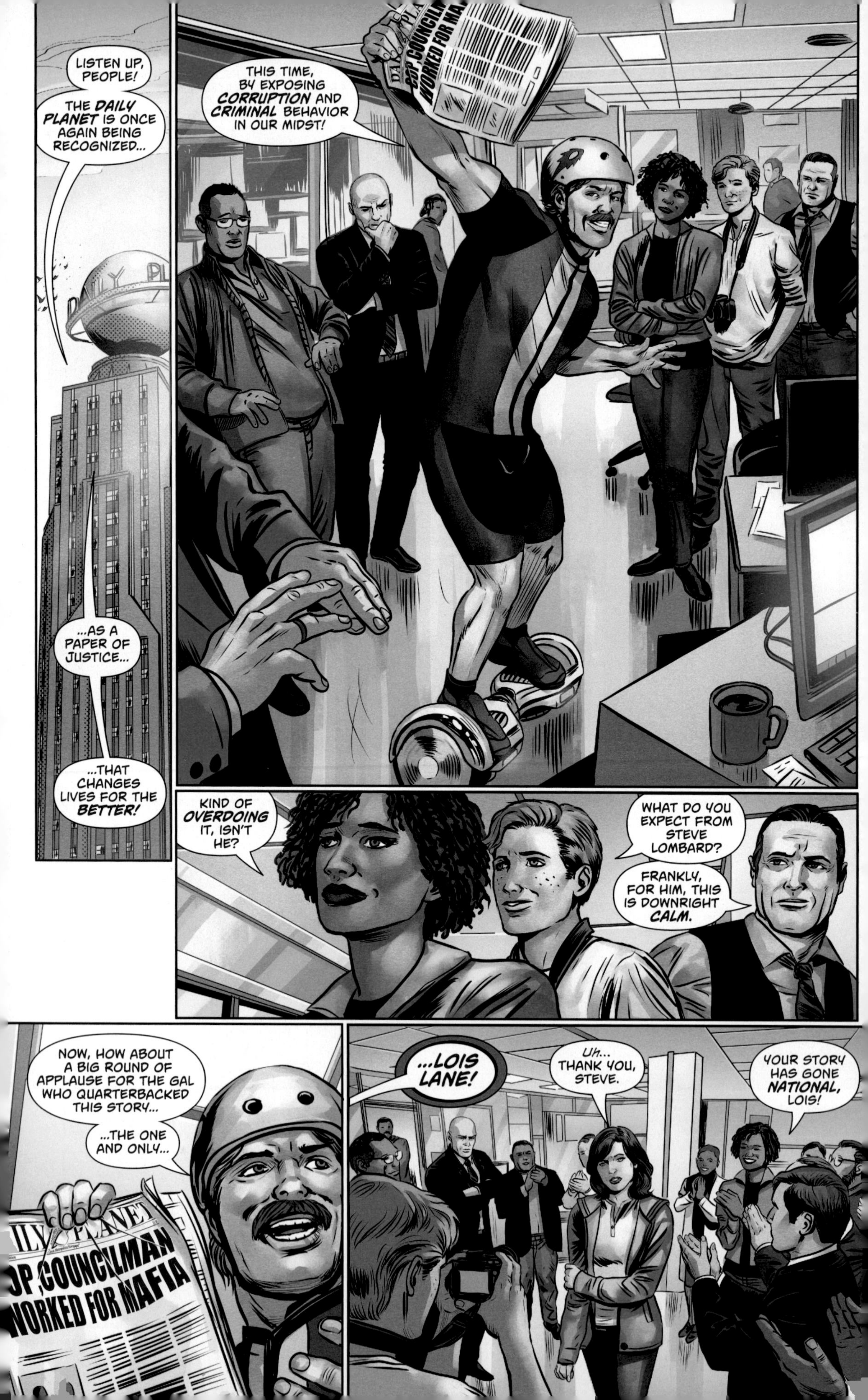
LISTEN UP, PEOPLE!
THE DAILY PLANET IS ONCE AGAIN BEING RECOGNIZED...
THIS TIME, BY EXPOSING CORRUPTION AND CRIMINAL BEHAVIOR IN OUR MIDST!
...AS A PAPER OF JUSTICE...
...THAT CHANGES LIVES FOR THE BETTER!
KIND OF OVERDOING IT, ISN'T HE?
WHAT DO YOU EXPECT FROM STEVE LOMBARD?
FRANKLY, FOR HIM, THIS IS DOWNRIGHT CALM.
NOW, HOW ABOUT A BIG ROUND OF APPLAUSE FOR THE GAL WHO QUARTERBACKED THIS STORY...
...THE ONE AND ONLY...
DAILY PLANET
COP COUNCILMAN WORKED FOR MAFIA
...LOIS LANE!
UH... THANK YOU, STEVE.
YOUR STORY HAS GONE NATIONAL, LOIS!

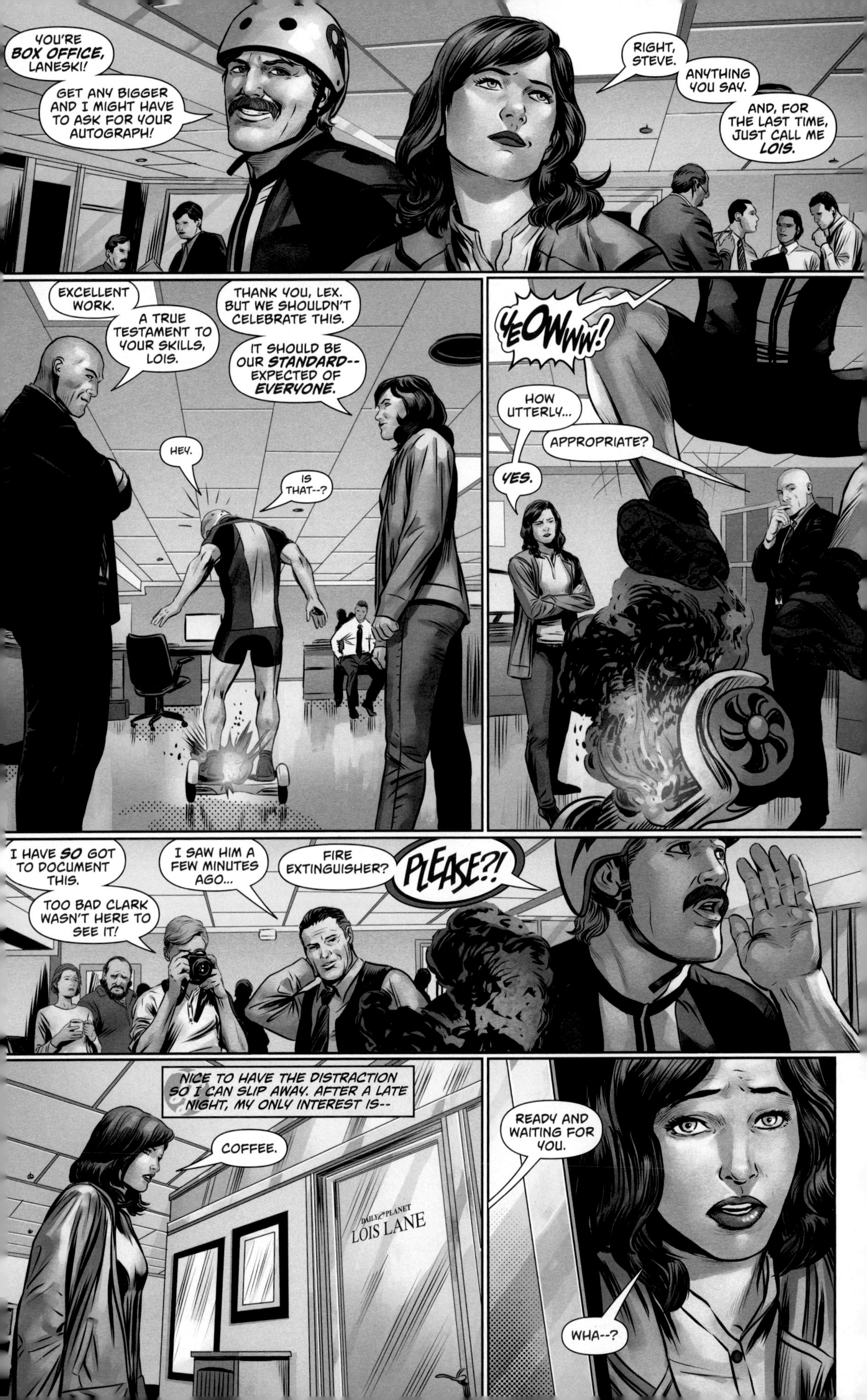

YOU'RE BOX OFFICE, LANESKI!
GET ANY BIGGER AND I MIGHT HAVE TO ASK FOR YOUR AUTOGRAPH!
RIGHT, STEVE.
ANYTHING YOU SAY.
AND, FOR THE LAST TIME, JUST CALL ME LOIS.
EXCELLENT WORK.
A TRUE TESTAMENT TO YOUR SKILLS, LOIS.
THANK YOU, LEX. BUT WE SHOULDN'T CELEBRATE THIS.
IT SHOULD BE OUR STANDARD-- EXPECTED OF EVERYONE.
HEY.
IS THAT--?
YEOWWW!
HOW UTTERLY...
APPROPRIATE?
YES.
I HAVE SO GOT TO DOCUMENT THIS.
TOO BAD CLARK WASN'T HERE TO SEE IT!
I SAW HIM A FEW MINUTES AGO...
FIRE EXTINGUISHER?
PLEASE?!
NICE TO HAVE THE DISTRACTION SO I CAN SLIP AWAY. AFTER A LATE NIGHT, MY ONLY INTEREST IS--
COFFEE.
DAILY PLANET
LOIS LANE
READY AND WAITING FOR YOU.
WHA--?

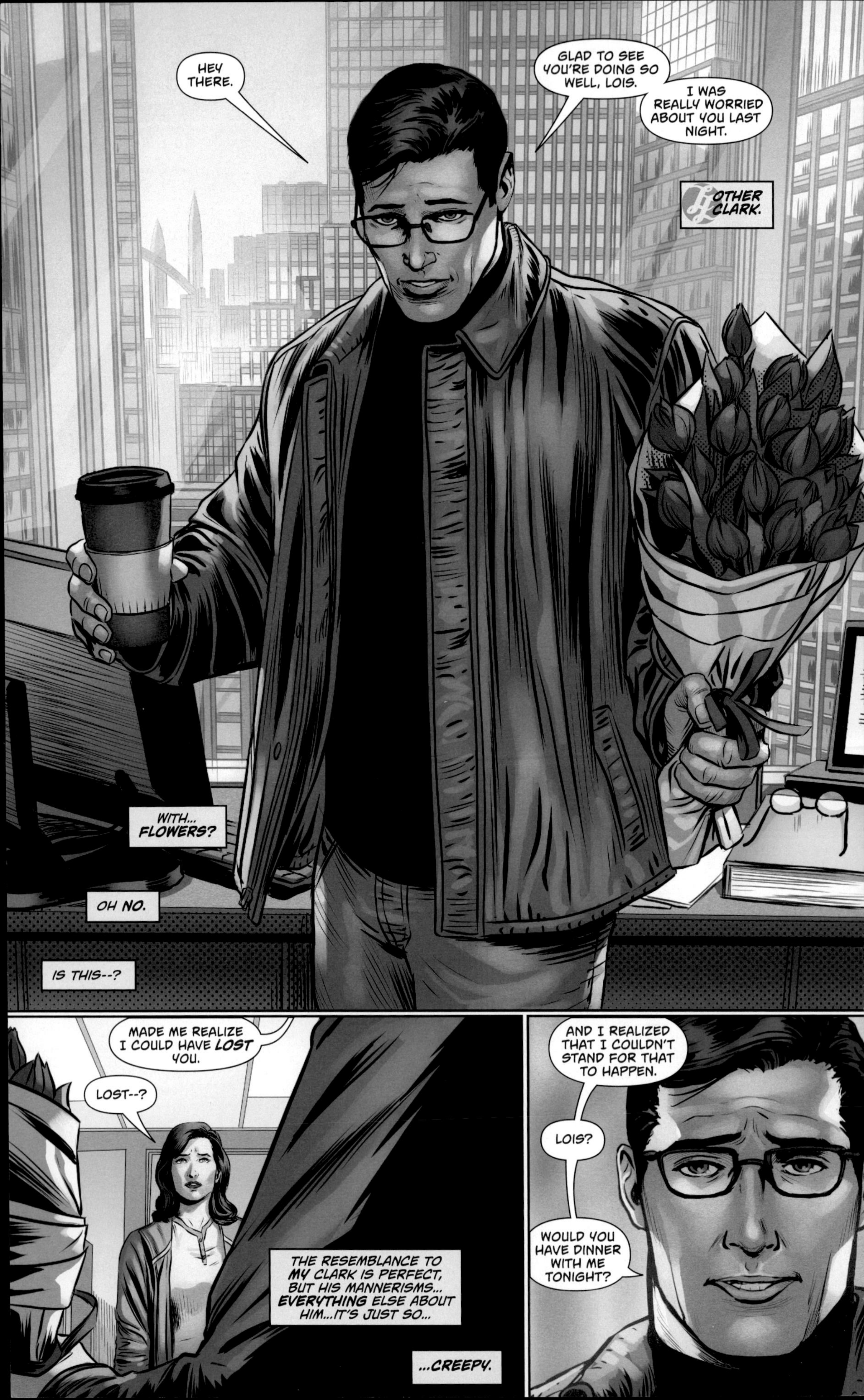
HEY THERE.
GLAD TO SEE YOU'RE DOING SO WELL, LOIS.
I WAS REALLY WORRIED ABOUT YOU LAST NIGHT.
OTHER CLARK.
WITH... FLOWERS?
OH NO.
IS THIS--?
MADE ME REALIZE I COULD HAVE LOST YOU.
LOST--?
THE RESEMBLANCE TO MY CLARK IS PERFECT, BUT HIS MANNERISMS... EVERYTHING ELSE ABOUT HIM...IT'S JUST SO...
...CREEPY.
AND I REALIZED THAT I COULDN'T STAND FOR THAT TO HAPPEN.
LOIS?
WOULD YOU HAVE DINNER WITH ME TONIGHT?

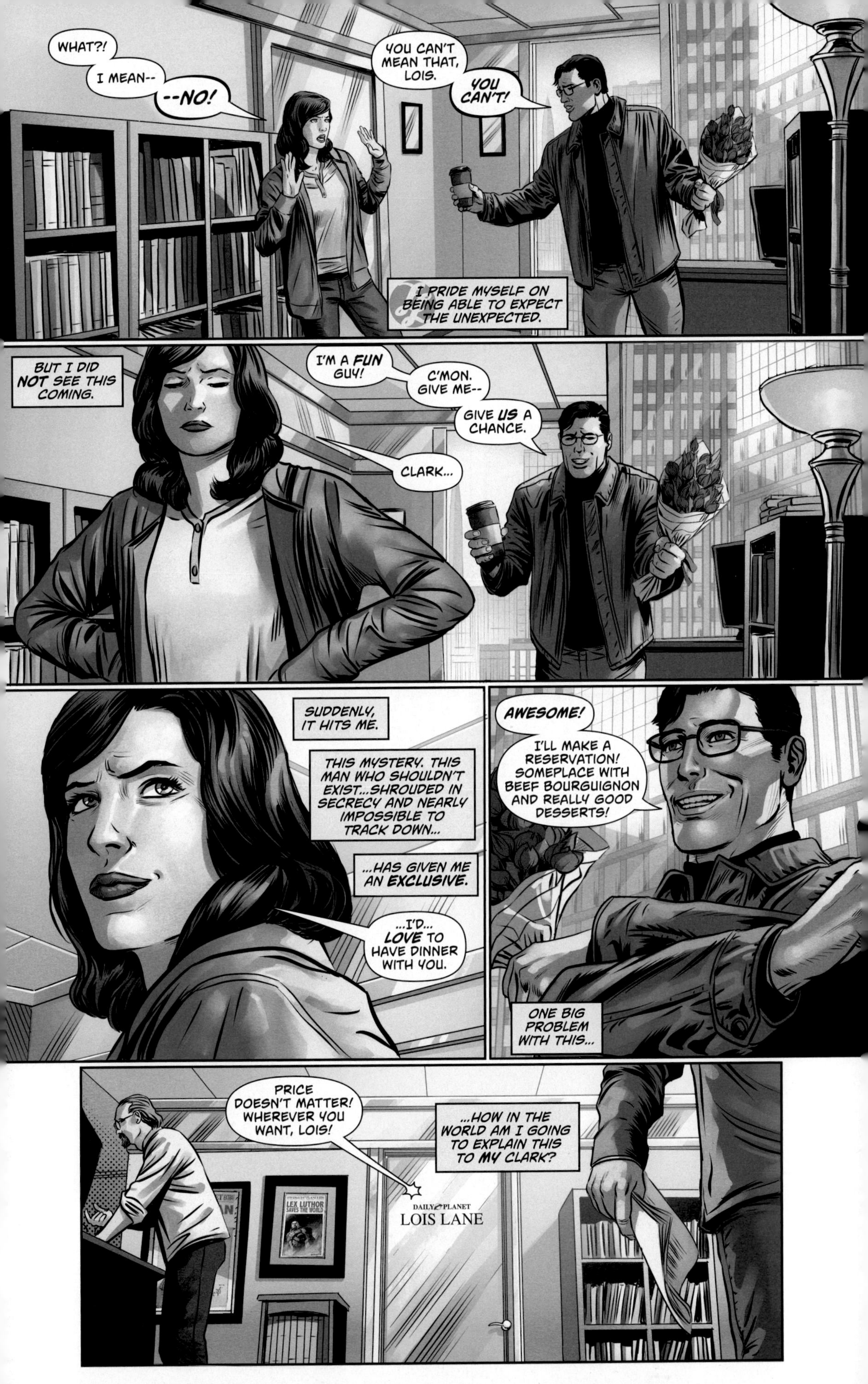
WHAT?!
I MEAN--
--NO!
YOU CAN'T MEAN THAT, LOIS.
YOU CAN'T!
I PRIDE MYSELF ON BEING ABLE TO EXPECT THE UNEXPECTED.
BUT I DID NOT SEE THIS COMING.
I'M A FUN GUY!
C'MON. GIVE ME--
GIVE US A CHANCE.
CLARK...
SUDDENLY, IT HITS ME.
THIS MYSTERY. THIS MAN WHO SHOULDN'T EXIST...SHROUDED IN SECRECY AND NEARLY IMPOSSIBLE TO TRACK DOWN...
...HAS GIVEN ME AN EXCLUSIVE.
...I'D... LOVE TO HAVE DINNER WITH YOU.
AWESOME!
I'LL MAKE A RESERVATION! SOMEPLACE WITH BEEF BOURGUIGNON AND REALLY GOOD DESSERTS!
ONE BIG PROBLEM WITH THIS...
PRICE DOESN'T MATTER! WHEREVER YOU WANT, LOIS!
...HOW IN THE WORLD AM I GOING TO EXPLAIN THIS TO MY CLARK?
LEX LUTHOR SAVES THE WORLD
DAILY PLANET
LOIS LANE

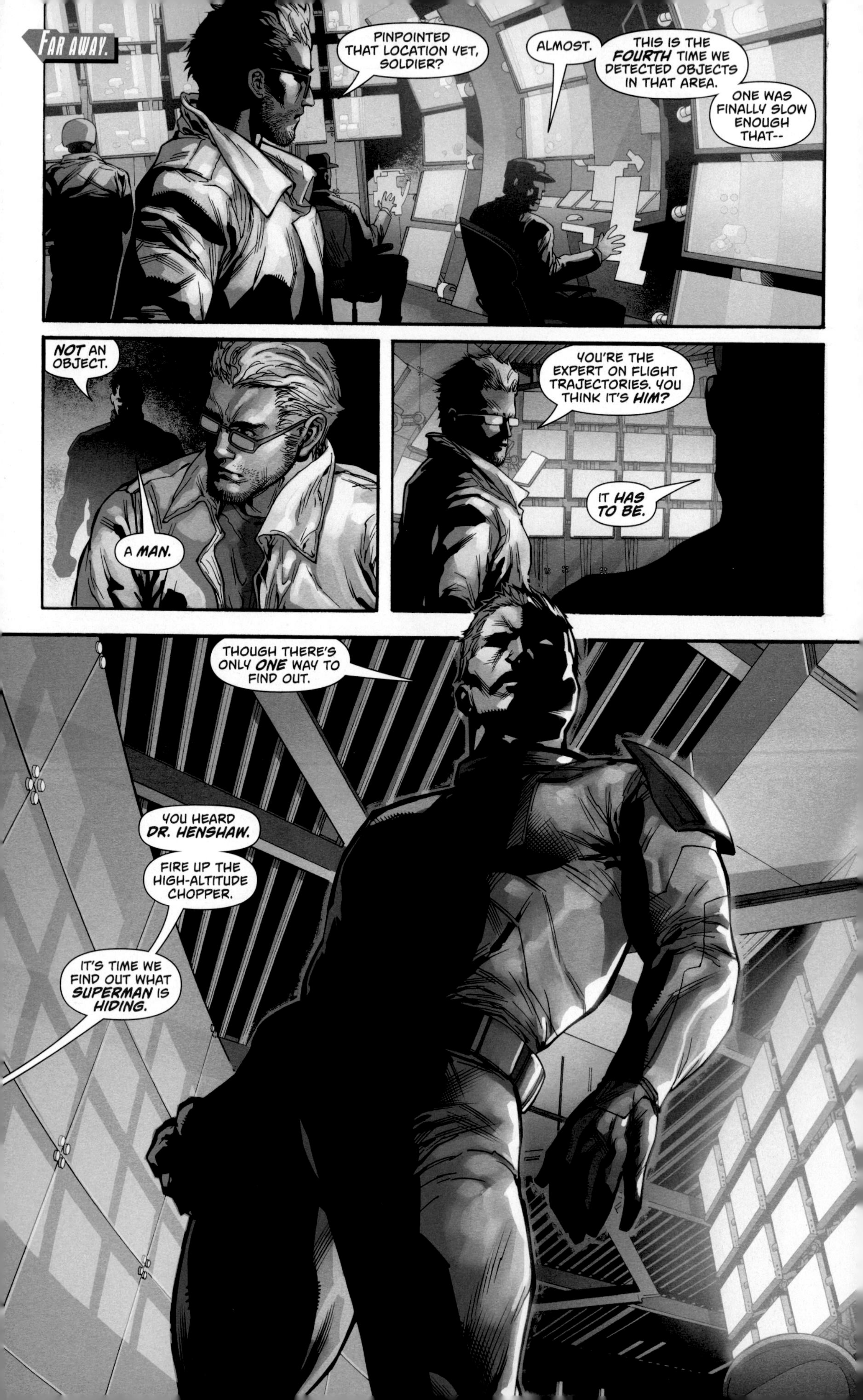
FAR AWAY.
PINPOINTED THAT LOCATION YET, SOLDIER?
ALMOST.
THIS IS THE FOURTH TIME WE DETECTED OBJECTS IN THAT AREA.
ONE WAS FINALLY SLOW ENOUGH THAT--
NOT AN OBJECT.
A MAN.
YOU'RE THE EXPERT ON FLIGHT TRAJECTORIES. YOU THINK IT'S HIM?
IT HAS TO BE.
THOUGH THERE'S ONLY ONE WAY TO FIND OUT.
YOU HEARD DR. HENSHAW.
FIRE UP THE HIGH-ALTITUDE CHOPPER.
IT'S TIME WE FIND OUT WHAT SUPERMAN IS HIDING.

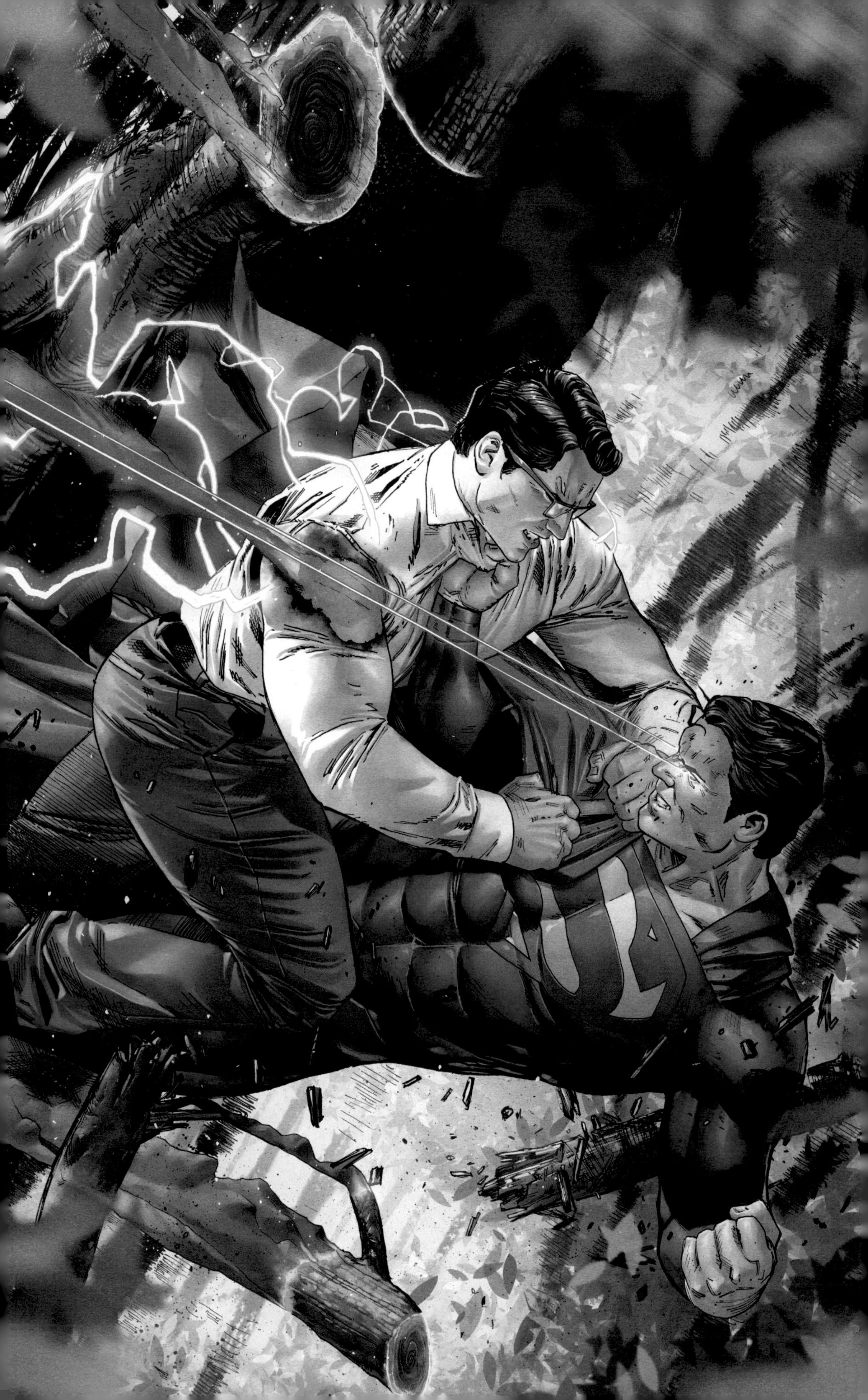

MILD MANNERED part two

DAN JURGENS writer * PATCH ZIRCHER & STEPHEN SEGOVIA pencillers
PATCH ZIRCHER & ART THIBERT inkers * ULISES ARREOLA colorist
CLAY MANN & TOMEU MOREY cover art

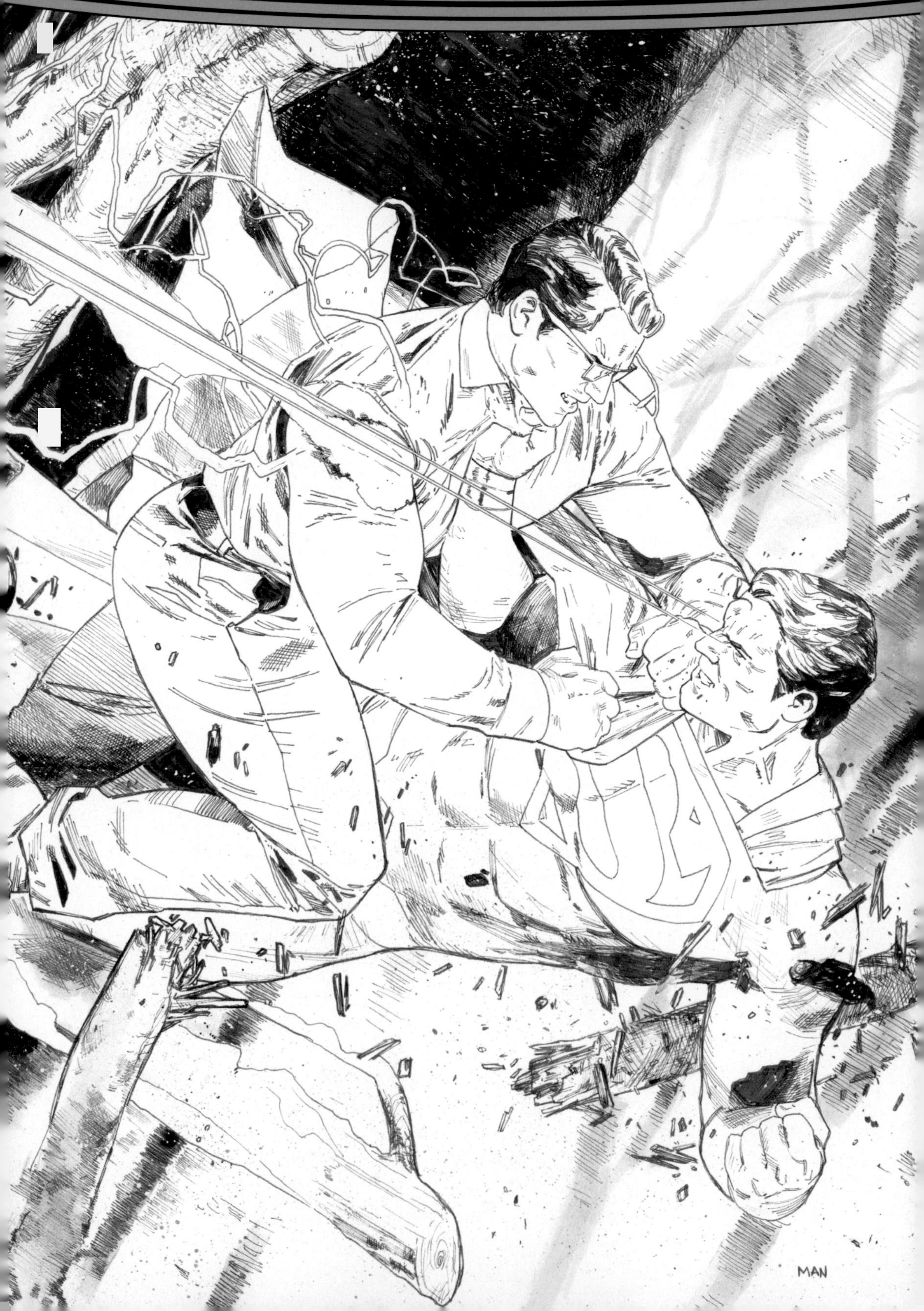
MAN

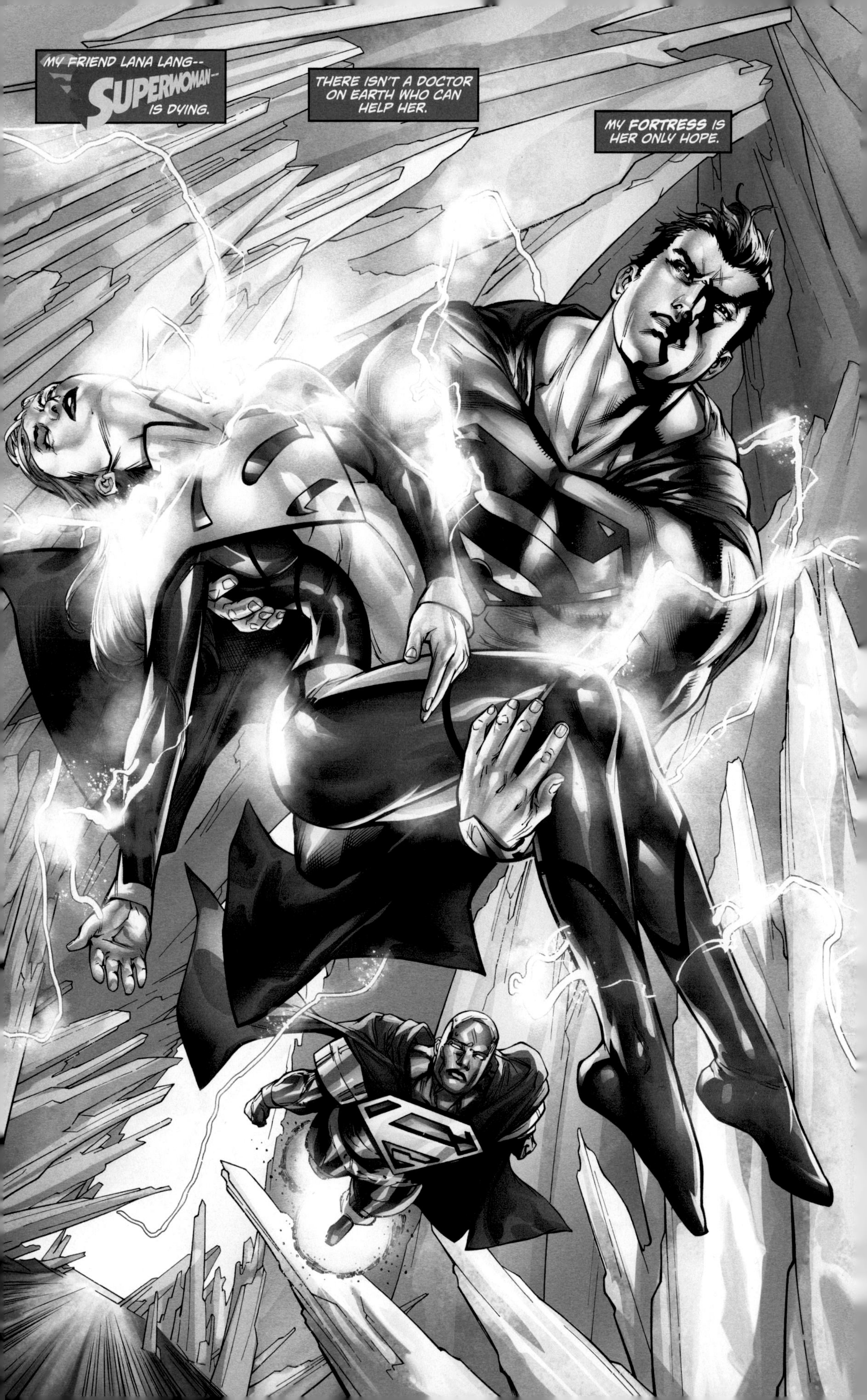
MY FRIEND LANA LANG-- SUPERWOMAN-- IS DYING.
THERE ISN'T A DOCTOR ON EARTH WHO CAN HELP HER.
MY FORTRESS IS HER ONLY HOPE.

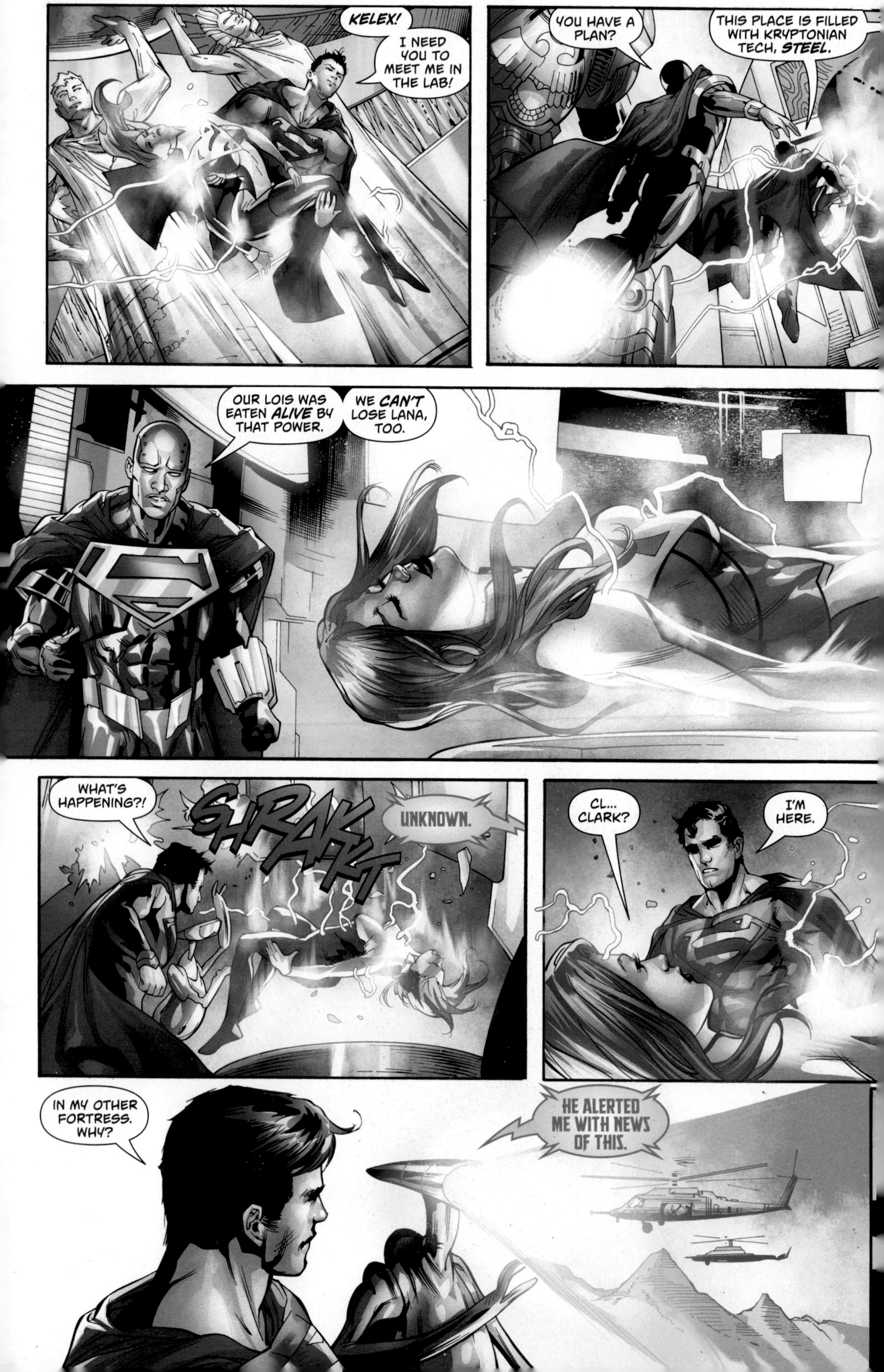
KELEX!
I NEED YOU TO MEET ME IN THE LAB!
YOU HAVE A PLAN?
THIS PLACE IS FILLED WITH KRYPTONIAN TECH, STEEL.
OUR LOIS WAS EATEN ALIVE BY THAT POWER.
WE CAN'T LOSE LANA, TOO.
WHAT'S HAPPENING?!
SHRAKAKT
UNKNOWN.
CL... CLARK?
I'M HERE.
IN MY OTHER FORTRESS. WHY?
HE ALERTED ME WITH NEWS OF THIS.

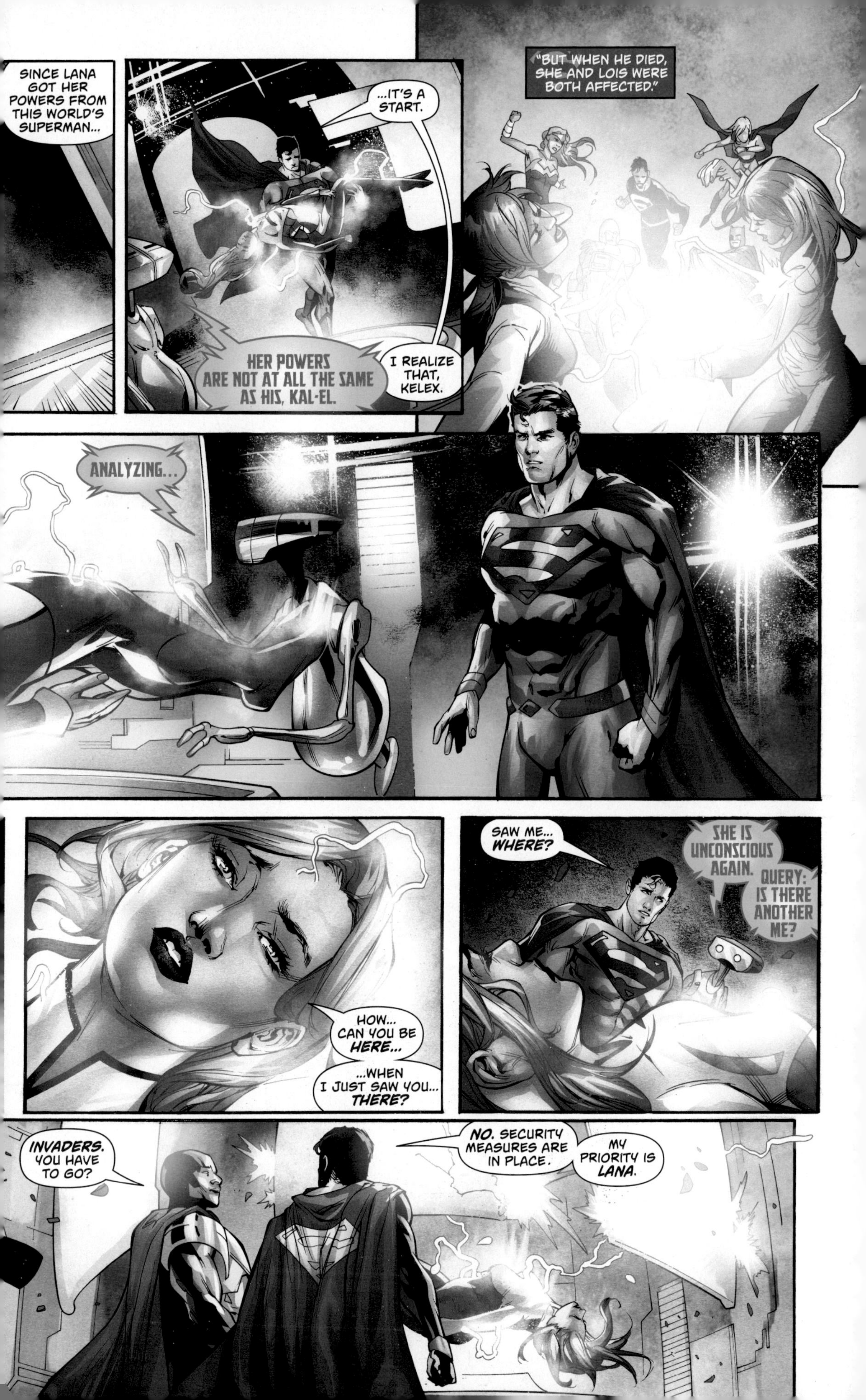

SINCE LANA GOT HER POWERS FROM THIS WORLD'S SUPERMAN...
...IT'S A START.
HER POWERS ARE NOT AT ALL THE SAME AS HIS, KAL-EL.
I REALIZE THAT, KELEX.
"BUT WHEN HE DIED, SHE AND LOIS WERE BOTH AFFECTED."
ANALYZING...
HOW... CAN YOU BE HERE...
...WHEN I JUST SAW YOU... THERE?
SAW ME... WHERE?
SHE IS UNCONSCIOUS AGAIN.
QUERY: IS THERE ANOTHER ME?
INVADERS. YOU HAVE TO GO?
NO. SECURITY MEASURES ARE IN PLACE.
MY PRIORITY IS LANA.

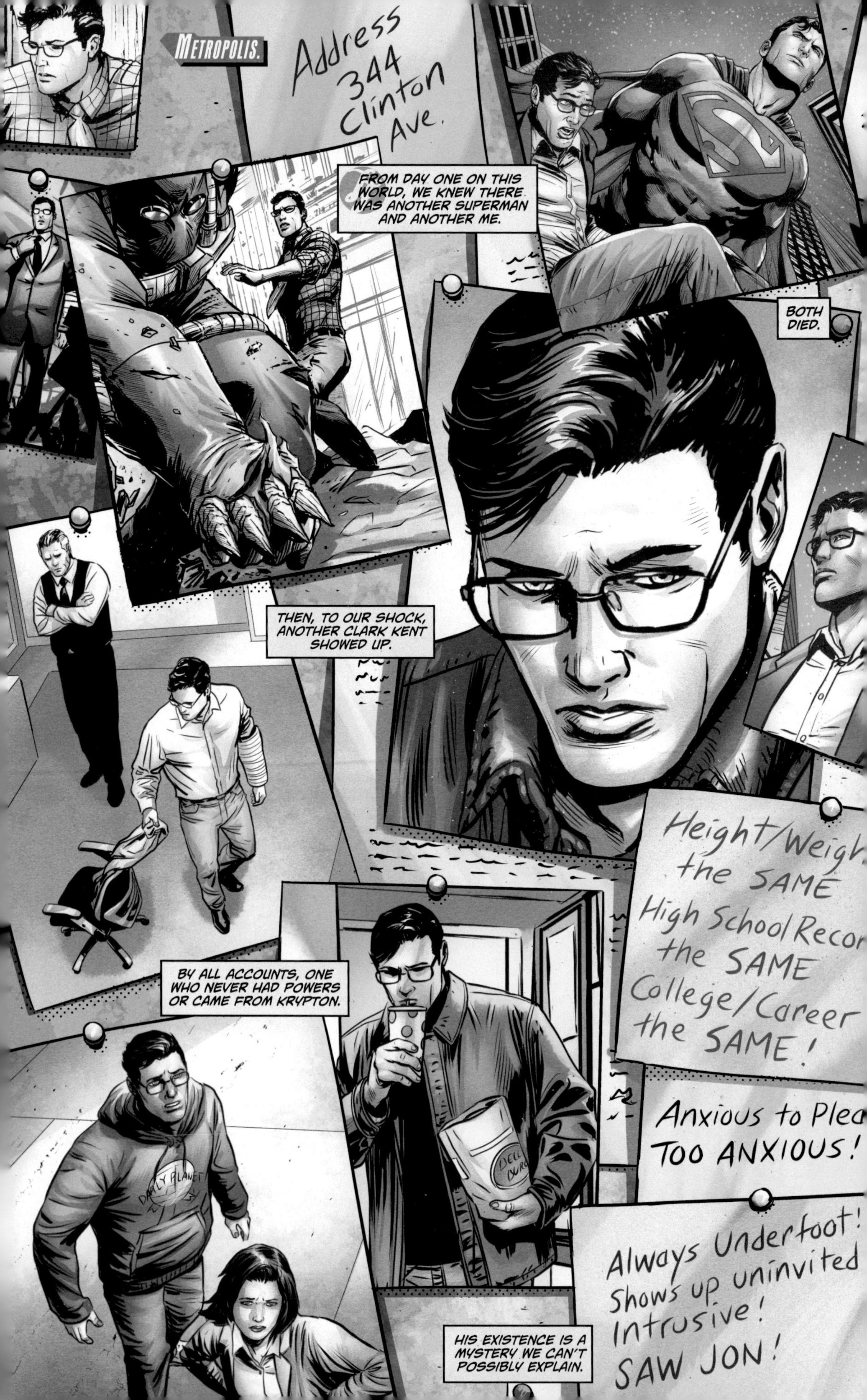
METROPOLIS.
Address 344 Clinton Ave.
FROM DAY ONE ON THIS WORLD, WE KNEW THERE WAS ANOTHER SUPERMAN AND ANOTHER ME.
BOTH DIED.
THEN, TO OUR SHOCK, ANOTHER CLARK KENT SHOWED UP.
Height/Weigh the SAME
High School Recor the SAME
College/Career the SAME!
BY ALL ACCOUNTS, ONE WHO NEVER HAD POWERS OR CAME FROM KRYPTON.
Anxious to Plea
TOO ANXIOUS!
Always Underfoot!
Shows up uninvited
Intrusive!
SAW JON!
HIS EXISTENCE IS A MYSTERY WE CAN'T POSSIBLY EXPLAIN.

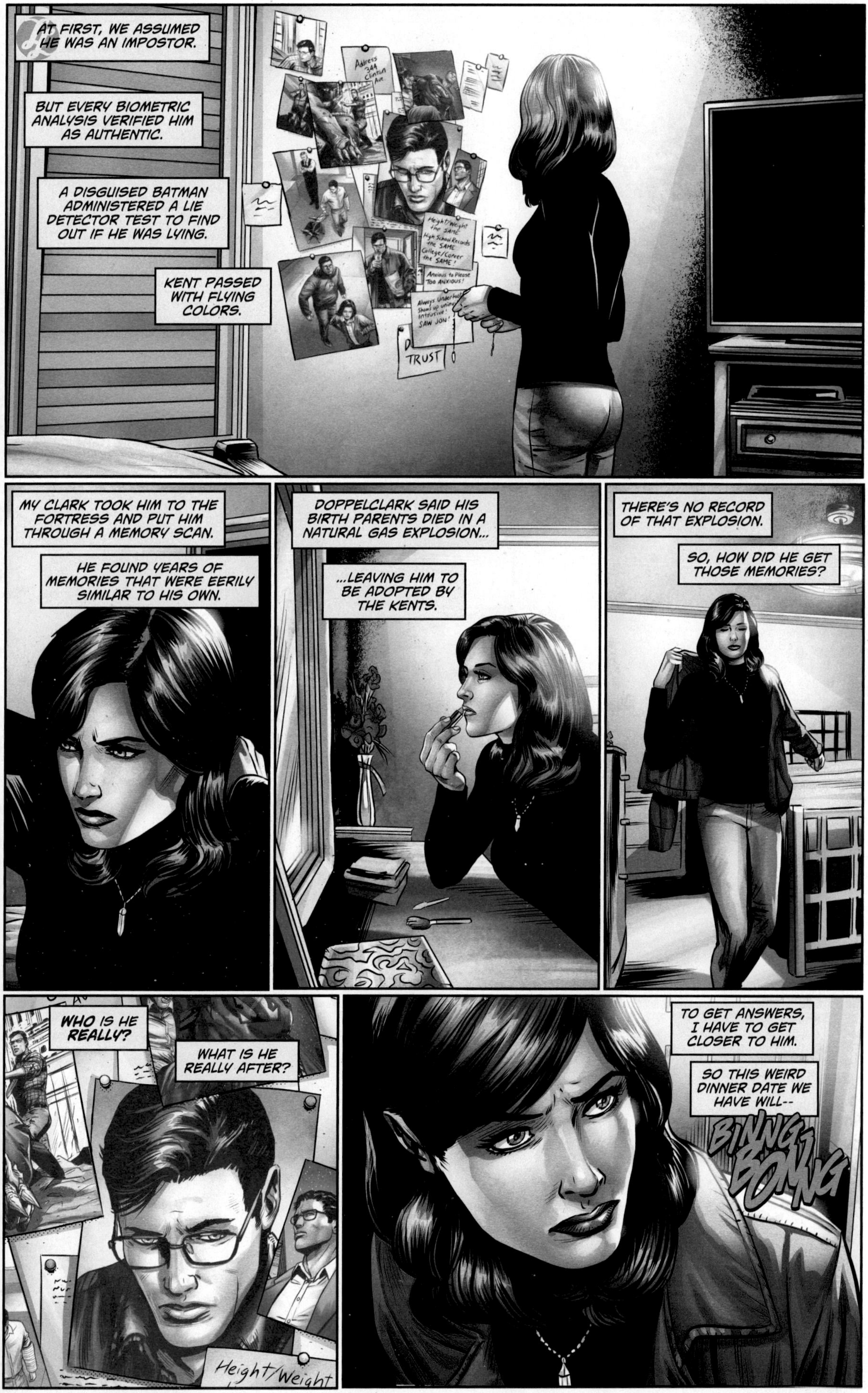

AT FIRST, WE ASSUMED HE WAS AN IMPOSTOR.
BUT EVERY BIOMETRIC ANALYSIS VERIFIED HIM AS AUTHENTIC.
A DISGUISED BATMAN ADMINISTERED A LIE DETECTOR TEST TO FIND OUT IF HE WAS LYING.
KENT PASSED WITH FLYING COLORS.
Address 344 Clinton Ave
Height/Weight the SAME
High School Records the SAME
College/Career the SAME!
Anxious to Please Too ANXIOUS!
SAW JON!
TRUST
MY CLARK TOOK HIM TO THE FORTRESS AND PUT HIM THROUGH A MEMORY SCAN.
HE FOUND YEARS OF MEMORIES THAT WERE EERILY SIMILAR TO HIS OWN.
DOPPELCLARK SAID HIS BIRTH PARENTS DIED IN A NATURAL GAS EXPLOSION...
...LEAVING HIM TO BE ADOPTED BY THE KENTS.
THERE'S NO RECORD OF THAT EXPLOSION.
SO, HOW DID HE GET THOSE MEMORIES?
WHO IS HE REALLY?
WHAT IS HE REALLY AFTER?
Height/Weight
TO GET ANSWERS, I HAVE TO GET CLOSER TO HIM.
SO THIS WEIRD DINNER DATE WE HAVE WILL--
BING BONG

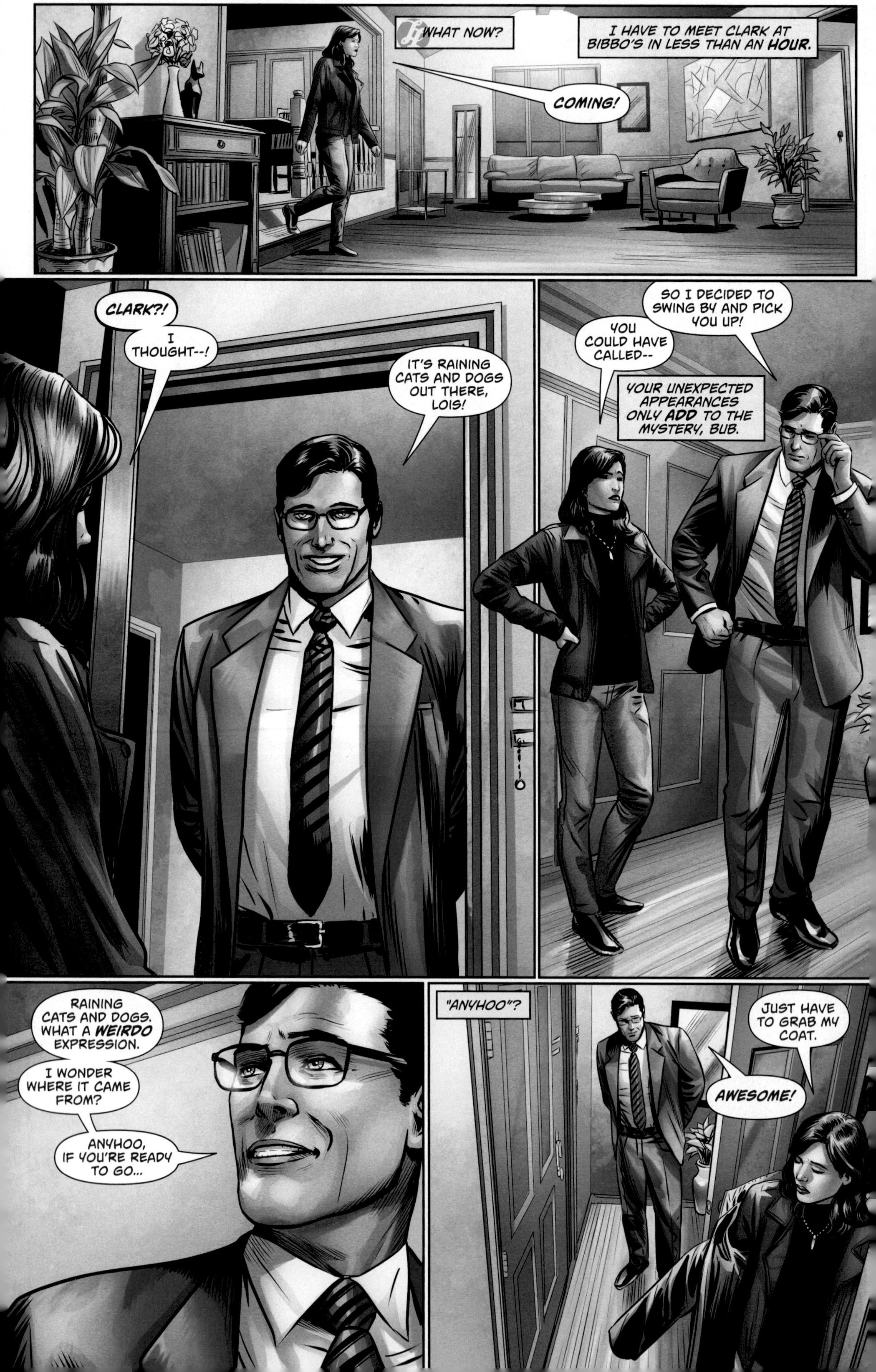
WHAT NOW?
I HAVE TO MEET CLARK AT BIBBO'S IN LESS THAN AN HOUR.
COMING!
CLARK?!
I THOUGHT--!
IT'S RAINING CATS AND DOGS OUT THERE, LOIS!
SO I DECIDED TO SWING BY AND PICK YOU UP!
YOU COULD HAVE CALLED--
YOUR UNEXPECTED APPEARANCES ONLY ADD TO THE MYSTERY, BUB.
RAINING CATS AND DOGS. WHAT A WEIRDO EXPRESSION.
I WONDER WHERE IT CAME FROM?
ANYHOO, IF YOU'RE READY TO GO...
"ANYHOO"?
JUST HAVE TO GRAB MY COAT.
AWESOME!

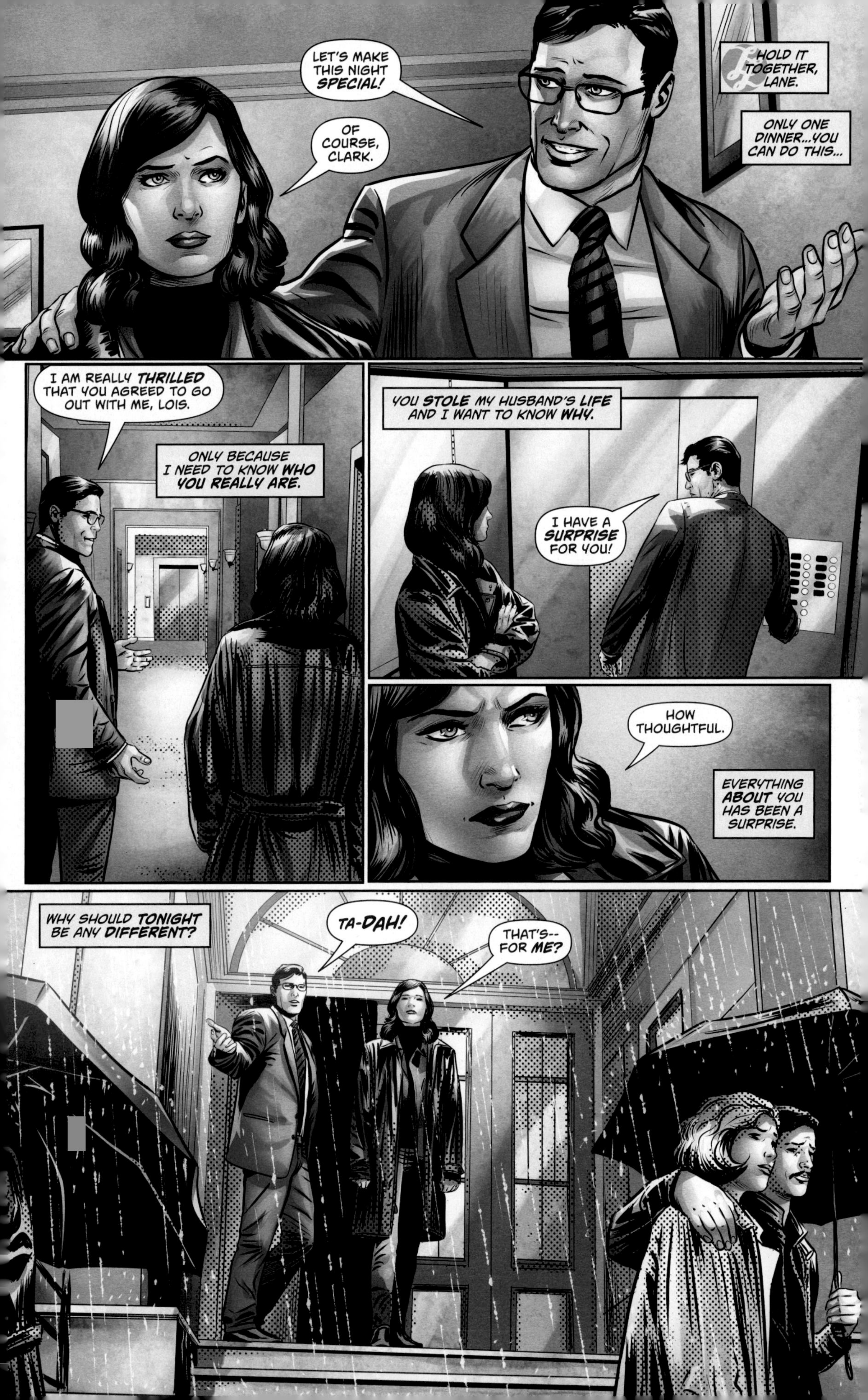
LET'S MAKE THIS NIGHT SPECIAL!
OF COURSE, CLARK.
HOLD IT TOGETHER, LANE.
ONLY ONE DINNER...YOU CAN DO THIS...
I AM REALLY THRILLED THAT YOU AGREED TO GO OUT WITH ME, LOIS.
ONLY BECAUSE I NEED TO KNOW WHO YOU REALLY ARE.
YOU STOLE MY HUSBAND'S LIFE AND I WANT TO KNOW WHY.
I HAVE A SURPRISE FOR YOU!
HOW THOUGHTFUL.
EVERYTHING ABOUT YOU HAS BEEN A SURPRISE.
WHY SHOULD TONIGHT BE ANY DIFFERENT?
TA-DAH!
THAT'S-- FOR ME?

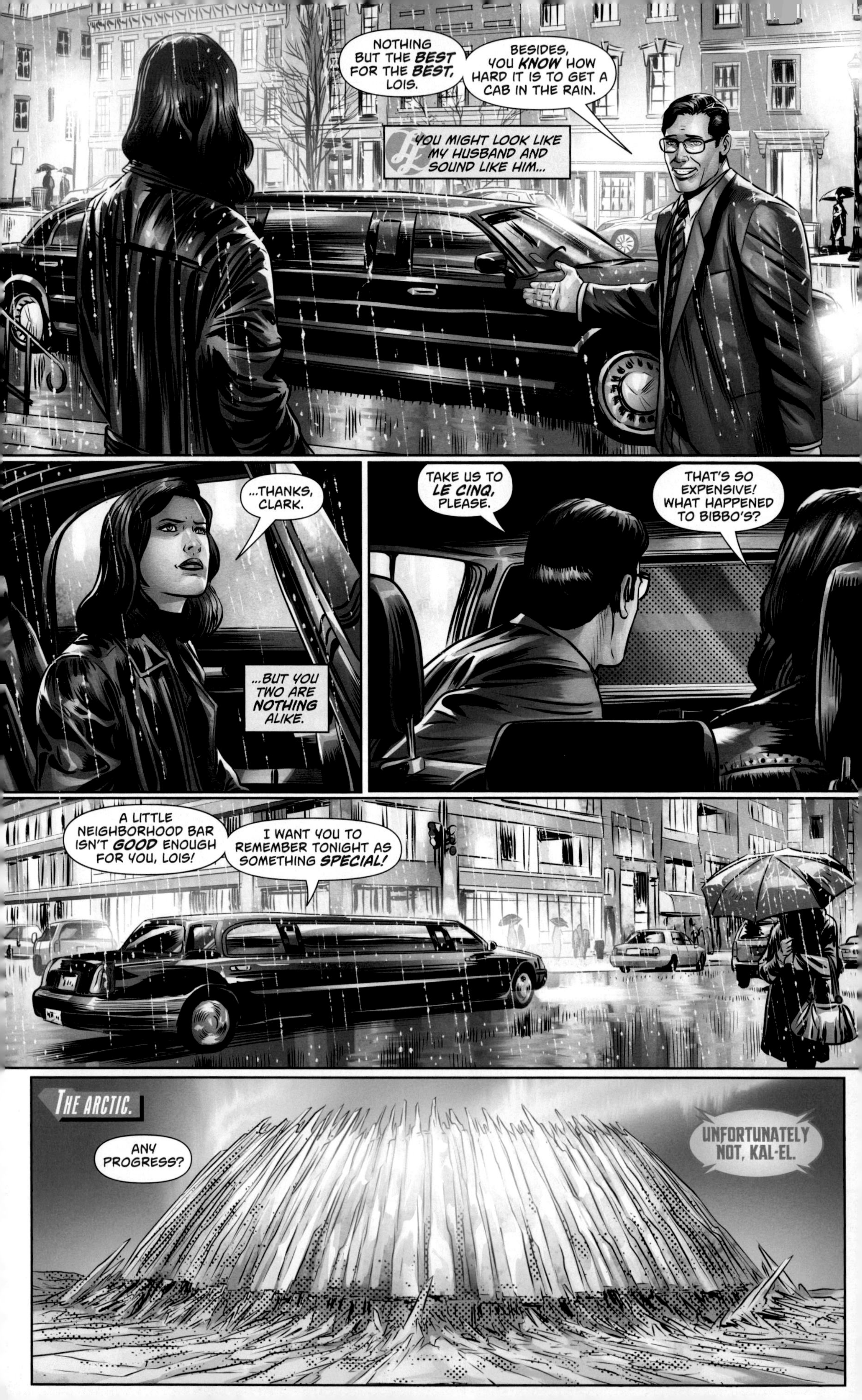
NOTHING BUT THE BEST FOR THE BEST, LOIS.
BESIDES, YOU KNOW HOW HARD IT IS TO GET A CAB IN THE RAIN.
YOU MIGHT LOOK LIKE MY HUSBAND AND SOUND LIKE HIM...
...THANKS, CLARK.
...BUT YOU TWO ARE NOTHING ALIKE.
TAKE US TO LE CINQ, PLEASE.
THAT'S SO EXPENSIVE! WHAT HAPPENED TO BIBBO'S?
A LITTLE NEIGHBORHOOD BAR ISN'T GOOD ENOUGH FOR YOU, LOIS!
I WANT YOU TO REMEMBER TONIGHT AS SOMETHING SPECIAL!
THE ARCTIC.
ANY PROGRESS?
UNFORTUNATELY NOT, KAL-EL.

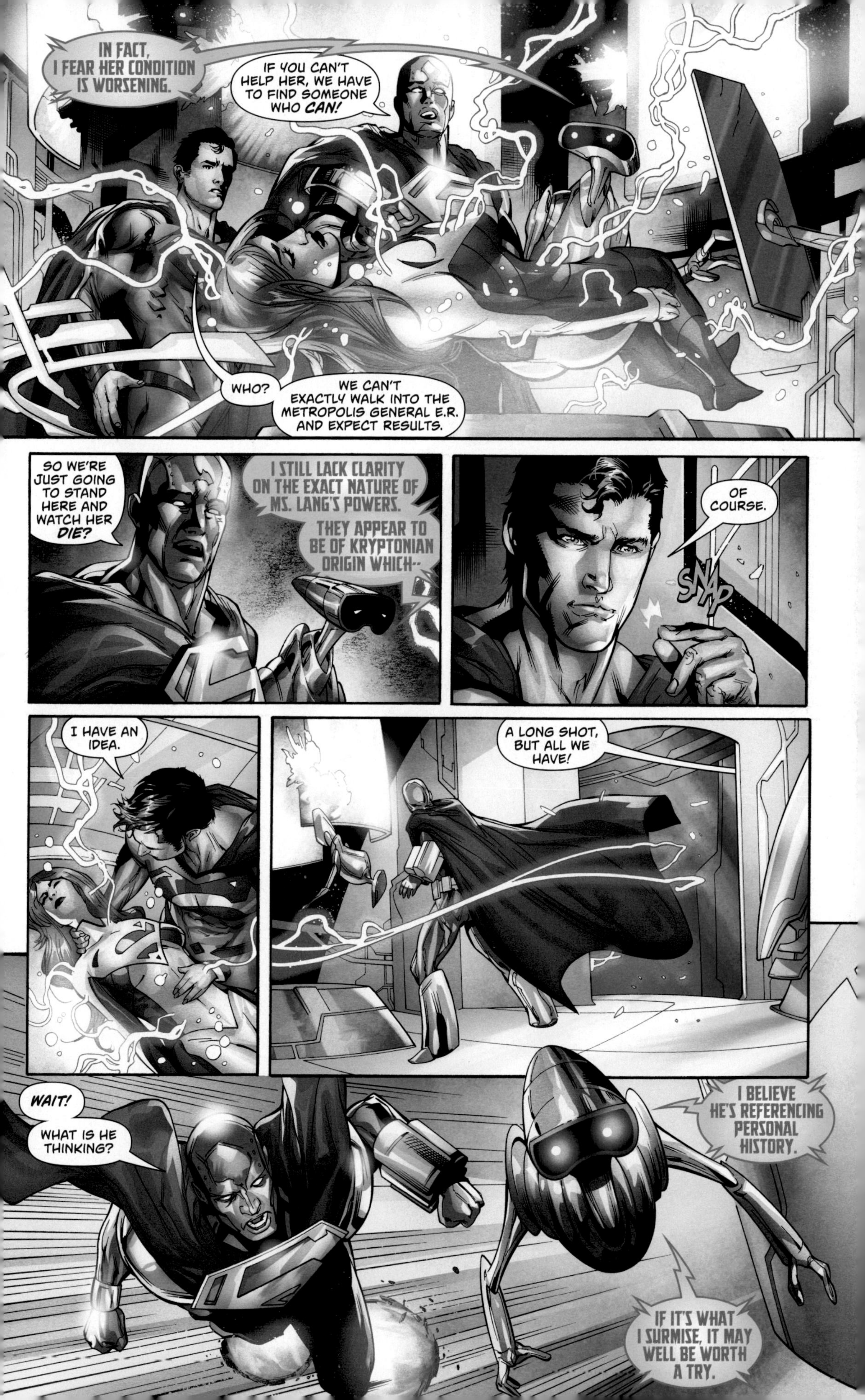
IN FACT, I FEAR HER CONDITION IS WORSENING.
IF YOU CAN'T HELP HER, WE HAVE TO FIND SOMEONE WHO CAN!
WHO?
WE CAN'T EXACTLY WALK INTO THE METROPOLIS GENERAL E.R. AND EXPECT RESULTS.
SO WE'RE JUST GOING TO STAND HERE AND WATCH HER DIE?
I STILL LACK CLARITY ON THE EXACT NATURE OF MS. LANG'S POWERS.
THEY APPEAR TO BE OF KRYPTONIAN ORIGIN WHICH--
OF COURSE.
SNAP
I HAVE AN IDEA.
A LONG SHOT, BUT ALL WE HAVE!
WAIT!
WHAT IS HE THINKING?
I BELIEVE HE'S REFERENCING PERSONAL HISTORY.
IF IT'S WHAT I SURMISE, IT MAY WELL BE WORTH A TRY.

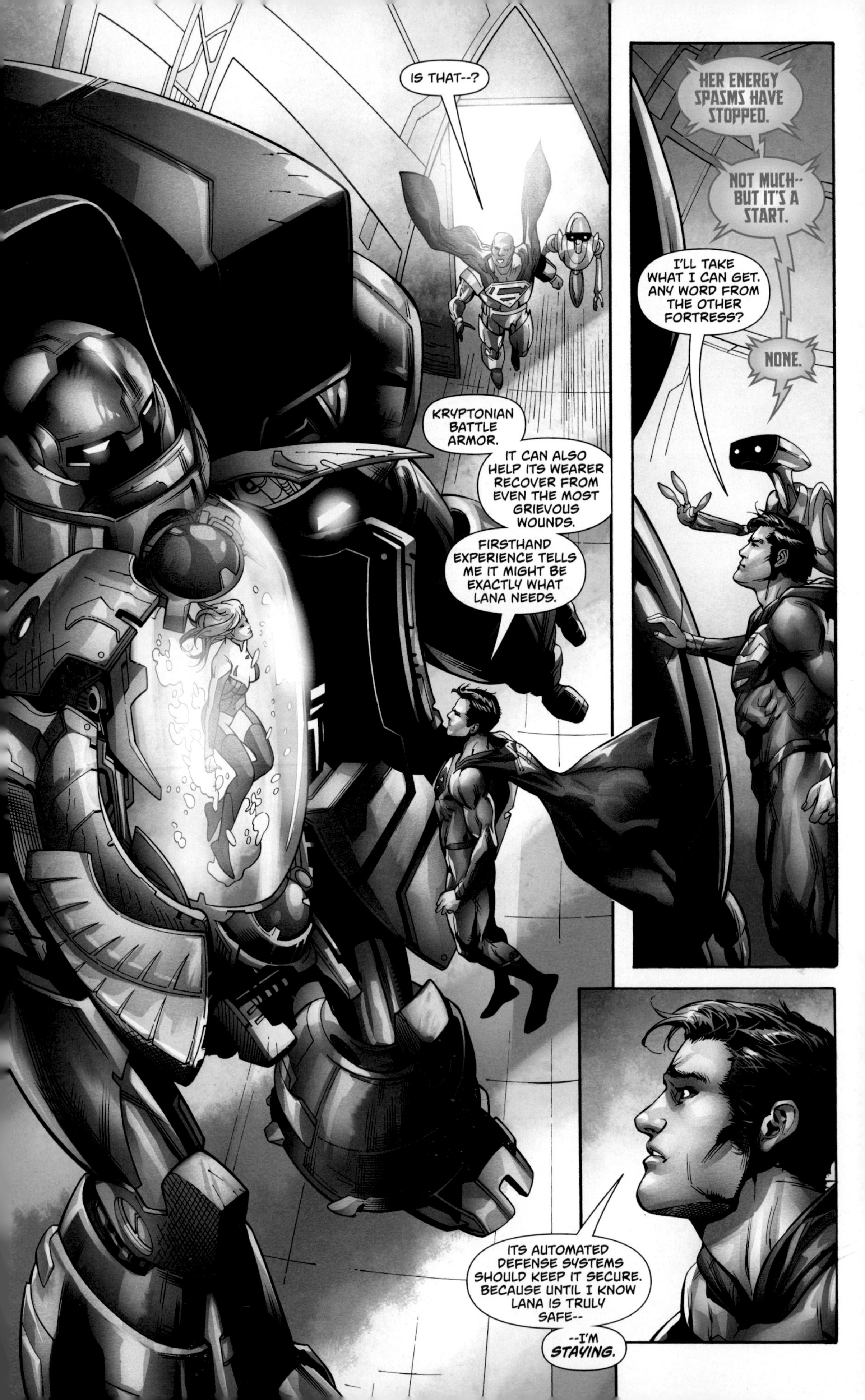
IS THAT--?
KRYPTONIAN BATTLE ARMOR.
IT CAN ALSO HELP ITS WEARER RECOVER FROM EVEN THE MOST GRIEVOUS WOUNDS.
FIRSTHAND EXPERIENCE TELLS ME IT MIGHT BE EXACTLY WHAT LANA NEEDS.
HER ENERGY SPASMS HAVE STOPPED.
NOT MUCH-- BUT IT'S A START.
I'LL TAKE WHAT I CAN GET. ANY WORD FROM THE OTHER FORTRESS?
NONE.
ITS AUTOMATED DEFENSE SYSTEMS SHOULD KEEP IT SECURE. BECAUSE UNTIL I KNOW LANA IS TRULY SAFE--
--I'M *STAYING*.

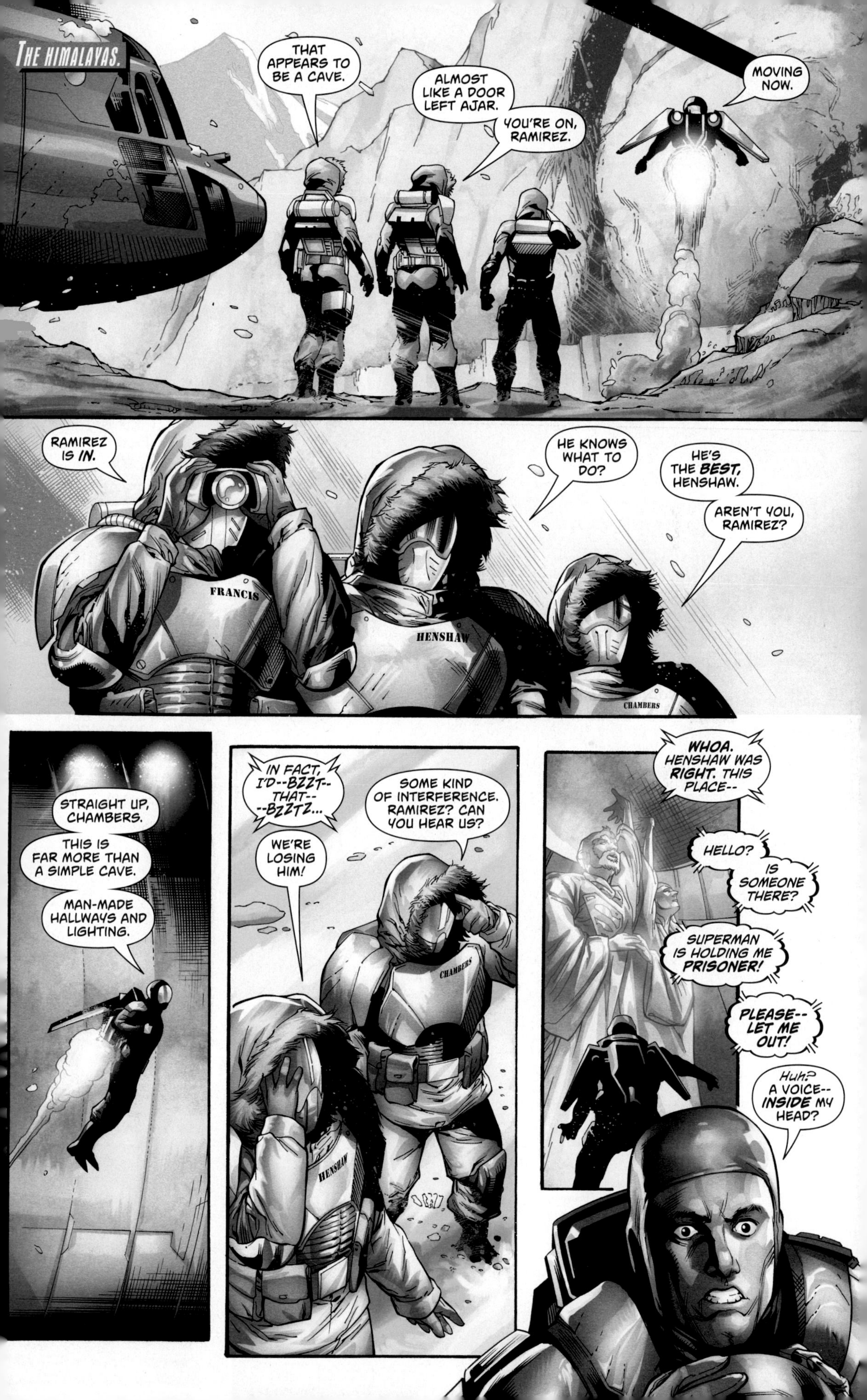
THE HIMALAYAS.
THAT APPEARS TO BE A CAVE.
ALMOST LIKE A DOOR LEFT AJAR.
YOU'RE ON, RAMIREZ.
MOVING NOW.
RAMIREZ IS IN.
HE KNOWS WHAT TO DO?
HE'S THE BEST, HENSHAW.
AREN'T YOU, RAMIREZ?
FRANCIS
HENSHAW
CHAMBERS
STRAIGHT UP, CHAMBERS.
THIS IS FAR MORE THAN A SIMPLE CAVE.
MAN-MADE HALLWAYS AND LIGHTING.
IN FACT, I'D--BZZT--THAT----BZZTZ...
WE'RE LOSING HIM!
SOME KIND OF INTERFERENCE. RAMIREZ? CAN YOU HEAR US?
CHAMBERS
HENSHAW
WHOA. HENSHAW WAS RIGHT. THIS PLACE--
HELLO?
IS SOMEONE THERE?
SUPERMAN IS HOLDING ME PRISONER!
PLEASE--LET ME OUT!
Huh? A VOICE--INSIDE MY HEAD?

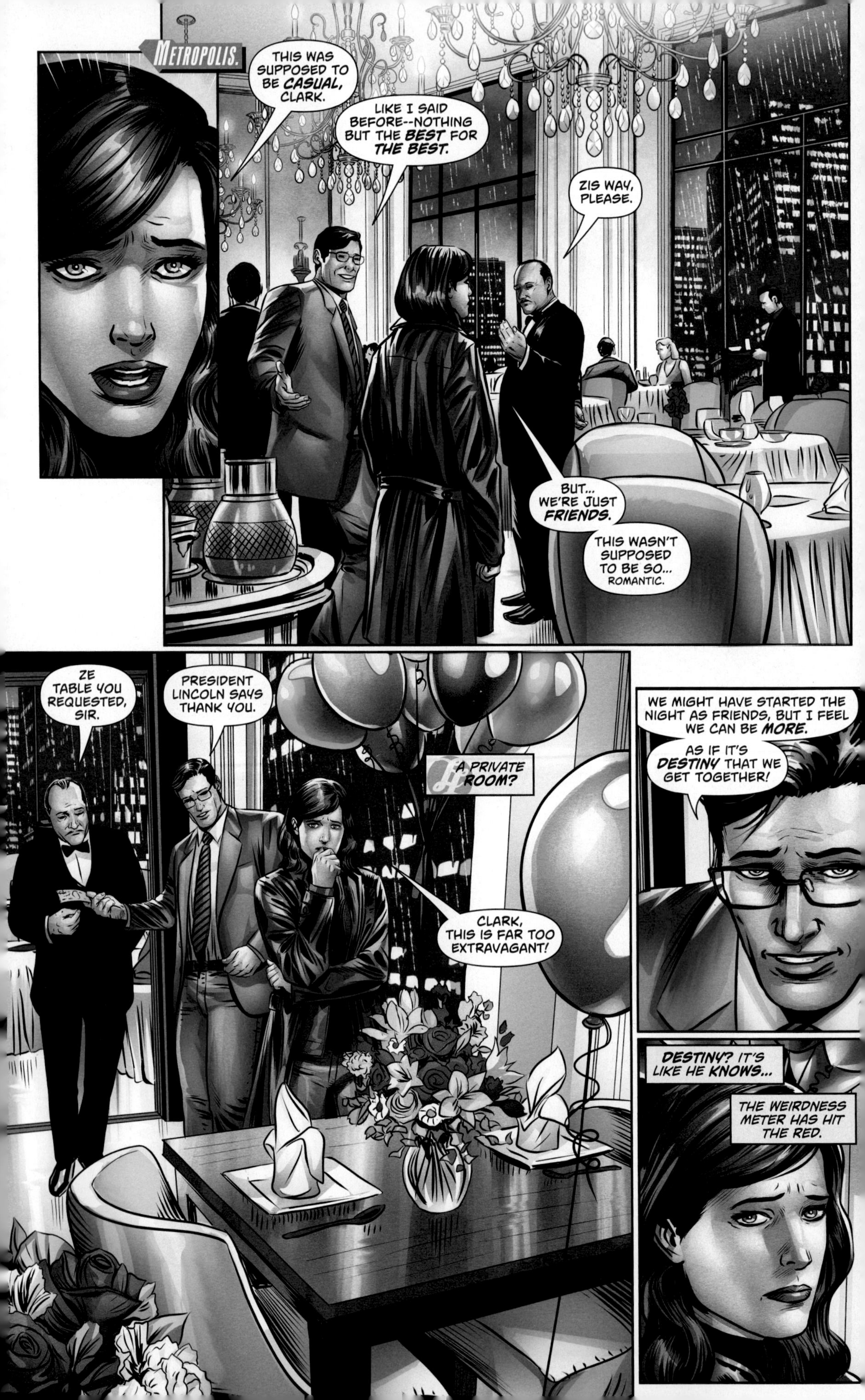
METROPOLIS.
THIS WAS SUPPOSED TO BE CASUAL, CLARK.
LIKE I SAID BEFORE--NOTHING BUT THE BEST FOR THE BEST.
ZIS WAY, PLEASE.
BUT... WE'RE JUST FRIENDS.
THIS WASN'T SUPPOSED TO BE SO... ROMANTIC.
ZE TABLE YOU REQUESTED, SIR.
PRESIDENT LINCOLN SAYS THANK YOU.
A PRIVATE ROOM?
CLARK, THIS IS FAR TOO EXTRAVAGANT!
WE MIGHT HAVE STARTED THE NIGHT AS FRIENDS, BUT I FEEL WE CAN BE MORE.
AS IF IT'S DESTINY THAT WE GET TOGETHER!
DESTINY? IT'S LIKE HE KNOWS...
THE WEIRDNESS METER HAS HIT THE RED.

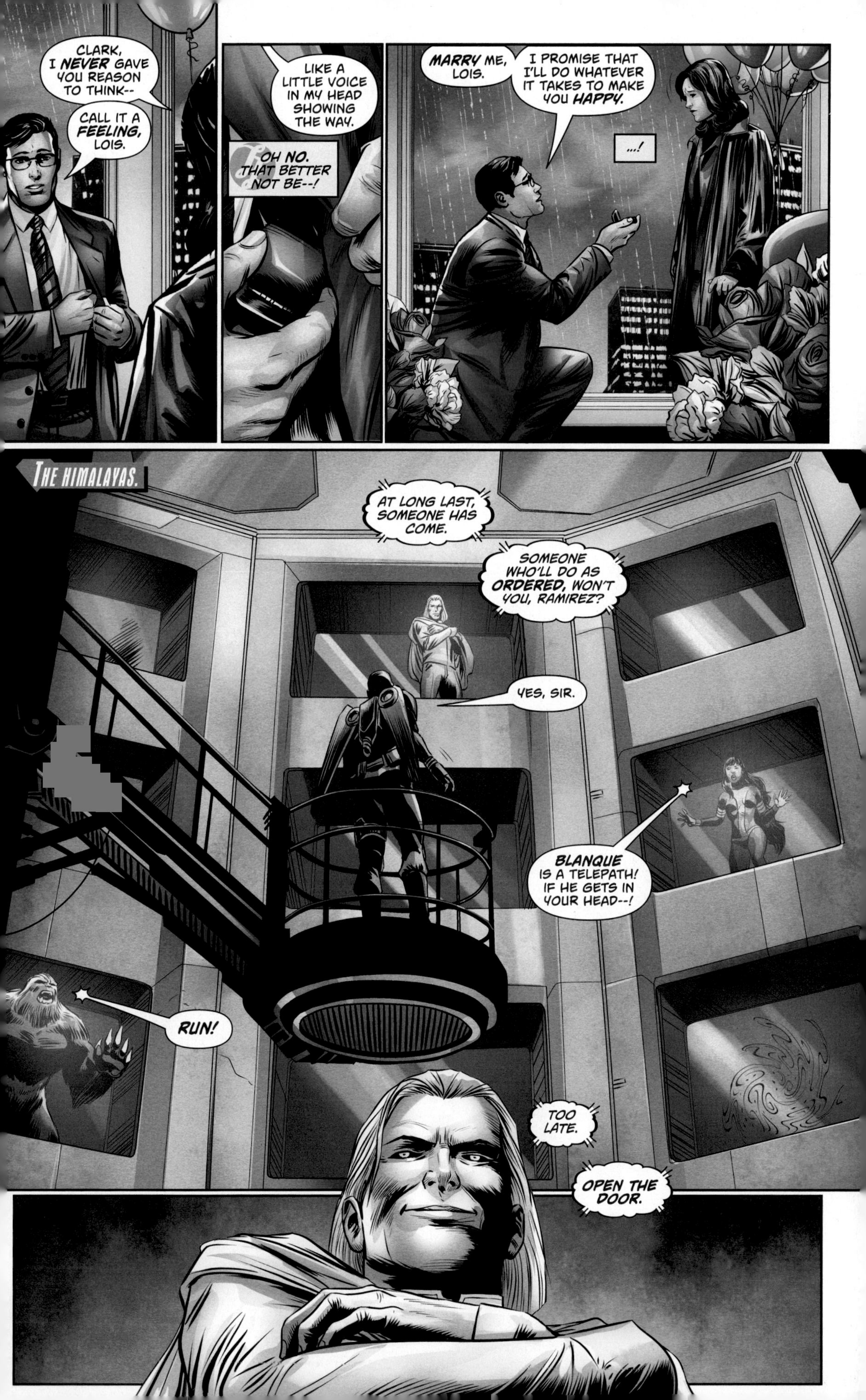
CLARK, I NEVER GAVE YOU REASON TO THINK--
CALL IT A FEELING, LOIS.
LIKE A LITTLE VOICE IN MY HEAD SHOWING THE WAY.
OH NO. THAT BETTER NOT BE--!
MARRY ME, LOIS.
I PROMISE THAT I'LL DO WHATEVER IT TAKES TO MAKE YOU HAPPY.
...!
THE HIMALAYAS.
AT LONG LAST, SOMEONE HAS COME.
SOMEONE WHO'LL DO AS ORDERED, WON'T YOU, RAMIREZ?
YES, SIR.
BLANQUE IS A TELEPATH! IF HE GETS IN YOUR HEAD--!
RUN!
TOO LATE.
OPEN THE DOOR.

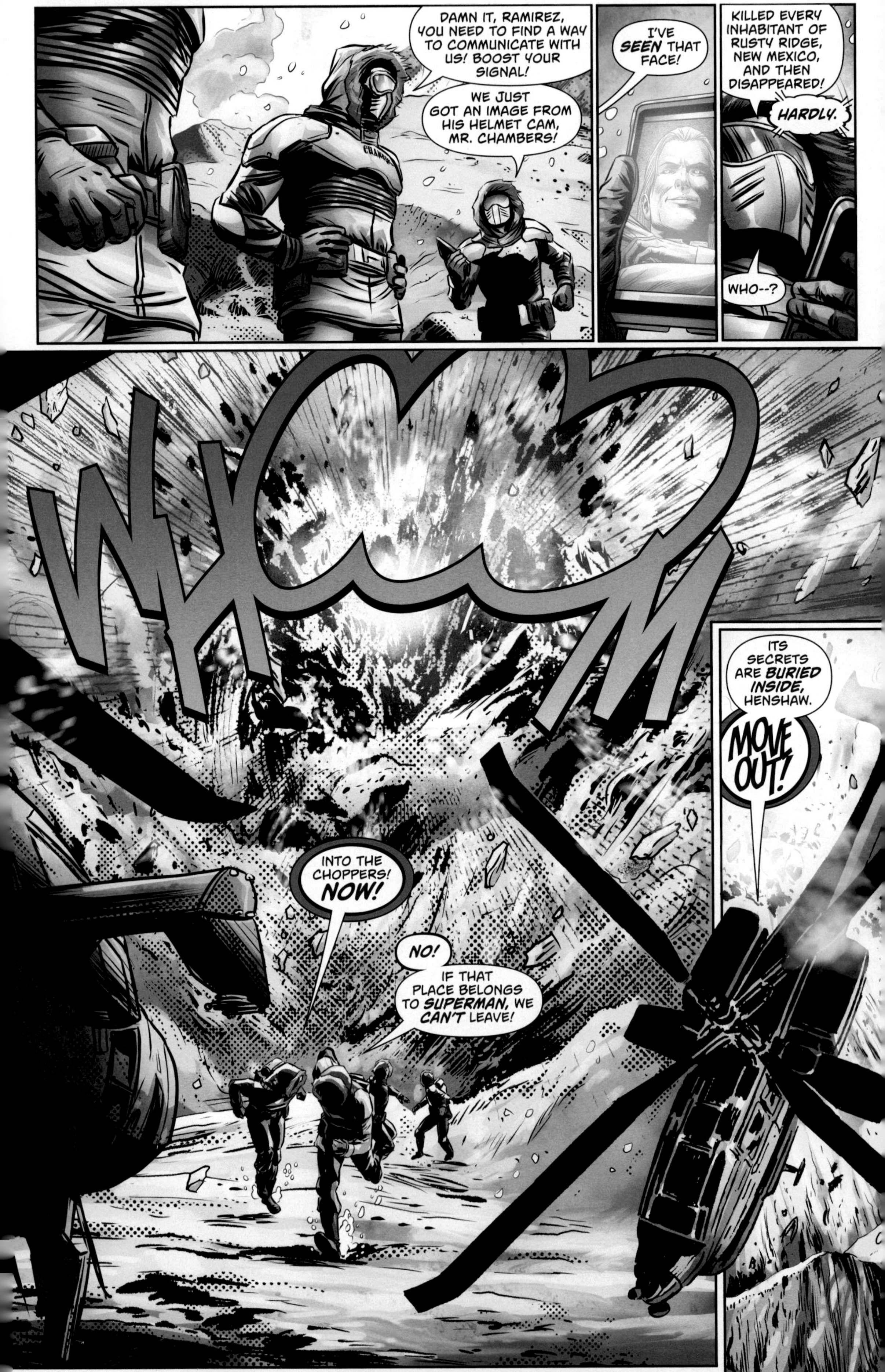

DAMN IT, RAMIREZ, YOU NEED TO FIND A WAY TO COMMUNICATE WITH US! BOOST YOUR SIGNAL!
WE JUST GOT AN IMAGE FROM HIS HELMET CAM, MR. CHAMBERS!
I'VE SEEN THAT FACE!
KILLED EVERY INHABITANT OF RUSTY RIDGE, NEW MEXICO, AND THEN DISAPPEARED!
HARDLY.
WHO--?
WHOOM
ITS SECRETS ARE BURIED INSIDE, HENSHAW.
MOVE OUT!
INTO THE CHOPPERS! NOW!
NO!
IF THAT PLACE BELONGS TO SUPERMAN, WE CAN'T LEAVE!

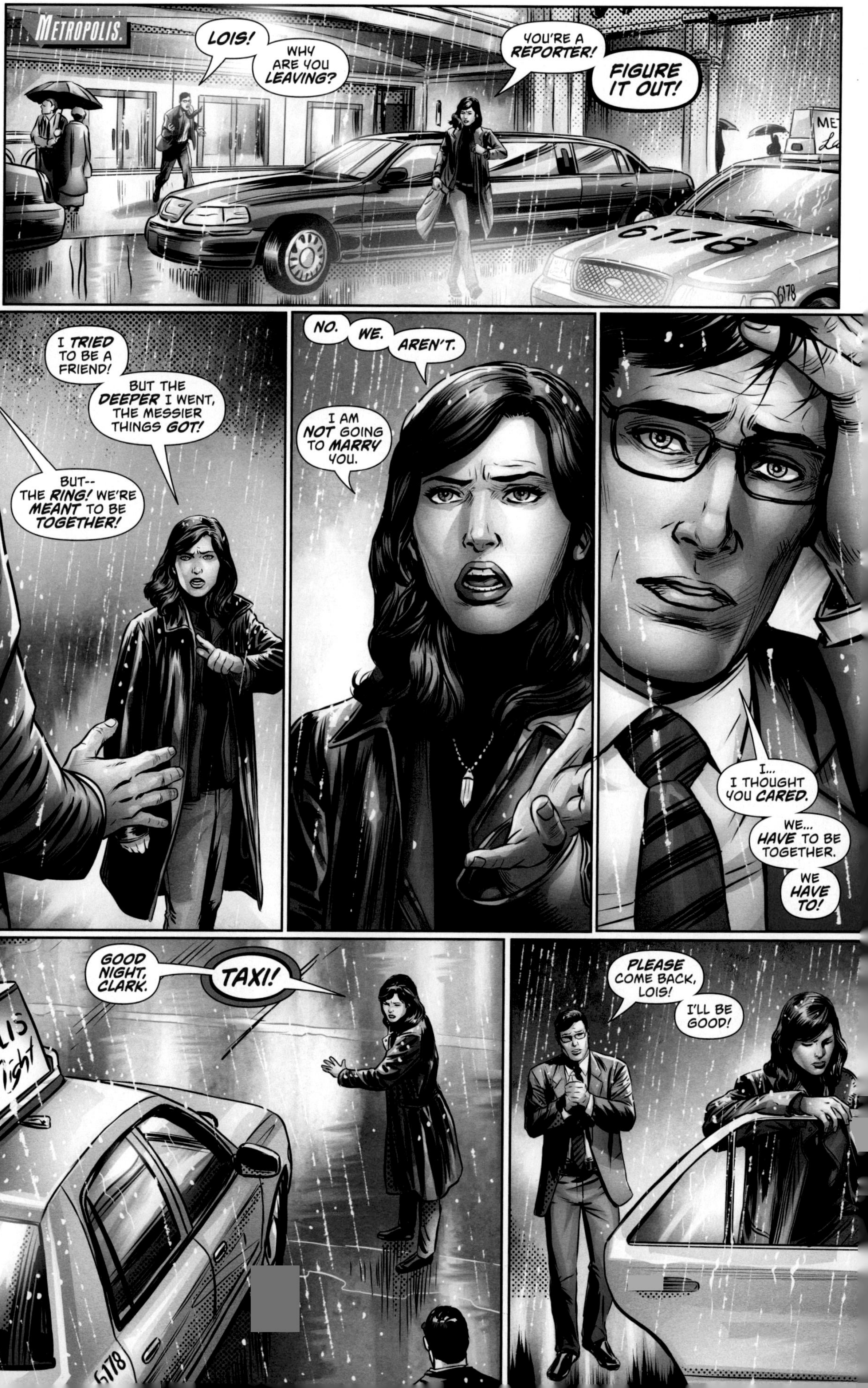
METROPOLIS.
LOIS!
WHY ARE YOU LEAVING?
YOU'RE A REPORTER!
FIGURE IT OUT!
6178
I TRIED TO BE A FRIEND!
BUT THE DEEPER I WENT, THE MESSIER THINGS GOT!
BUT-- THE RING! WE'RE MEANT TO BE TOGETHER!
NO.
WE.
AREN'T.
I AM NOT GOING TO MARRY YOU.
I... I THOUGHT YOU CARED.
WE... HAVE TO BE TOGETHER.
WE HAVE TO!
GOOD NIGHT, CLARK.
TAXI!
PLEASE COME BACK, LOIS!
I'LL BE GOOD!

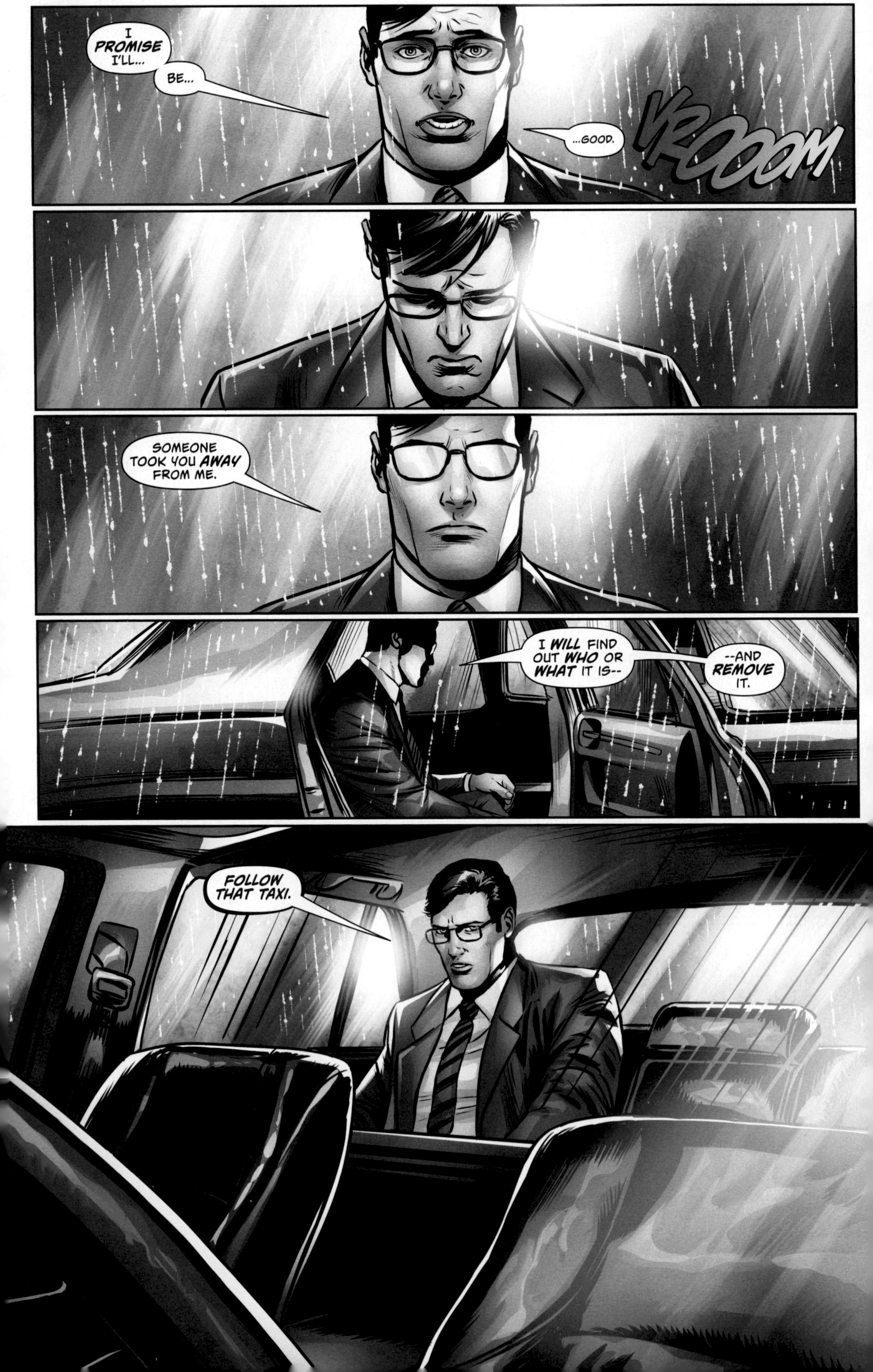
I PROMISE I'LL...
BE...
...GOOD.
VROOOOM
SOMEONE TOOK YOU AWAY FROM ME.
I WILL FIND OUT WHO OR WHAT IT IS--
--AND REMOVE IT.
FOLLOW THAT TAXI.

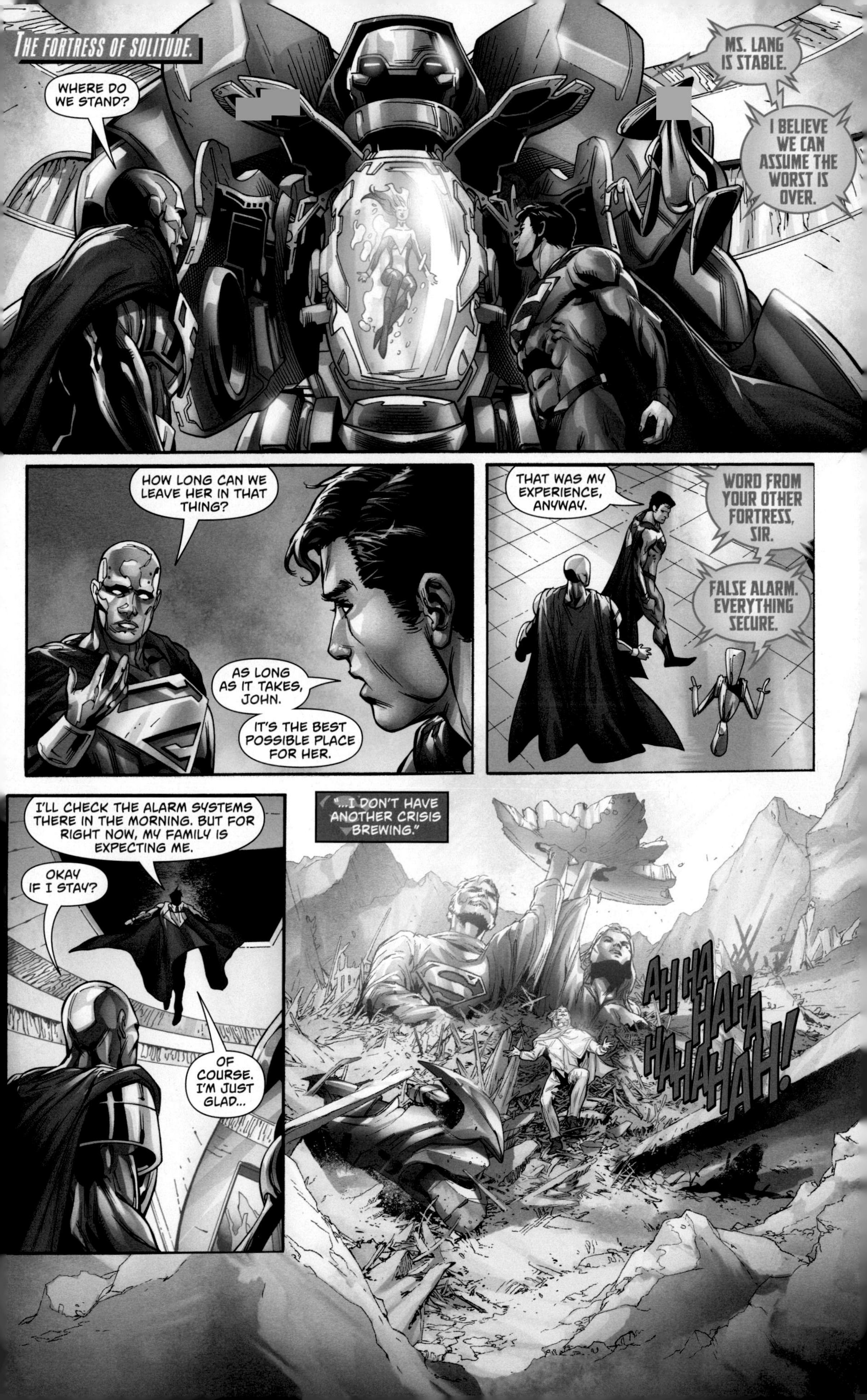
THE FORTRESS OF SOLITUDE.
WHERE DO WE STAND?
MS. LANG IS STABLE.
I BELIEVE WE CAN ASSUME THE WORST IS OVER.
HOW LONG CAN WE LEAVE HER IN THAT THING?
AS LONG AS IT TAKES, JOHN.
IT'S THE BEST POSSIBLE PLACE FOR HER.
THAT WAS MY EXPERIENCE, ANYWAY.
WORD FROM YOUR OTHER FORTRESS, SIR.
FALSE ALARM. EVERYTHING SECURE.
I'LL CHECK THE ALARM SYSTEMS THERE IN THE MORNING. BUT FOR RIGHT NOW, MY FAMILY IS EXPECTING ME.
OKAY IF I STAY?
OF COURSE. I'M JUST GLAD...
"...I DON'T HAVE ANOTHER CRISIS BREWING."
AH HA HAHA HAHAHAH!

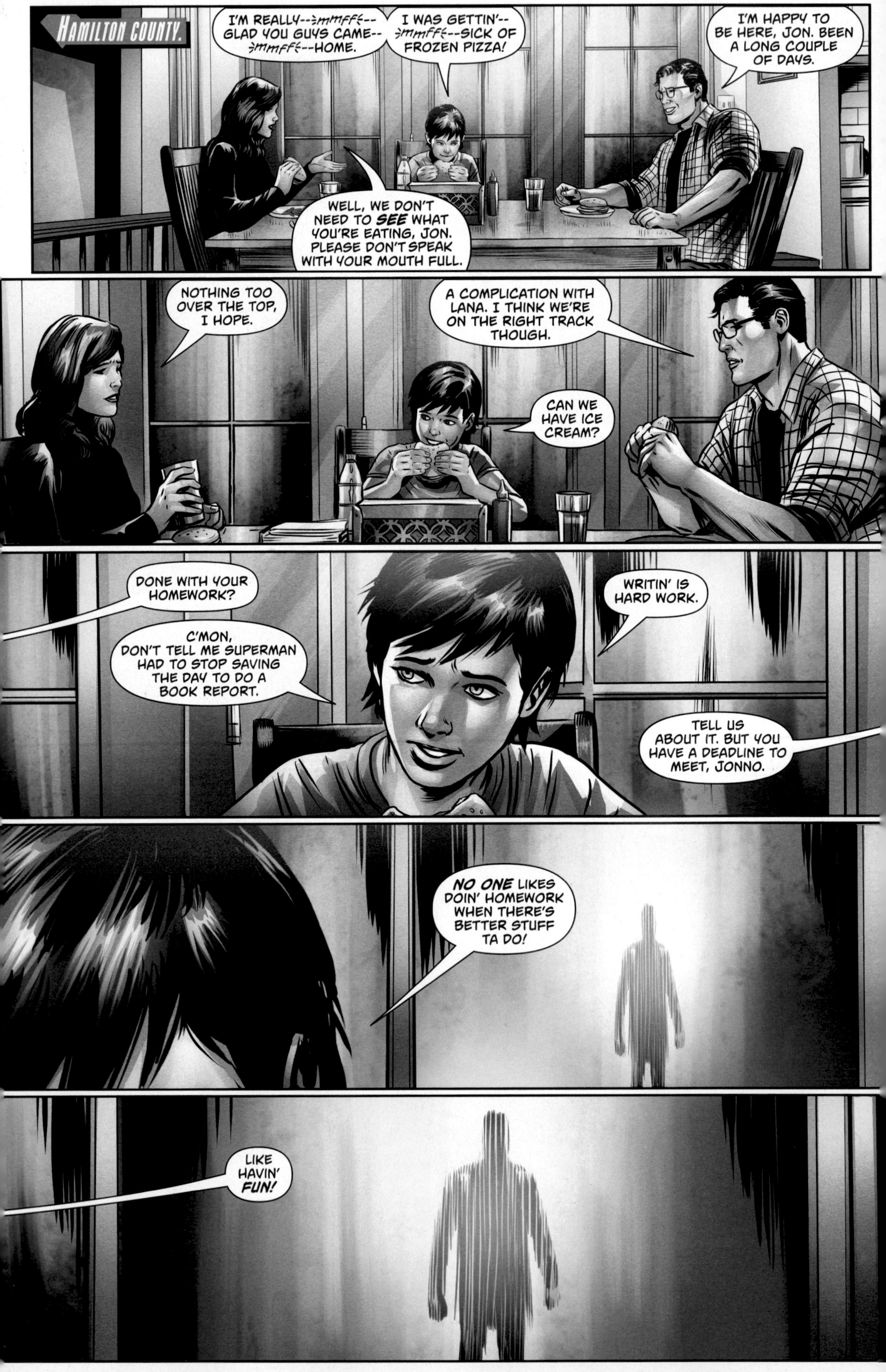
HAMILTON COUNTY.
I'M REALLY--*MMFF*--GLAD YOU GUYS CAME--*MMFF*--HOME.
I WAS GETTIN'--*MMFF*--SICK OF FROZEN PIZZA!
I'M HAPPY TO BE HERE, JON. BEEN A LONG COUPLE OF DAYS.
WELL, WE DON'T NEED TO SEE WHAT YOU'RE EATING, JON. PLEASE DON'T SPEAK WITH YOUR MOUTH FULL.
NOTHING TOO OVER THE TOP, I HOPE.
A COMPLICATION WITH LANA. I THINK WE'RE ON THE RIGHT TRACK THOUGH.
CAN WE HAVE ICE CREAM?
DONE WITH YOUR HOMEWORK?
C'MON, DON'T TELL ME SUPERMAN HAD TO STOP SAVING THE DAY TO DO A BOOK REPORT.
WRITIN' IS HARD WORK.
TELL US ABOUT IT. BUT YOU HAVE A DEADLINE TO MEET, JONNO.
NO ONE LIKES DOIN' HOMEWORK WHEN THERE'S BETTER STUFF TA DO!
LIKE HAVIN' FUN!

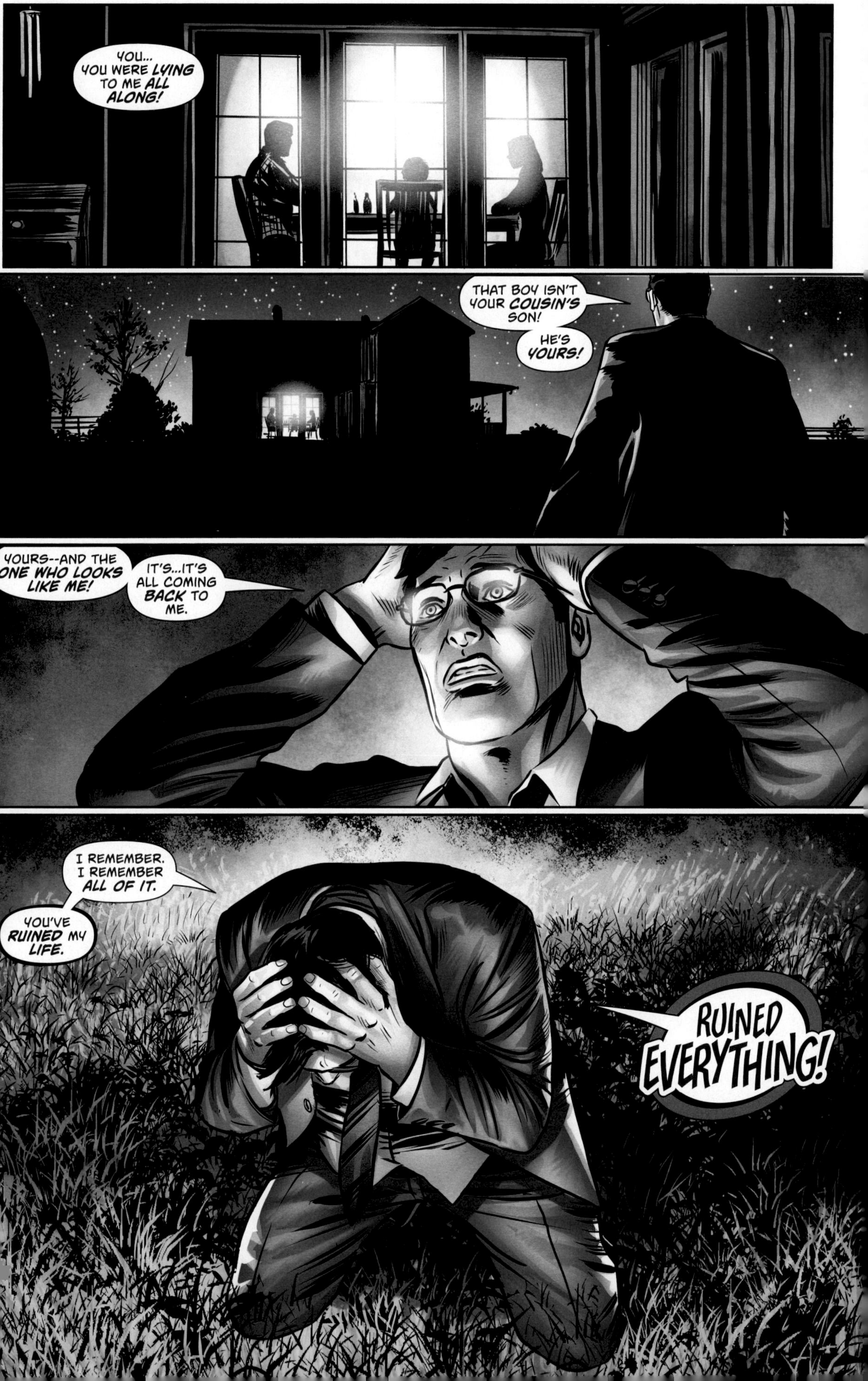
YOU... YOU WERE LYING TO ME ALL ALONG!
THAT BOY ISN'T YOUR COUSIN'S SON!
HE'S YOURS!
YOURS--AND THE ONE WHO LOOKS LIKE ME!
IT'S...IT'S ALL COMING BACK TO ME.
I REMEMBER. I REMEMBER ALL OF IT.
YOU'VE RUINED MY LIFE.
RUINED EVERYTHING!

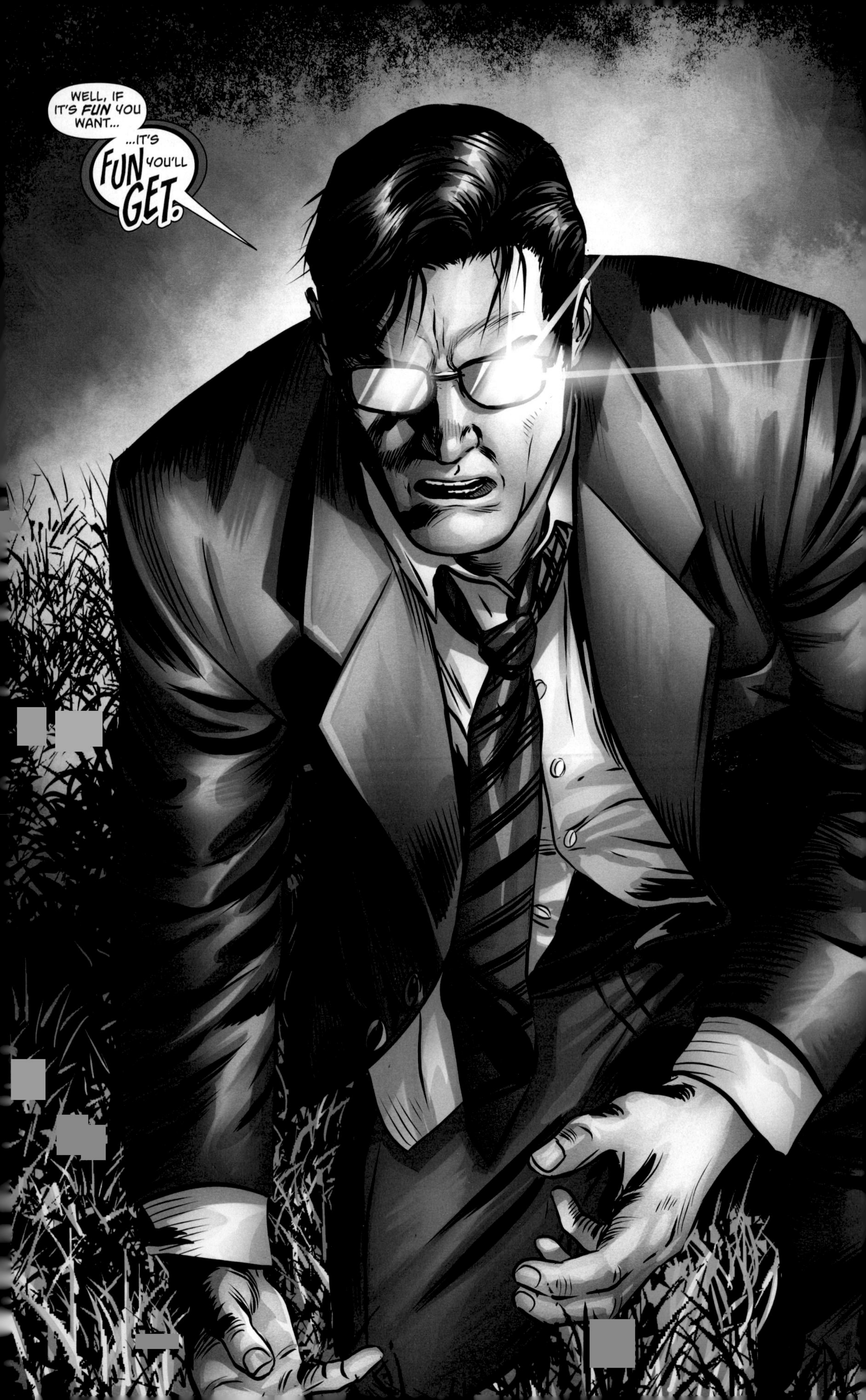
WELL, IF IT'S FUN YOU WANT...
...IT'S FUN YOU'LL GET.

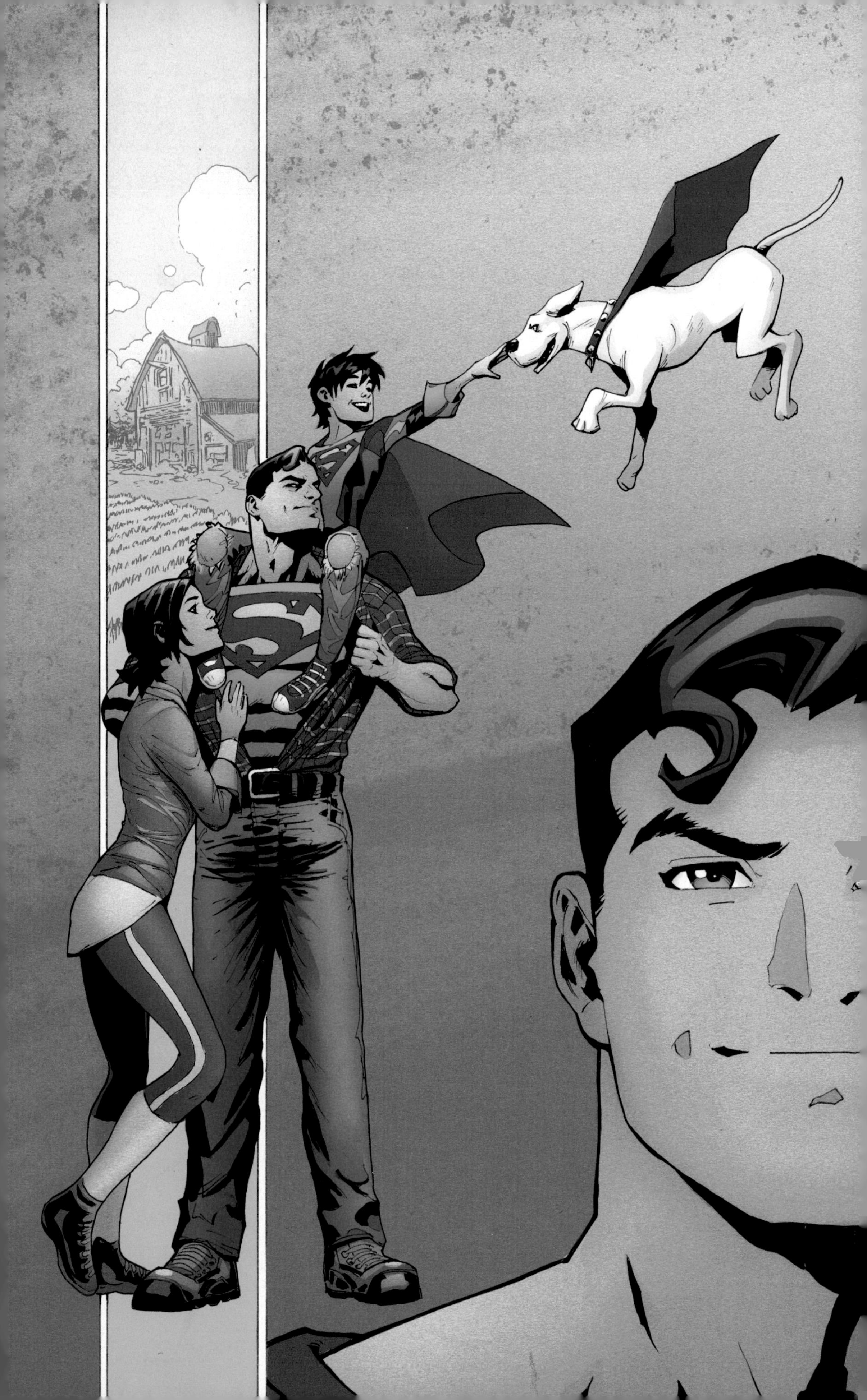

SUPERMAN: REBORN part one

PETER J. TOMASI & PATRICK GLEASON writers * PATRICK GLEASON penciller

MICK GRAY inker * JOHN KALISZ colorist

PATRICK GLEASON & JOHN KALISZ cover art

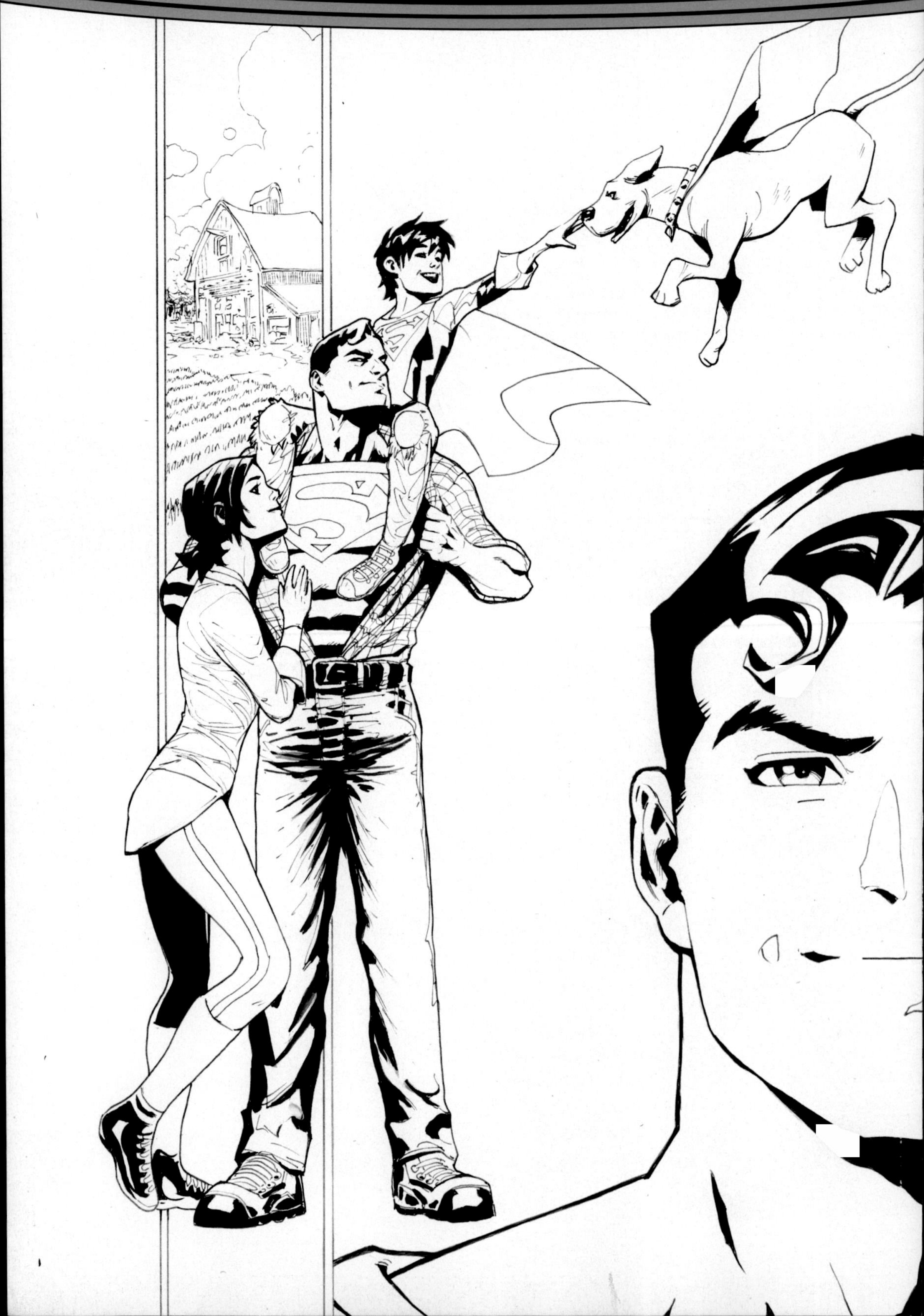

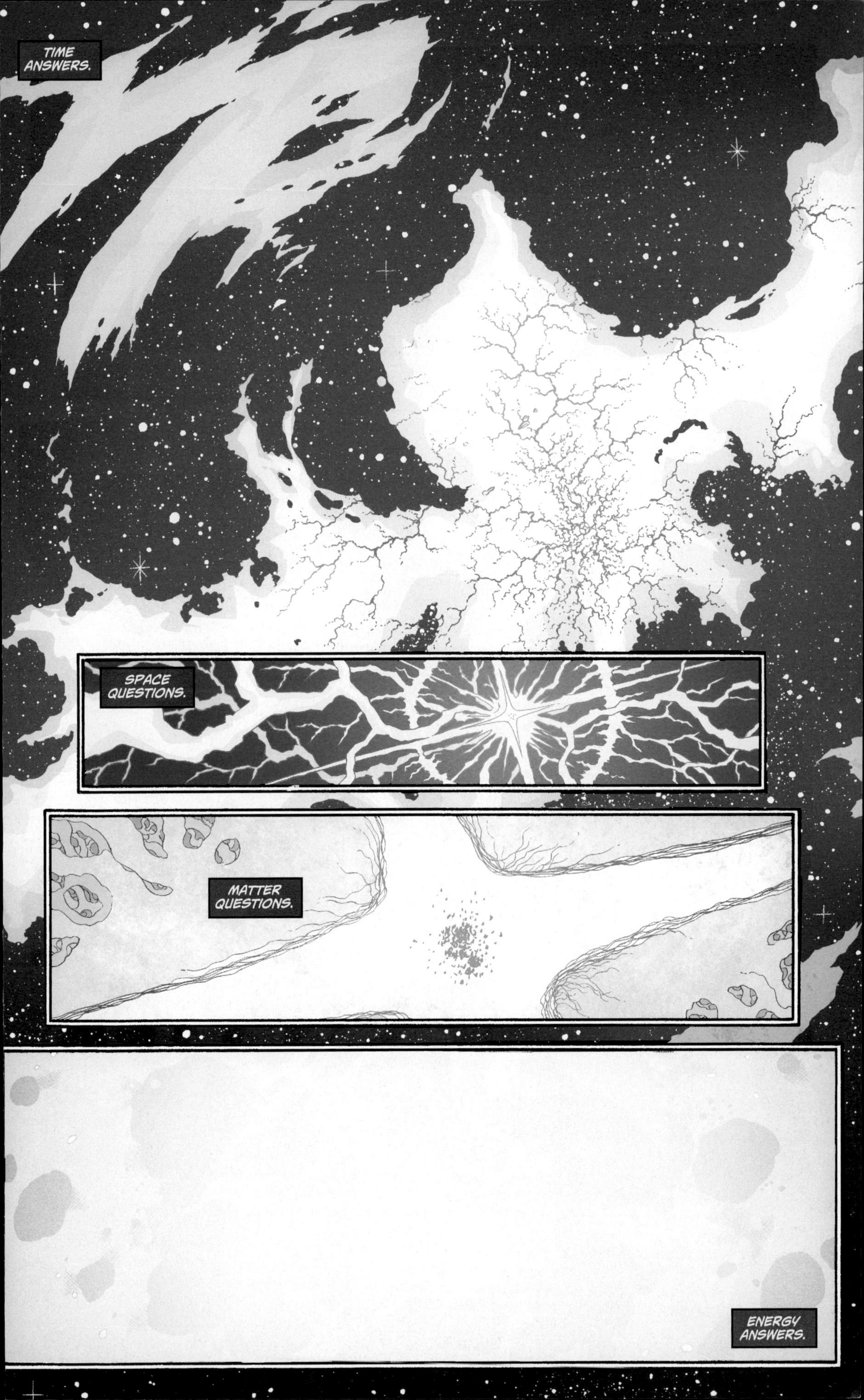
TIME
ANSWERS.
SPACE
QUESTIONS.
MATTER
QUESTIONS.
ENERGY
ANSWERS.

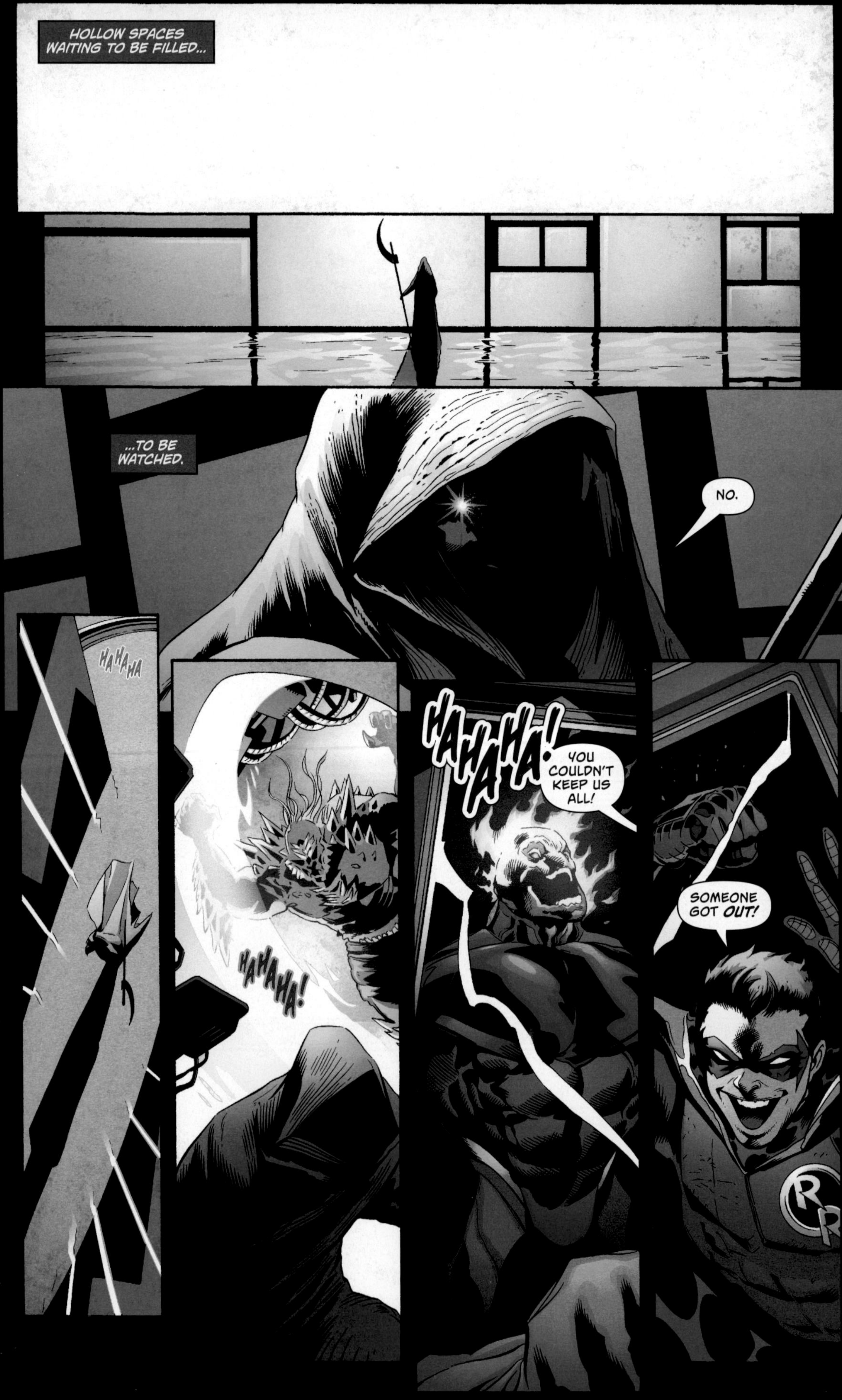
HOLLOW SPACES WAITING TO BE FILLED...
...TO BE WATCHED.
NO.
HA HA HA
HA HA HA!
HAHAHA!
YOU COULDN'T KEEP US ALL!
SOMEONE GOT OUT!

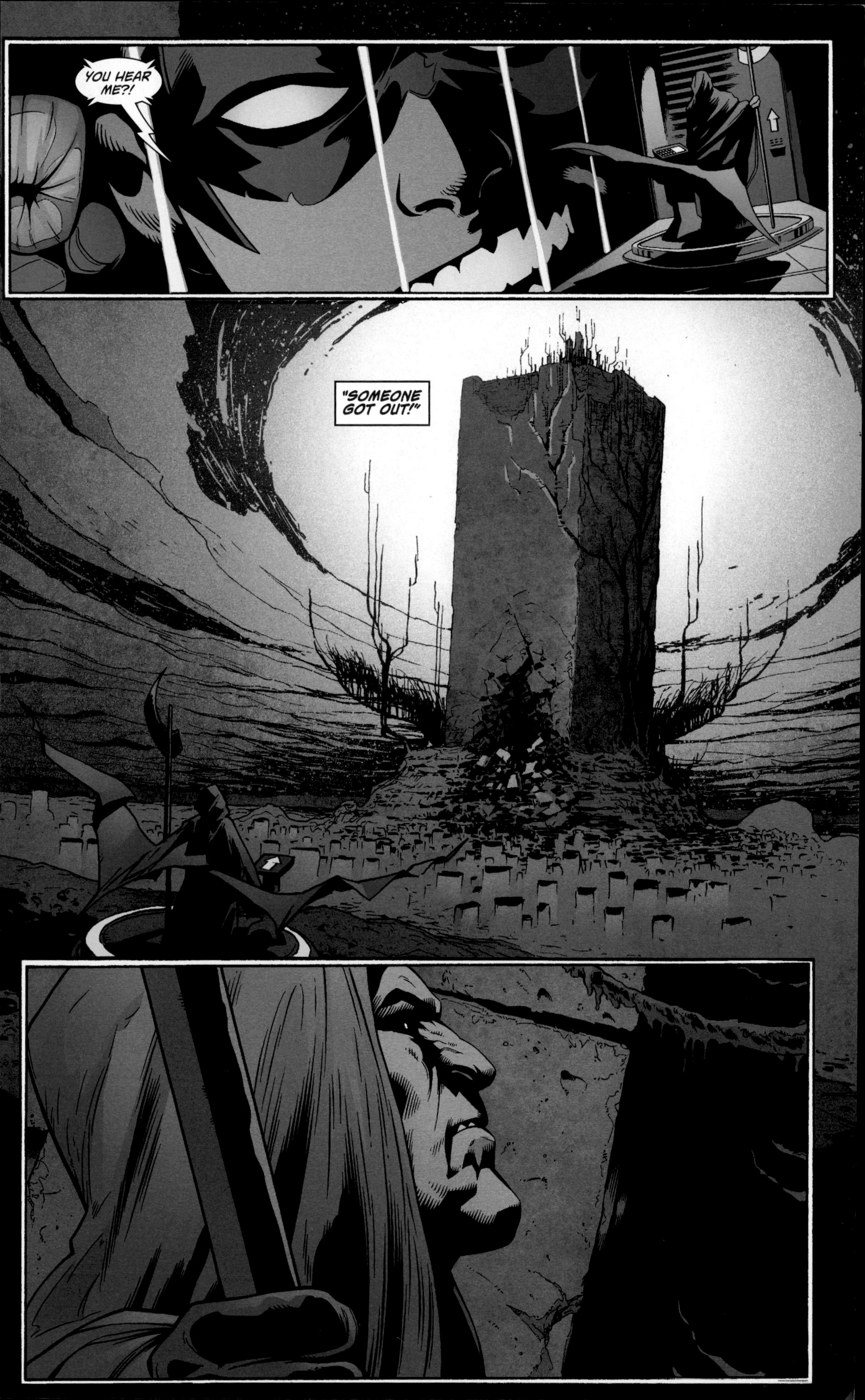
YOU HEAR ME?!
"SOMEONE GOT OUT!"

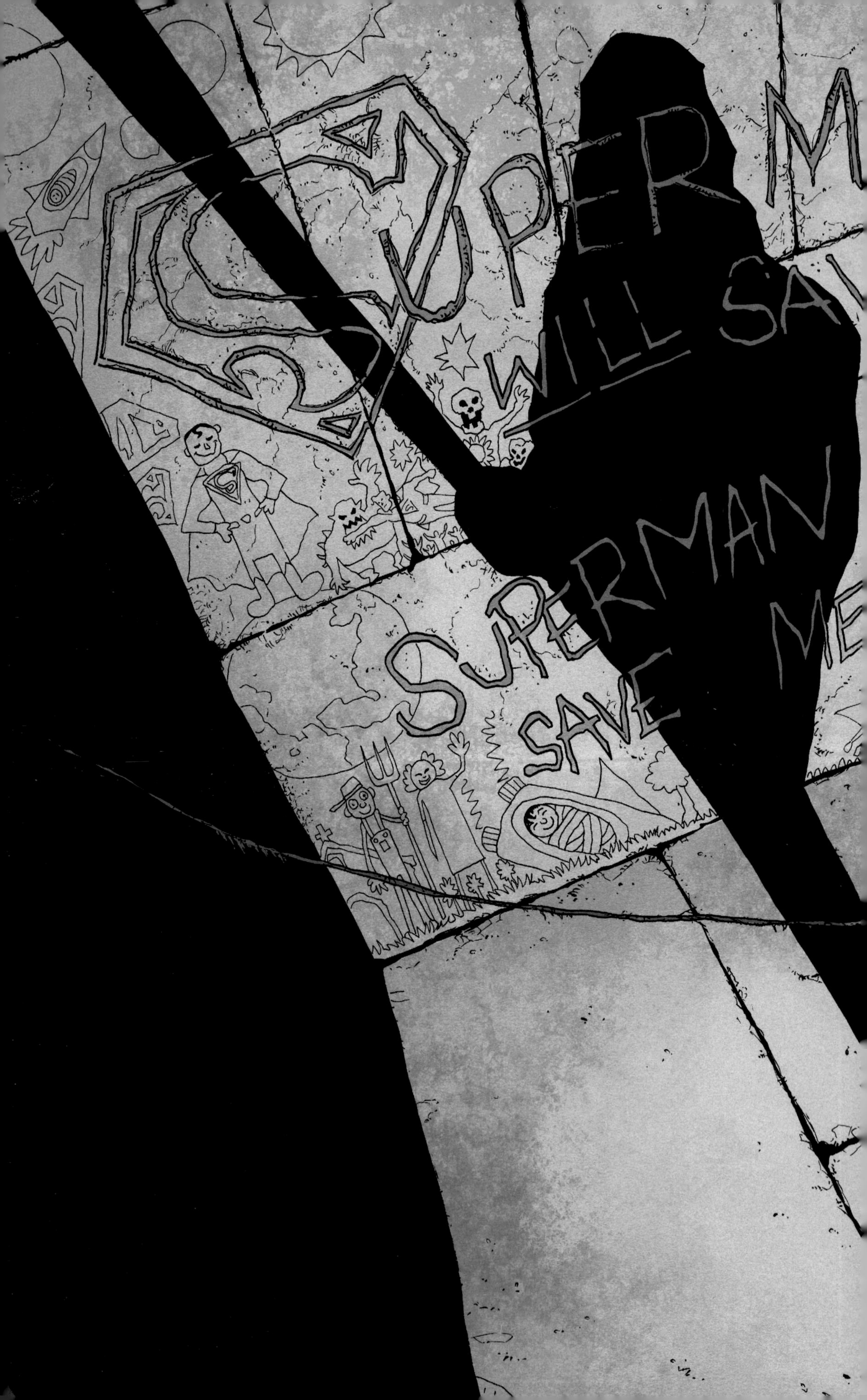

SUPER M
WILL SA
SUPERMAN
SAVE ME

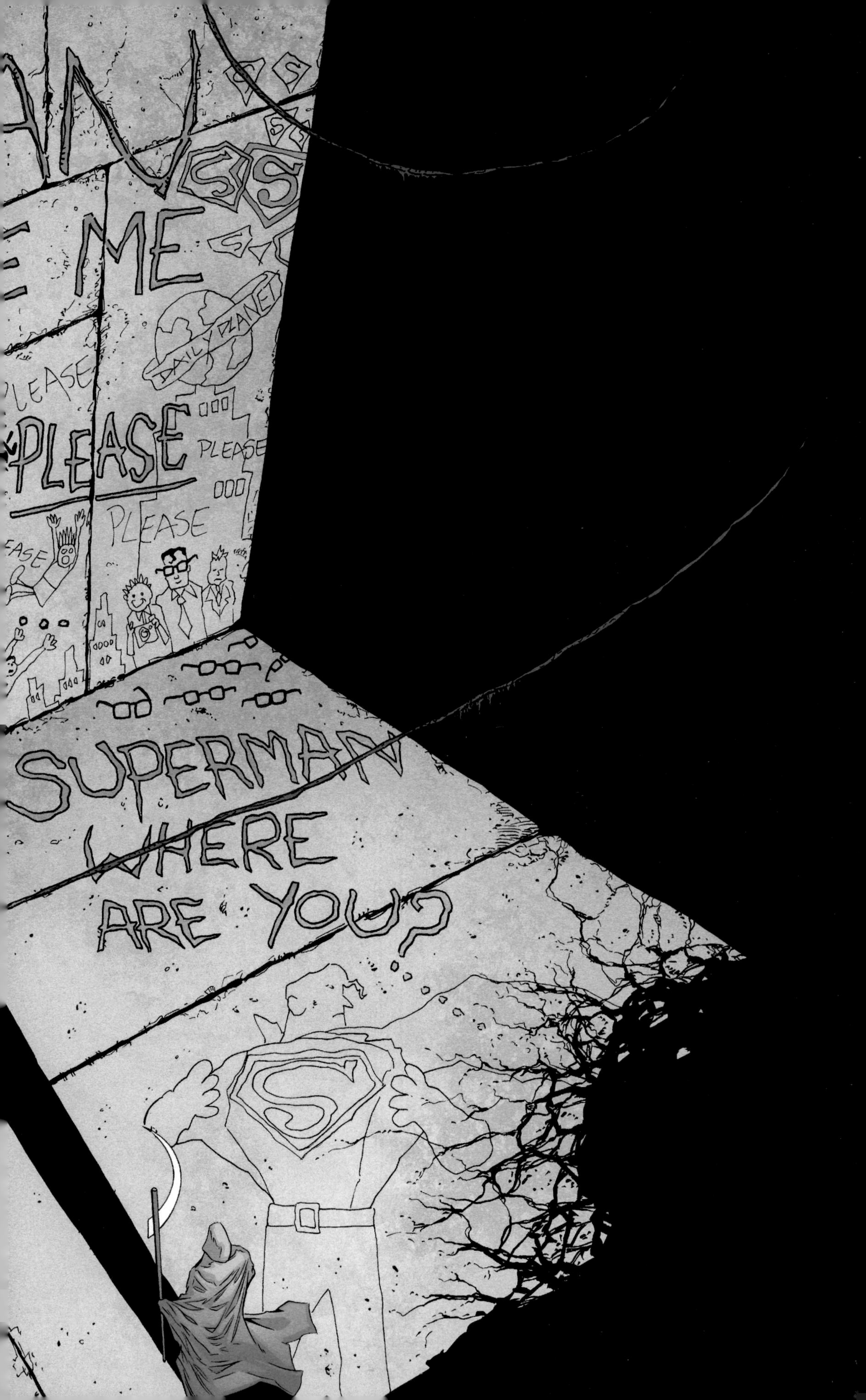
ME
DAILY PLANET
PLEASE
PLEASE
PLEASE
SUPERMAN
WHERE
ARE YOU?

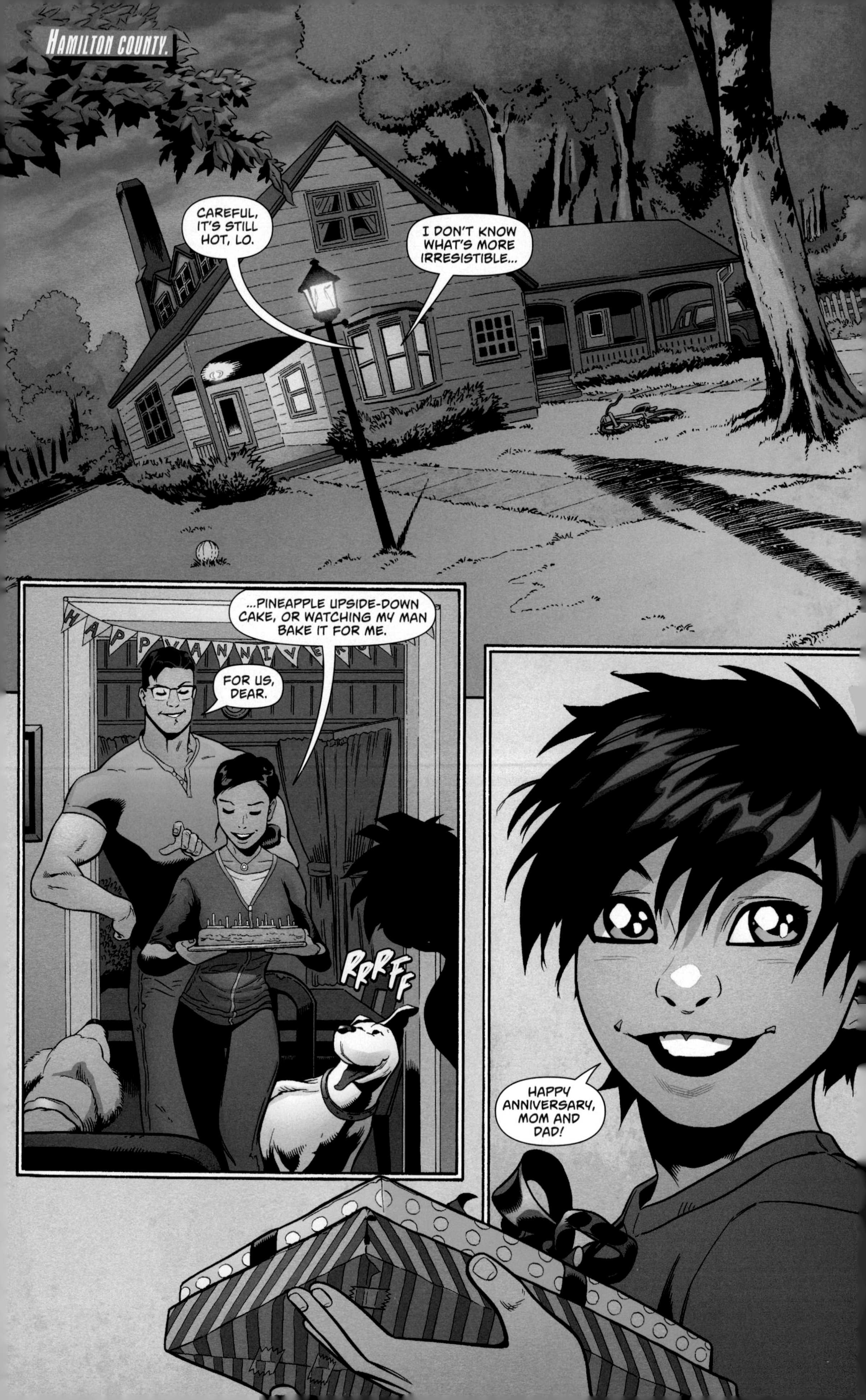
HAMILTON COUNTY.
CAREFUL, IT'S STILL HOT, LO.
I DON'T KNOW WHAT'S MORE IRRESISTIBLE...
...PINEAPPLE UPSIDE-DOWN CAKE, OR WATCHING MY MAN BAKE IT FOR ME.
FOR US, DEAR.
RRRFF
HAPPY ANNIVERSARY, MOM AND DAD!

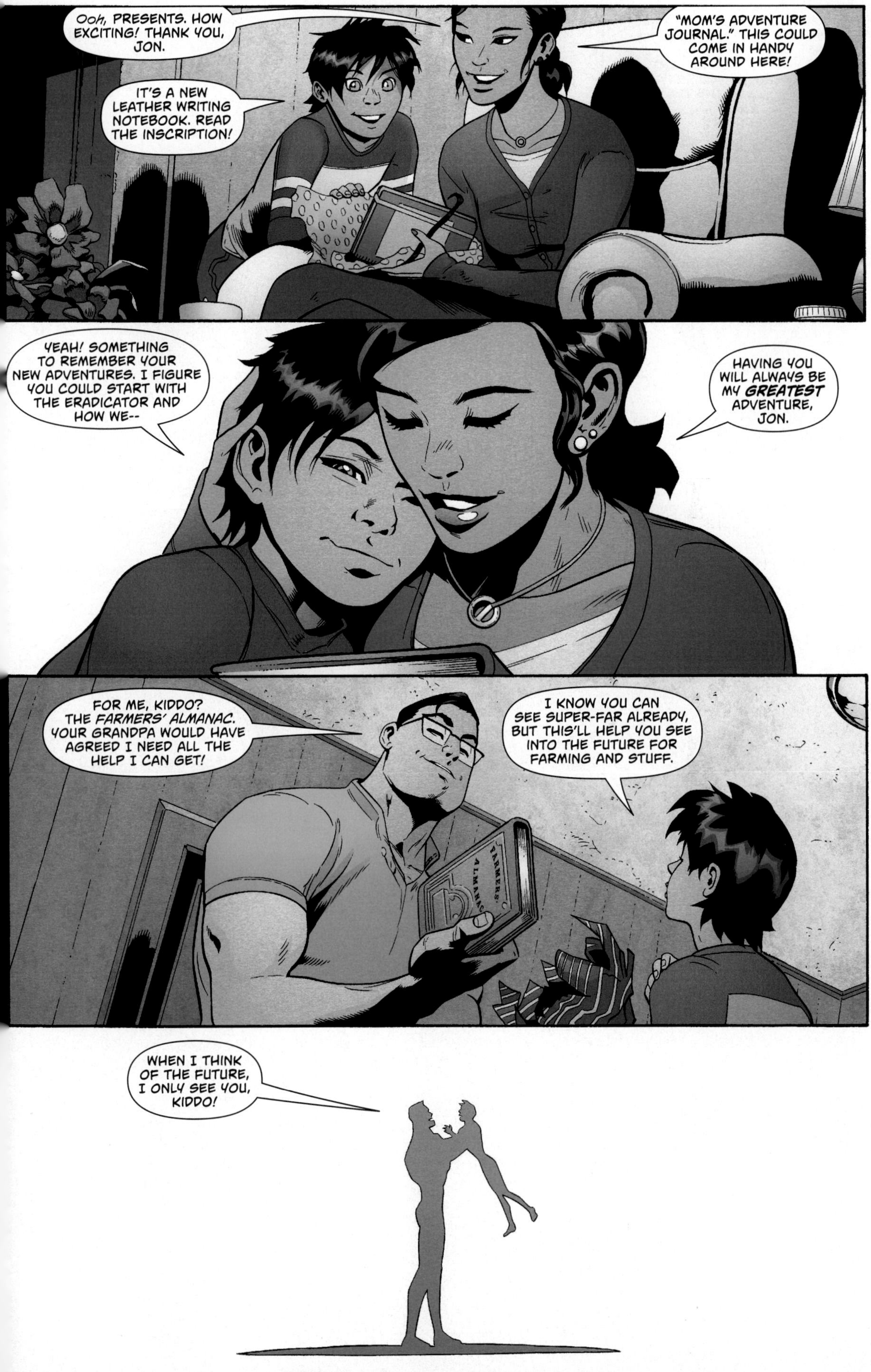

Ooh, PRESENTS. HOW EXCITING! THANK YOU, JON.
"MOM'S ADVENTURE JOURNAL." THIS COULD COME IN HANDY AROUND HERE!
IT'S A NEW LEATHER WRITING NOTEBOOK. READ THE INSCRIPTION!
YEAH! SOMETHING TO REMEMBER YOUR NEW ADVENTURES. I FIGURE YOU COULD START WITH THE ERADICATOR AND HOW WE--
HAVING YOU WILL ALWAYS BE MY **GREATEST** ADVENTURE, JON.
FOR ME, KIDDO? THE *FARMERS' ALMANAC*. YOUR GRANDPA WOULD HAVE AGREED I NEED ALL THE HELP I CAN GET!
I KNOW YOU CAN SEE SUPER-FAR ALREADY, BUT THIS'LL HELP YOU SEE INTO THE FUTURE FOR FARMING AND STUFF.
FARMERS' ALMANAC
WHEN I THINK OF THE FUTURE, I ONLY SEE YOU, KIDDO!

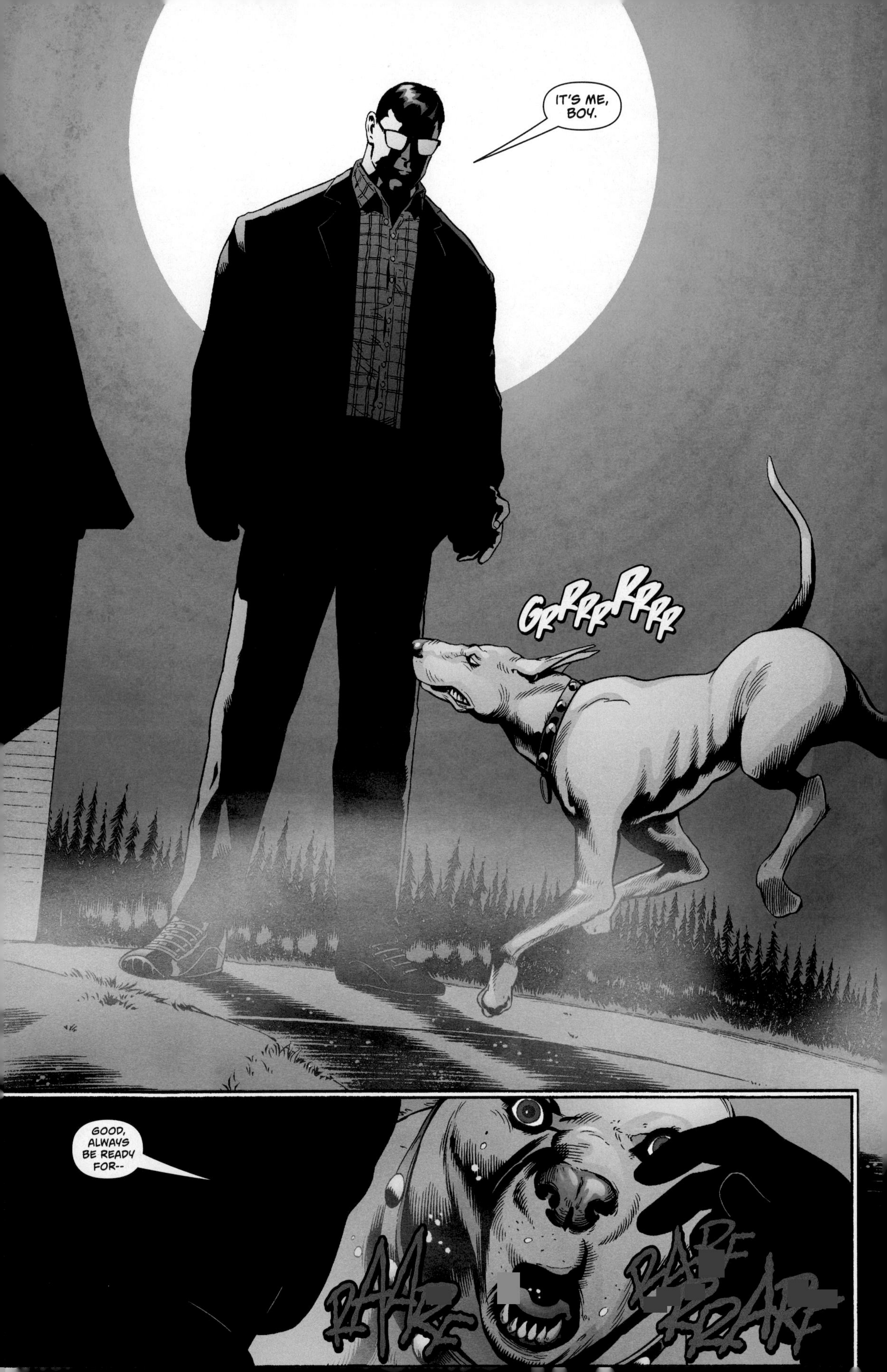
IT'S ME, BOY.
GRRRRRRRR
GOOD, ALWAYS BE READY FOR--

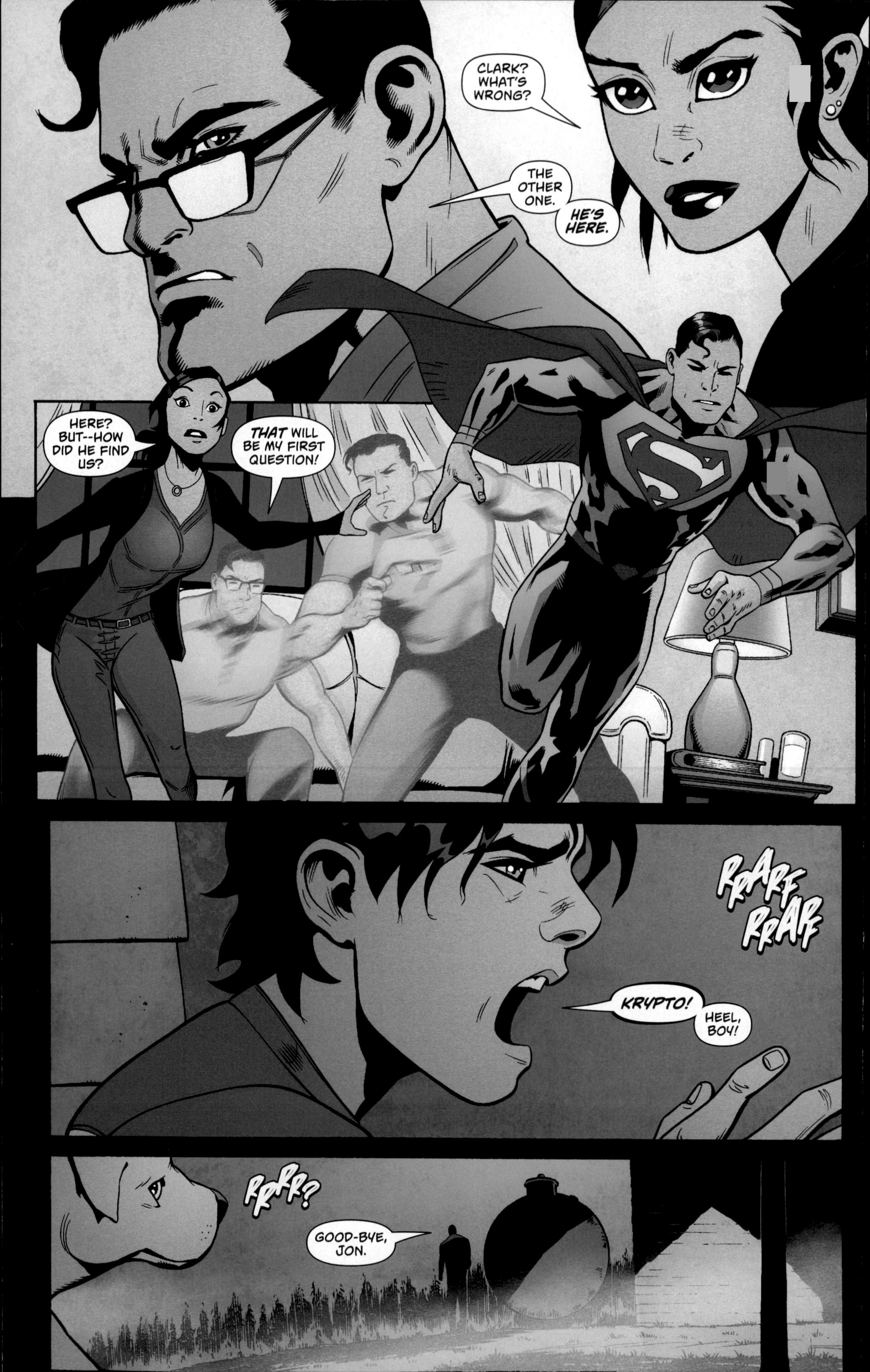
CLARK? WHAT'S WRONG?
THE OTHER ONE.
HE'S HERE.
HERE? BUT--HOW DID HE FIND US?
THAT WILL BE MY FIRST QUESTION!
RRARF RRARF
KRYPTO!
HEEL, BOY!
RRRR?
GOOD-BYE, JON.

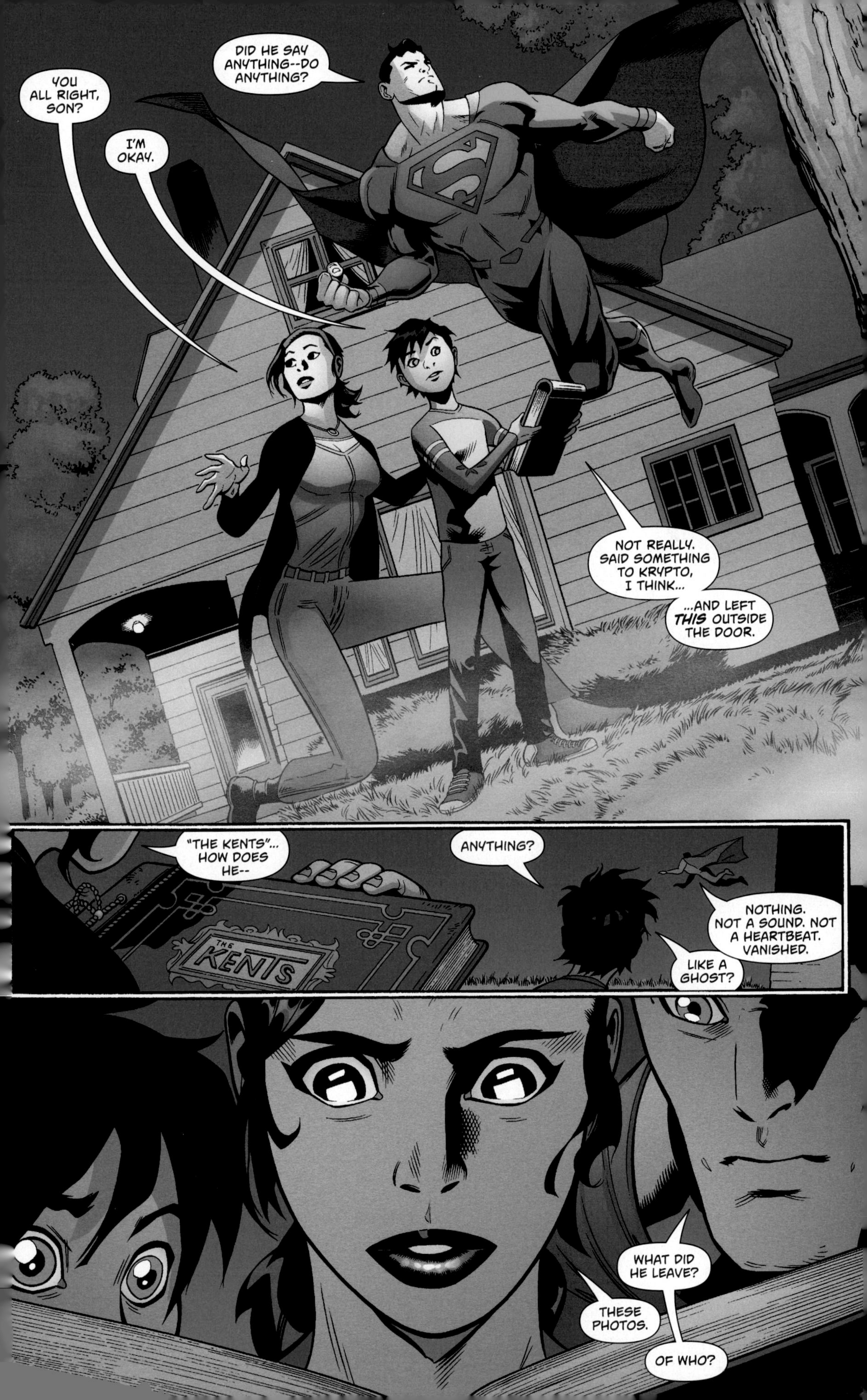
DID HE SAY ANYTHING--DO ANYTHING?
YOU ALL RIGHT, SON?
I'M OKAY.
NOT REALLY. SAID SOMETHING TO KRYPTO, I THINK...
...AND LEFT THIS OUTSIDE THE DOOR.
"THE KENTS"... HOW DOES HE--
THE KENTS
ANYTHING?
NOTHING. NOT A SOUND. NOT A HEARTBEAT. VANISHED.
LIKE A GHOST?
WHAT DID HE LEAVE?
THESE PHOTOS.
OF WHO?

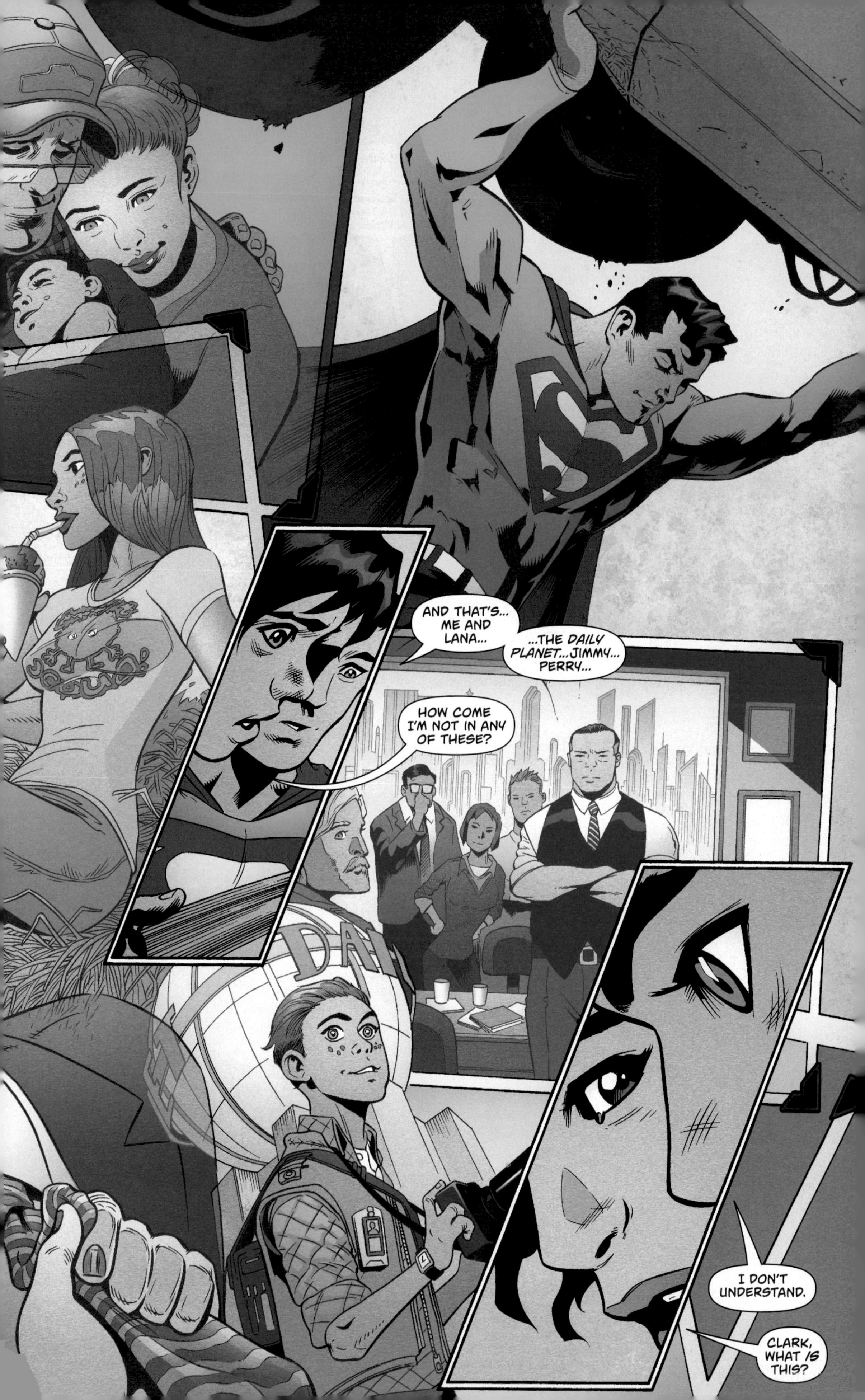
AND THAT'S... ME AND LANA...
...THE DAILY PLANET...JIMMY... PERRY...
HOW COME I'M NOT IN ANY OF THESE?
I DON'T UNDERSTAND.
CLARK, WHAT IS THIS?

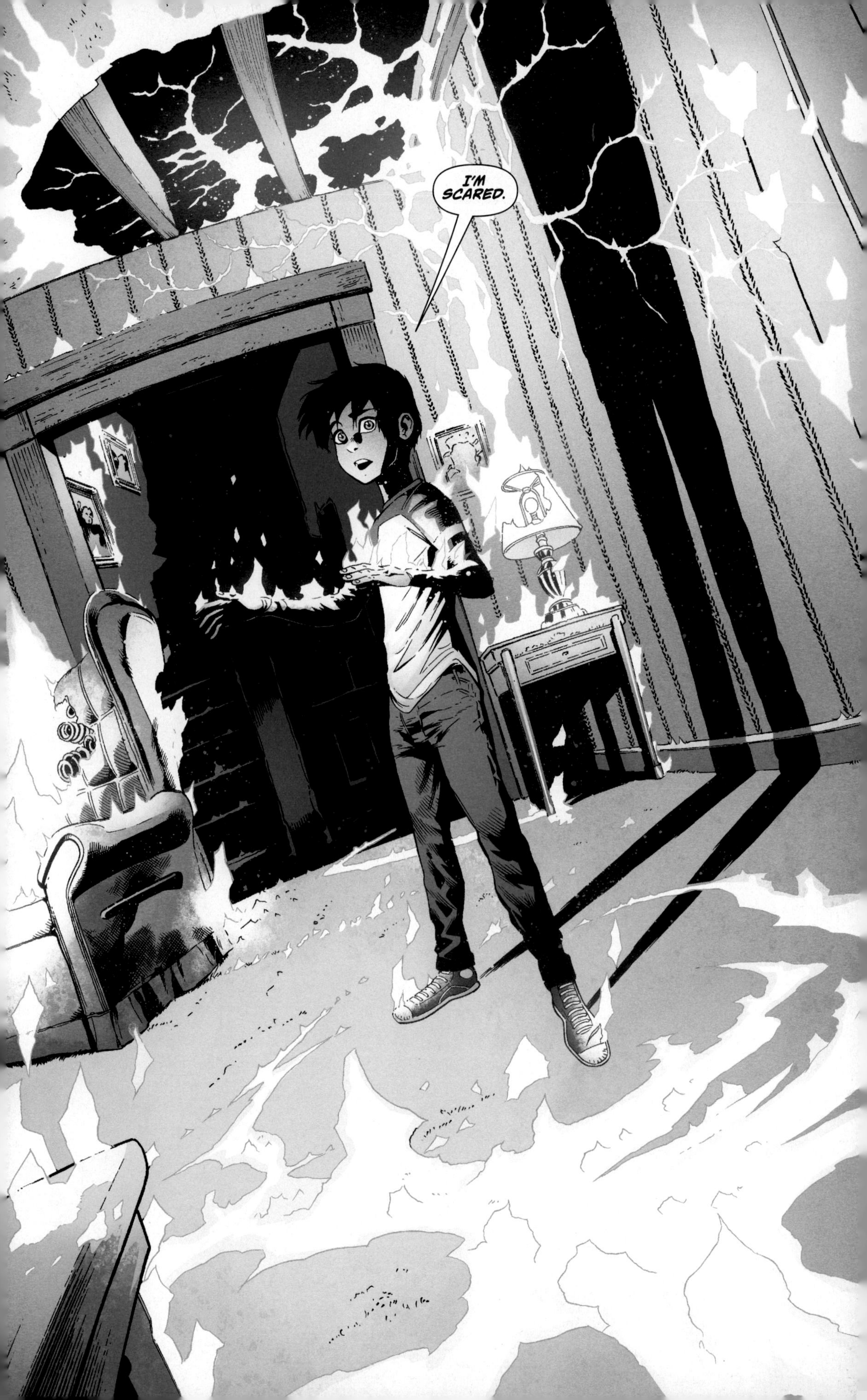
I'M SCARED.

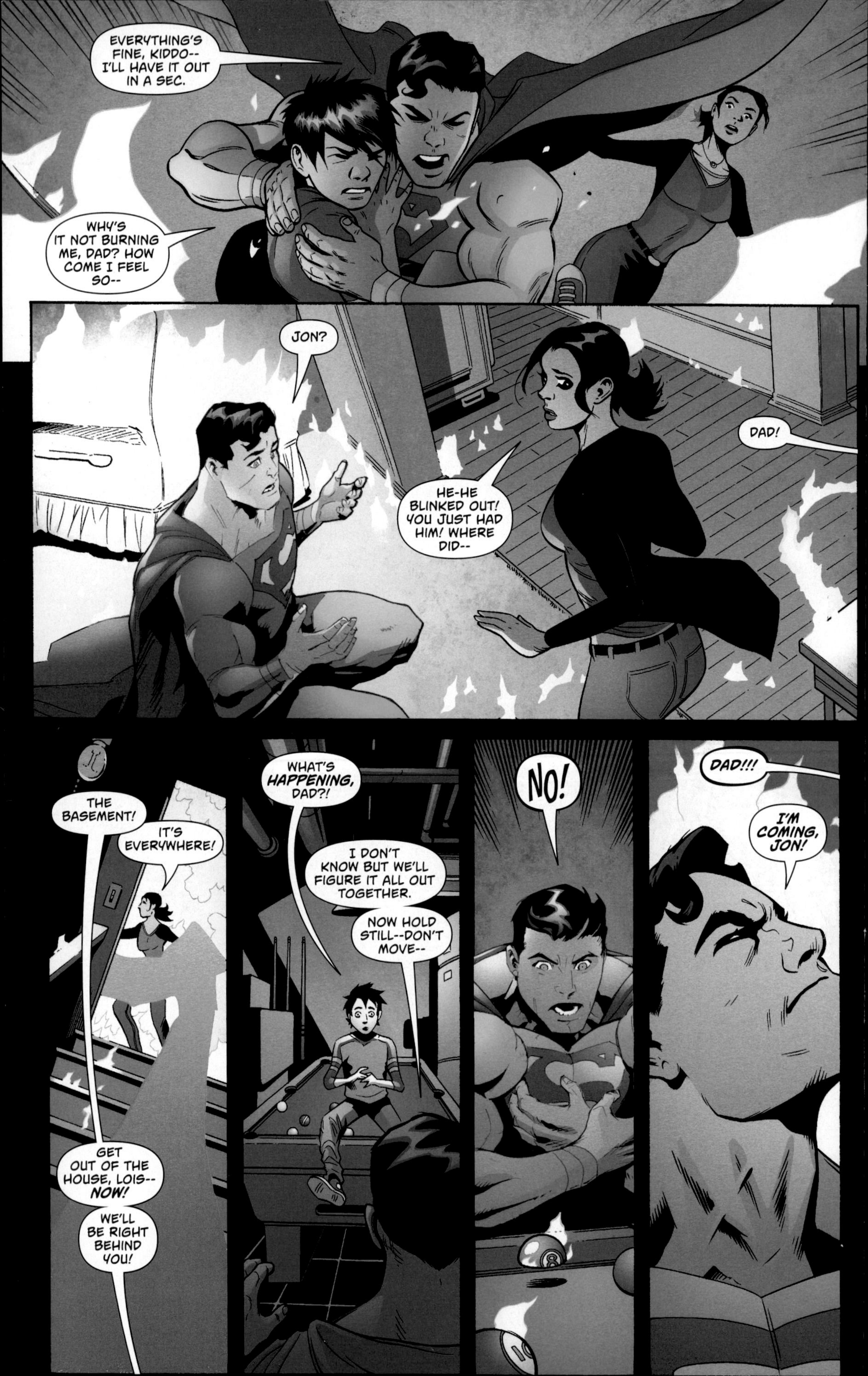
EVERYTHING'S FINE, KIDDO-- I'LL HAVE IT OUT IN A SEC.
WHY'S IT NOT BURNING ME, DAD? HOW COME I FEEL SO--
JON?
HE-HE BLINKED OUT! YOU JUST HAD HIM! WHERE DID--
DAD!
THE BASEMENT!
IT'S EVERYWHERE!
GET OUT OF THE HOUSE, LOIS-- NOW!
WE'LL BE RIGHT BEHIND YOU!
WHAT'S HAPPENING, DAD?!
I DON'T KNOW BUT WE'LL FIGURE IT ALL OUT TOGETHER.
NOW HOLD STILL--DON'T MOVE--
NO!
DAD!!!
I'M COMING, JON!

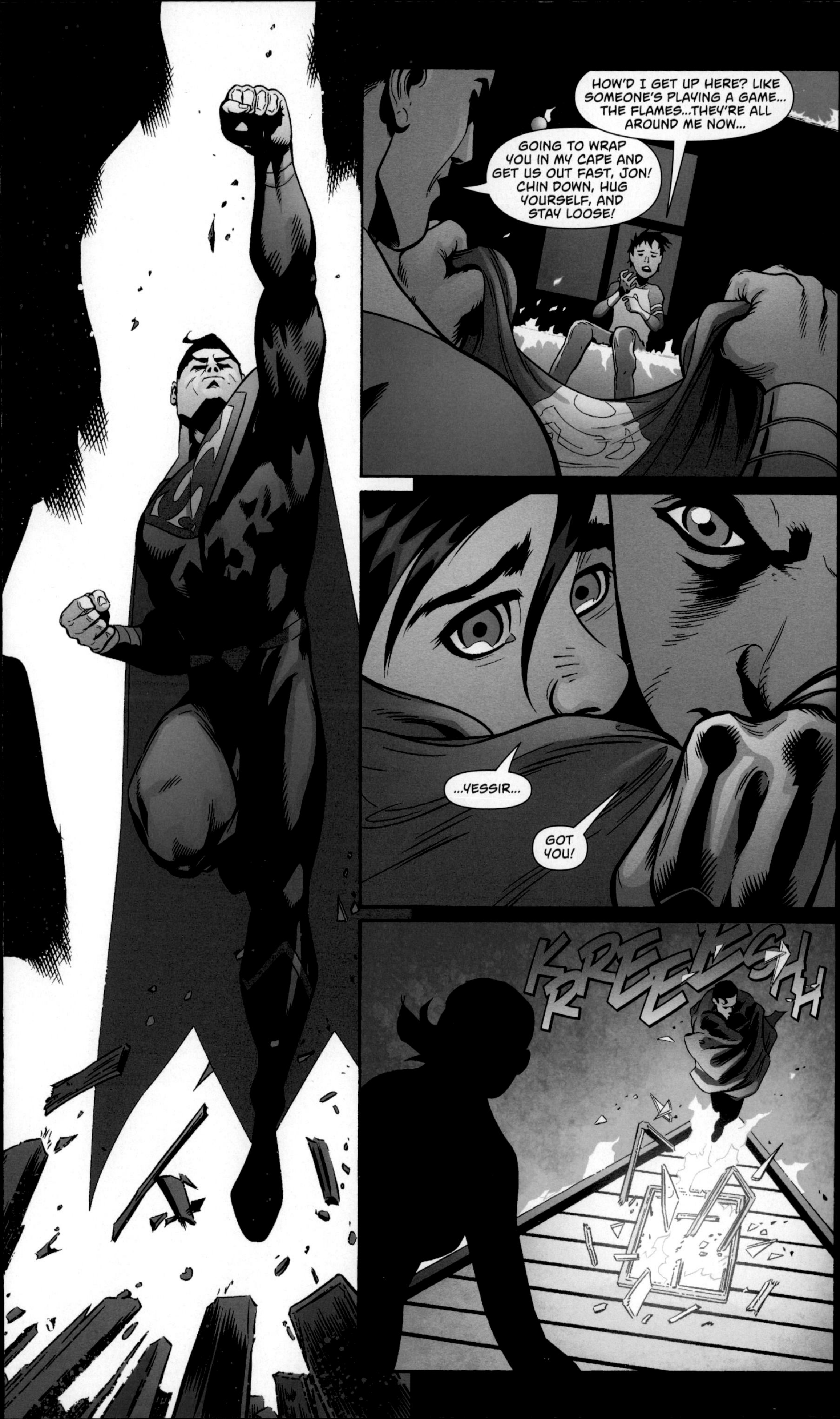
HOW'D I GET UP HERE? LIKE SOMEONE'S PLAYING A GAME... THE FLAMES...THEY'RE ALL AROUND ME NOW...
GOING TO WRAP YOU IN MY CAPE AND GET US OUT FAST, JON! CHIN DOWN, HUG YOURSELF, AND STAY LOOSE!
...YESSIR...
GOT YOU!
KREEESH

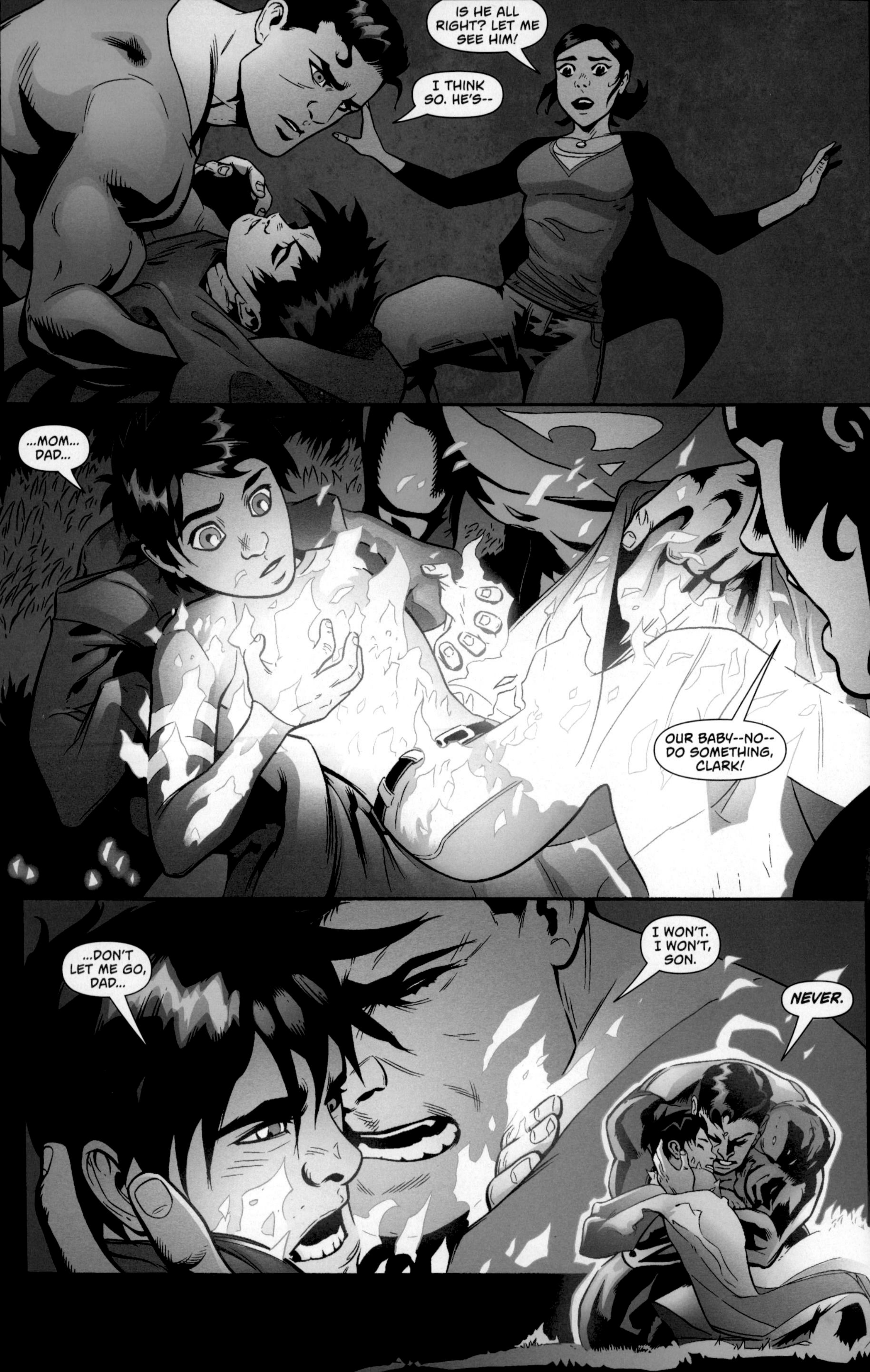
IS HE ALL RIGHT? LET ME SEE HIM!
I THINK SO. HE'S--
...MOM... DAD...
OUR BABY--NO-- DO SOMETHING, CLARK!
...DON'T LET ME GO, DAD...
I WON'T. I WON'T, SON.
NEVER.

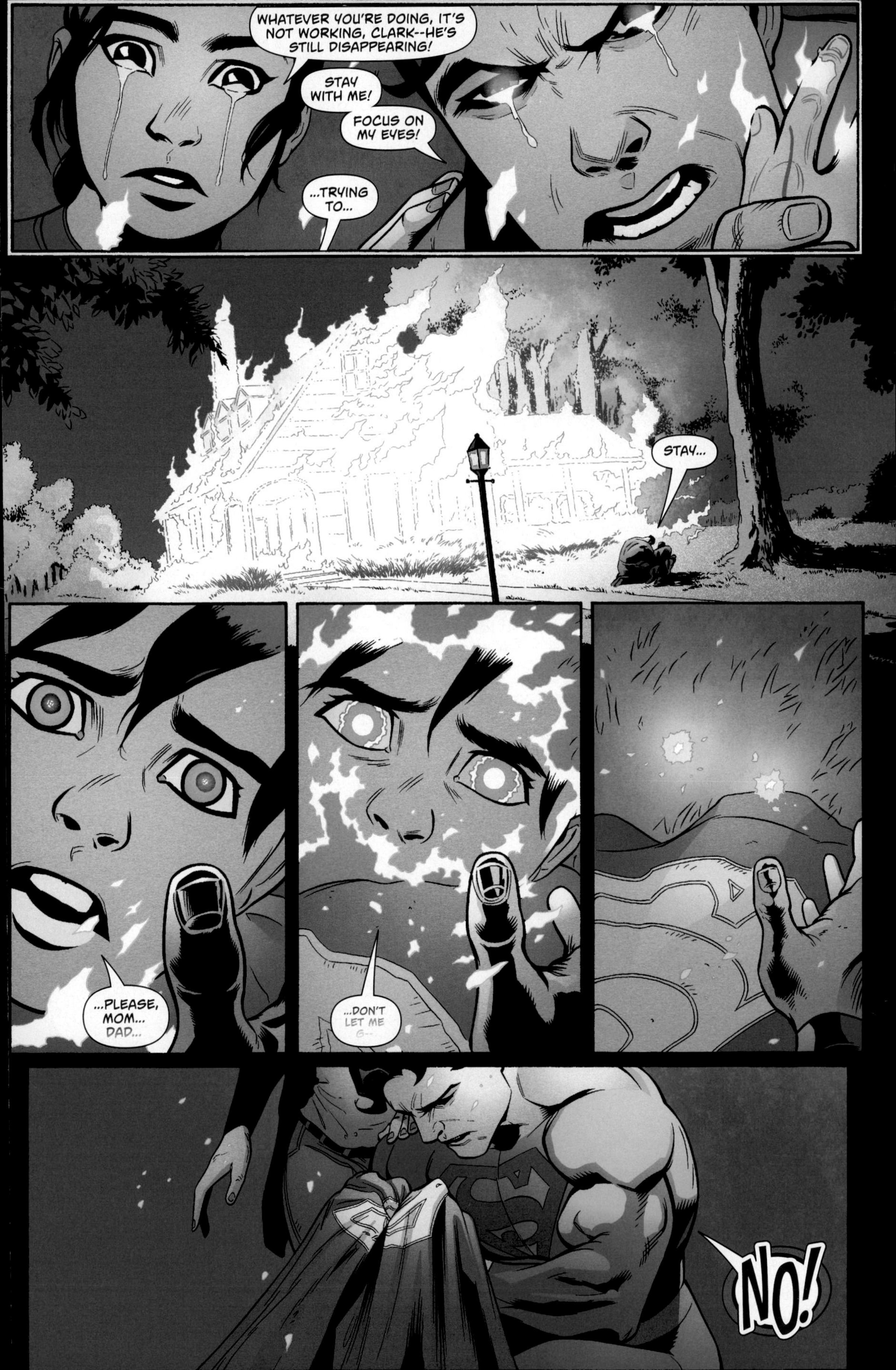
WHATEVER YOU'RE DOING, IT'S NOT WORKING, CLARK--HE'S STILL DISAPPEARING!
STAY WITH ME!
FOCUS ON MY EYES!
...TRYING TO...
STAY...
...PLEASE, MOM... DAD...
...DON'T LET ME G--
NO!

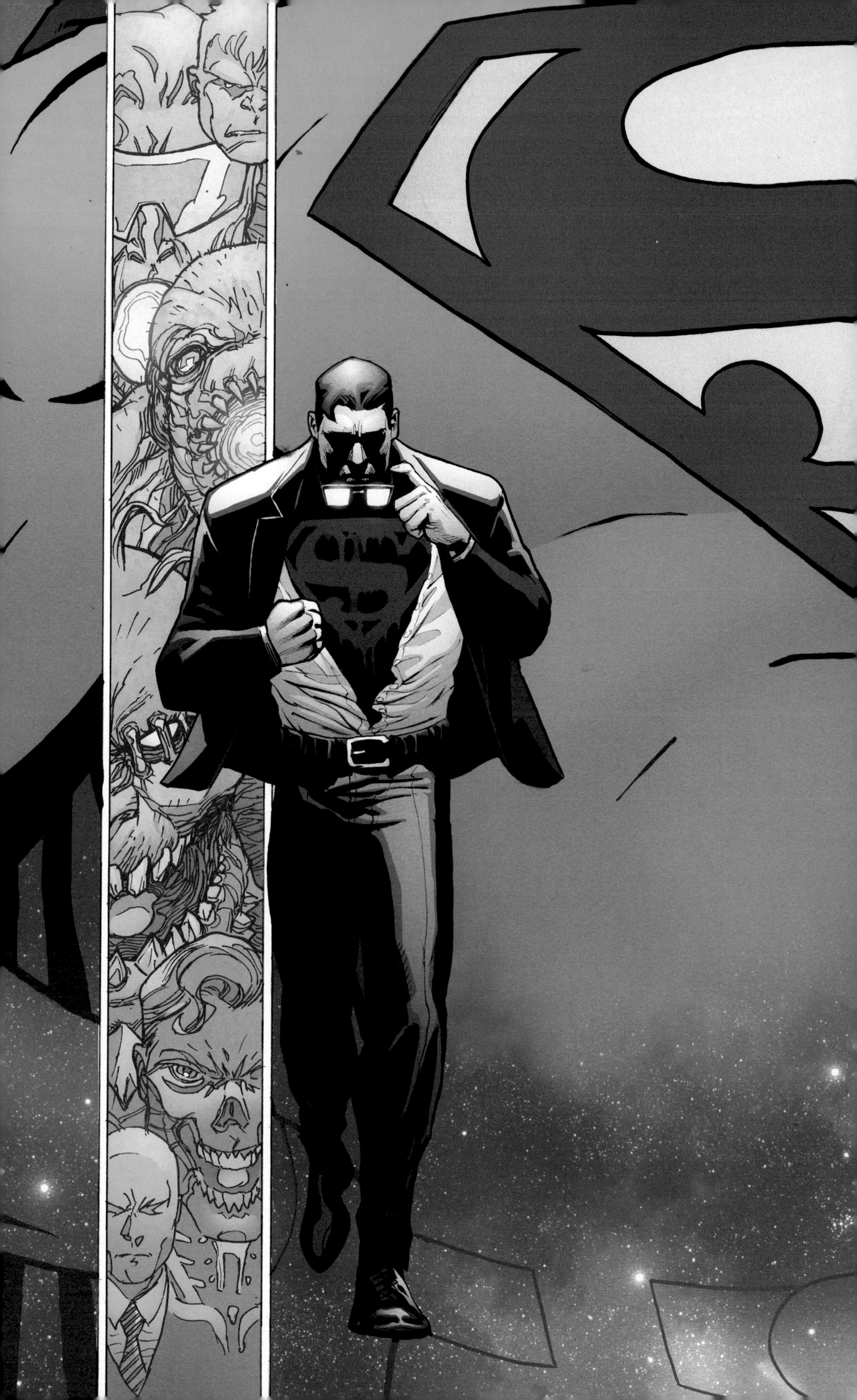

SUPERMAN: REBORN part two

DAN JURGENS writer * DOUG MAHNKE penciller
JAIME MENDOZA inker * WIL QUINTANA colorist
PATRICK GLEASON & JOHN KALISZ cover art

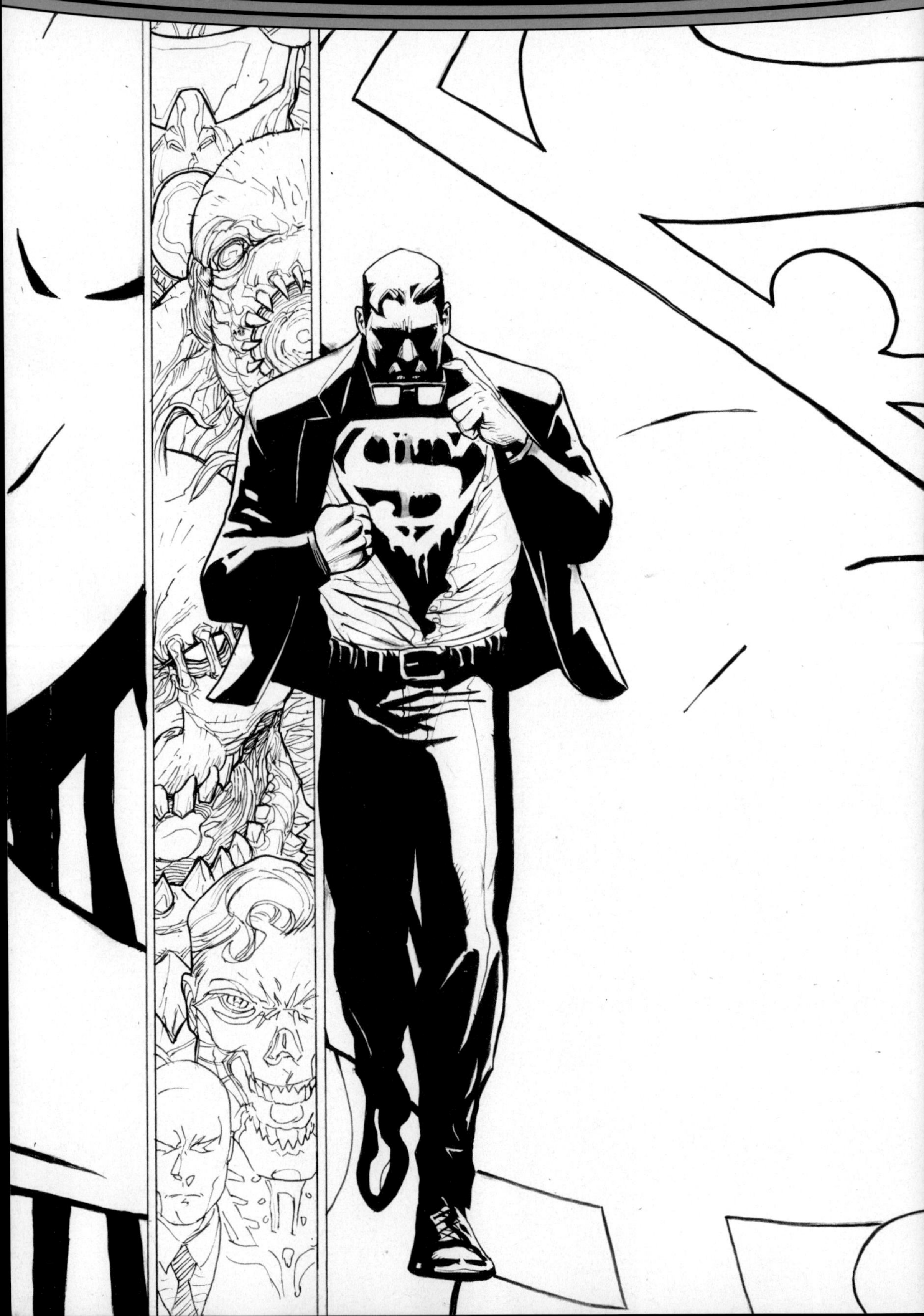

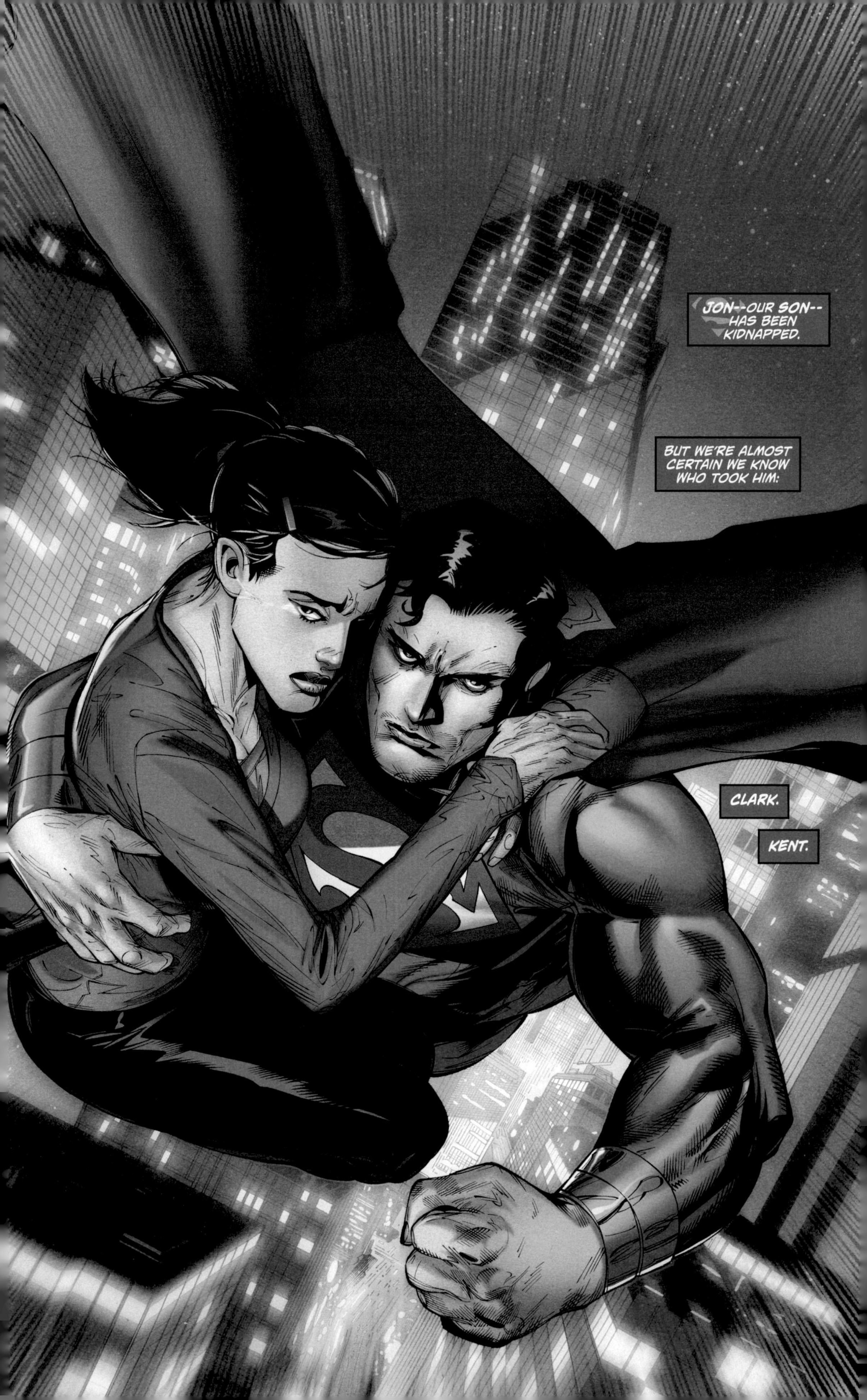
JON--OUR SON--HAS BEEN KIDNAPPED.
BUT WE'RE ALMOST CERTAIN WE KNOW WHO TOOK HIM:
CLARK.
KENT.

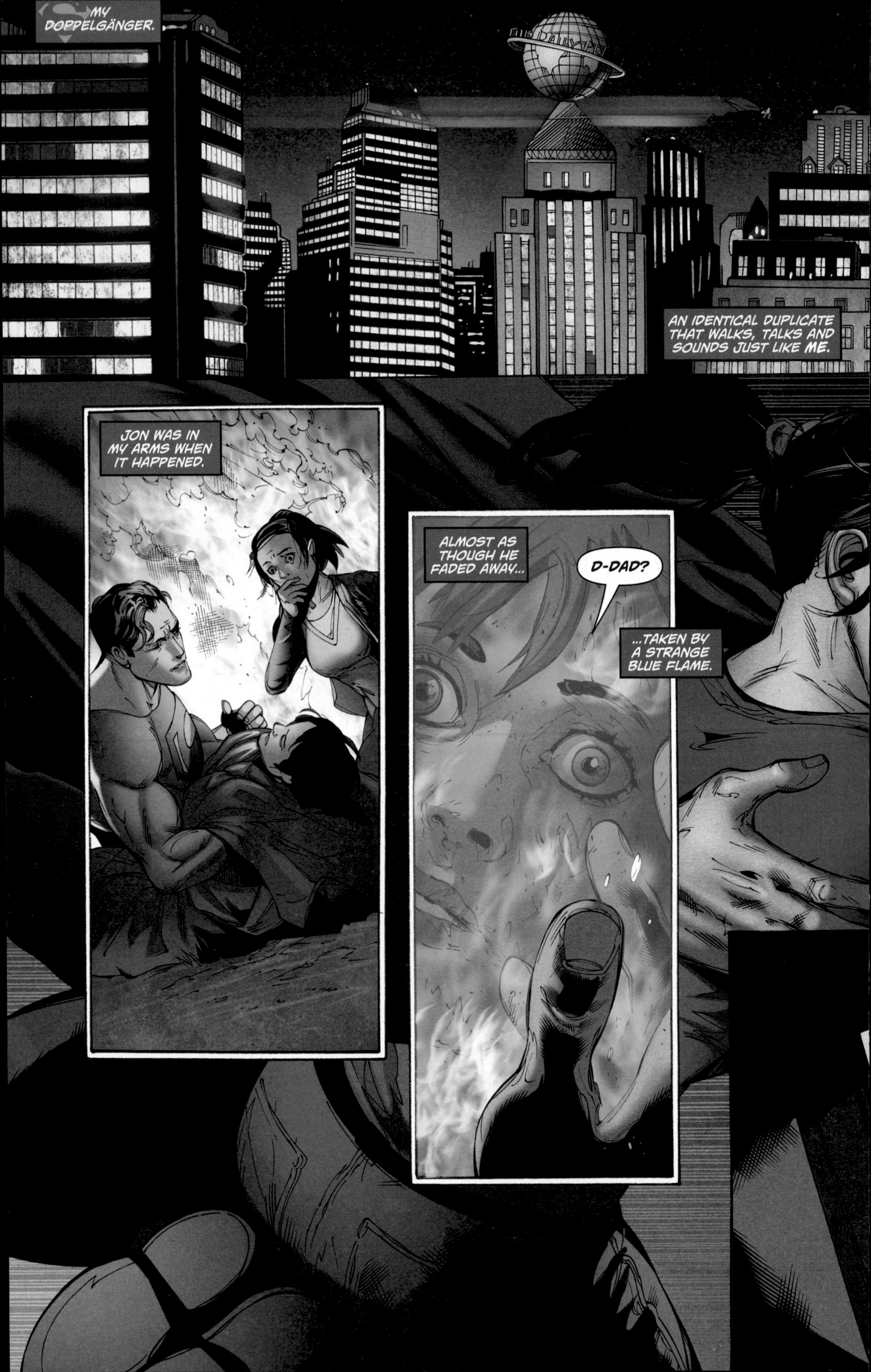

MY DOPPELGÄNGER.
AN IDENTICAL DUPLICATE THAT WALKS, TALKS AND SOUNDS JUST LIKE ME.
JON WAS IN MY ARMS WHEN IT HAPPENED.
ALMOST AS THOUGH HE FADED AWAY...
D-DAD?
...TAKEN BY A STRANGE BLUE FLAME.

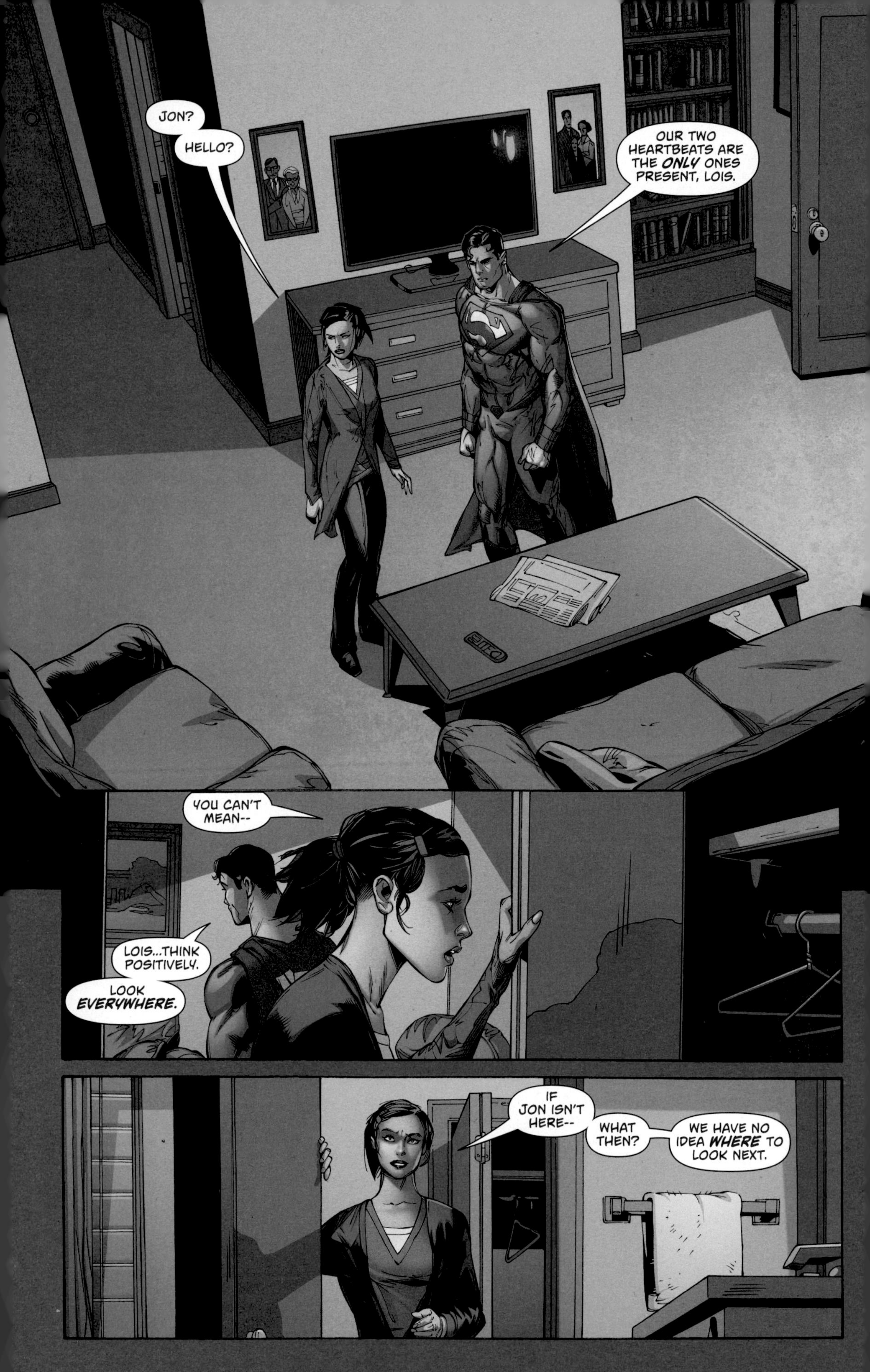
JON?
HELLO?
OUR TWO HEARTBEATS ARE THE ONLY ONES PRESENT, LOIS.
YOU CAN'T MEAN--
LOIS...THINK POSITIVELY.
LOOK EVERYWHERE.
IF JON ISN'T HERE--
WHAT THEN?
WE HAVE NO IDEA WHERE TO LOOK NEXT.

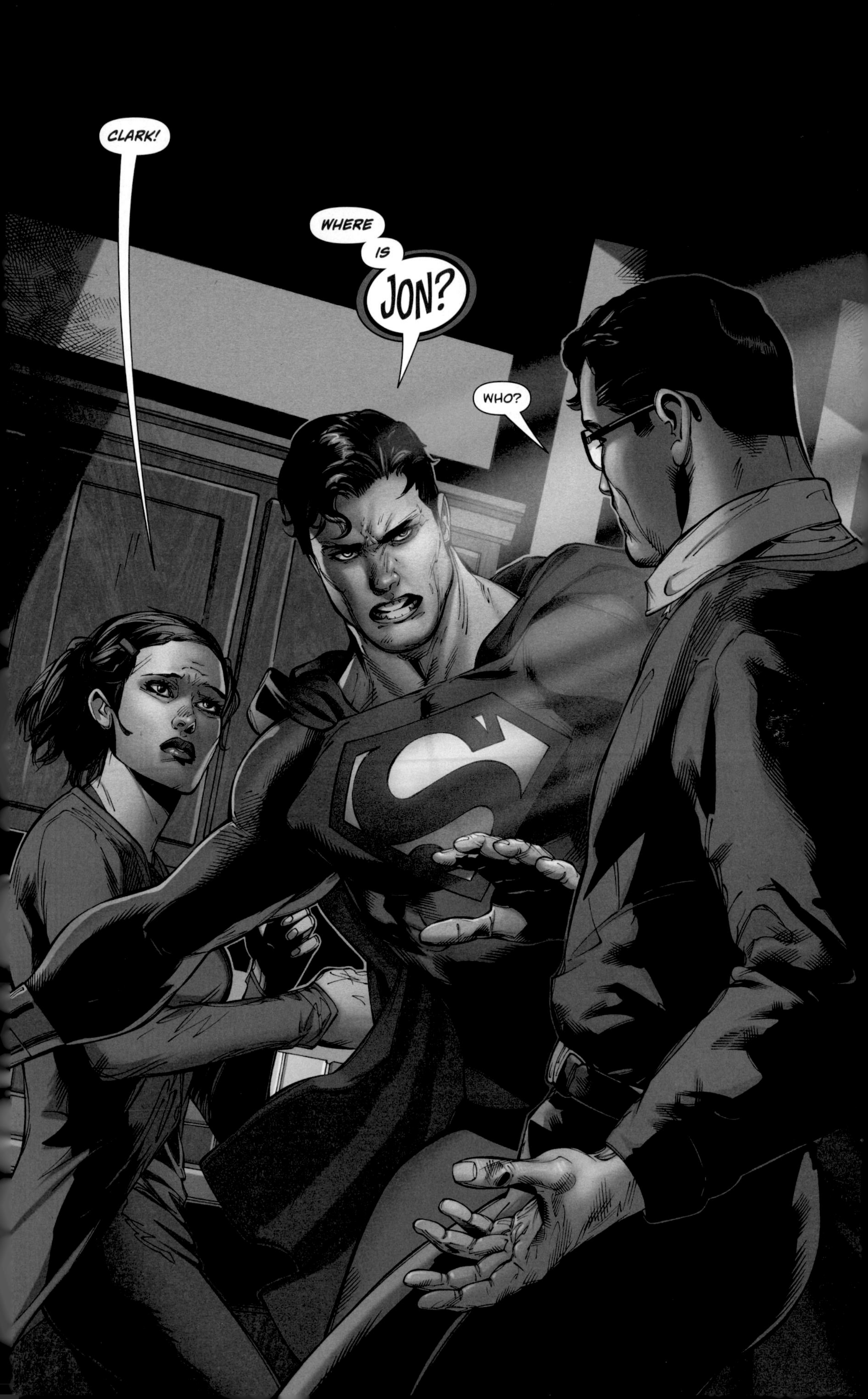
CLARK!
WHERE IS JON?
WHO?

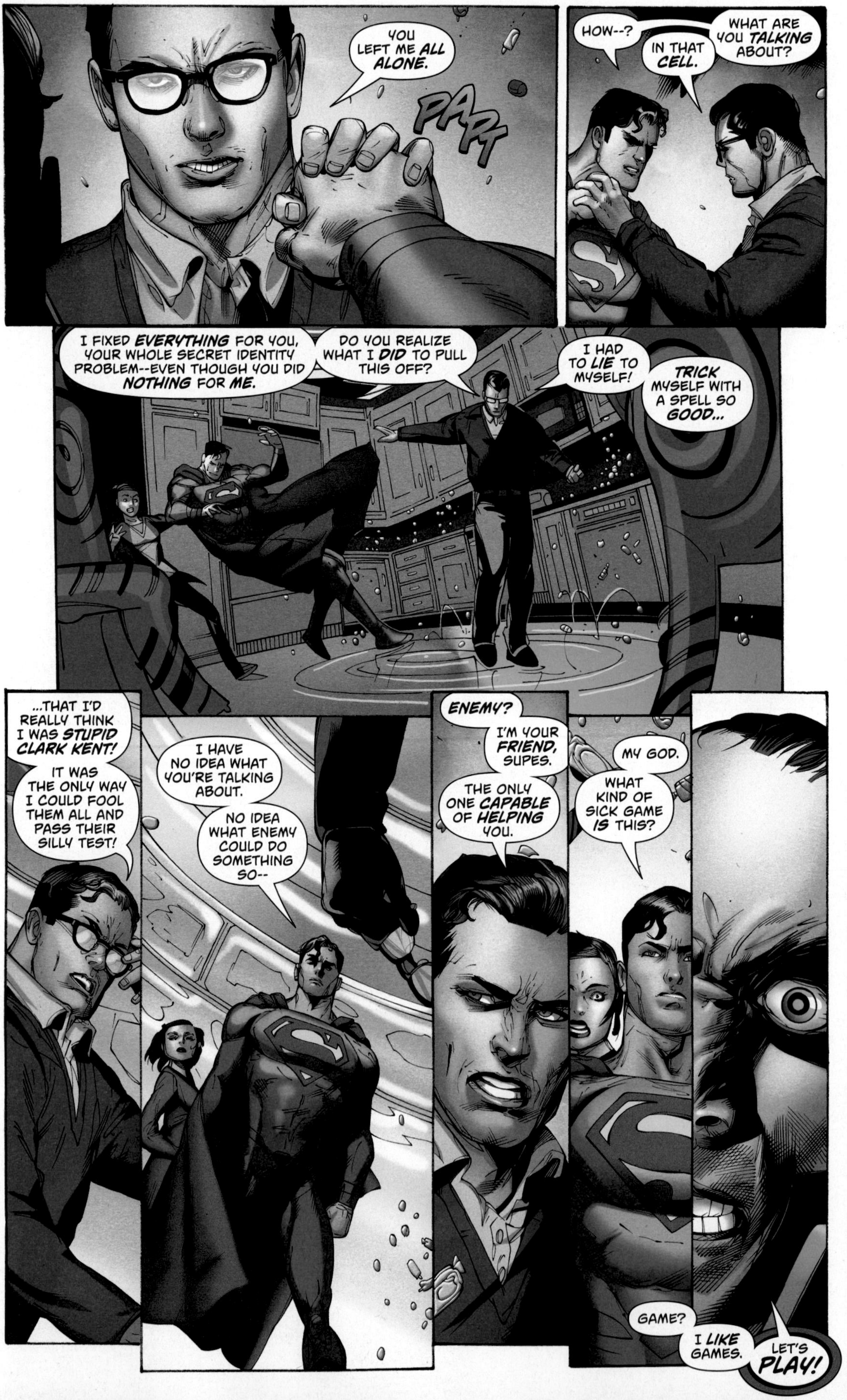

YOU LEFT ME ALL ALONE.
PAP!
HOW--?
IN THAT CELL.
WHAT ARE YOU TALKING ABOUT?
I FIXED EVERYTHING FOR YOU, YOUR WHOLE SECRET IDENTITY PROBLEM--EVEN THOUGH YOU DID NOTHING FOR ME.
DO YOU REALIZE WHAT I DID TO PULL THIS OFF?
I HAD TO LIE TO MYSELF!
TRICK MYSELF WITH A SPELL SO GOOD...
...THAT I'D REALLY THINK I WAS STUPID CLARK KENT!
IT WAS THE ONLY WAY I COULD FOOL THEM ALL AND PASS THEIR SILLY TEST!
I HAVE NO IDEA WHAT YOU'RE TALKING ABOUT.
NO IDEA WHAT ENEMY COULD DO SOMETHING SO--
ENEMY?
I'M YOUR FRIEND, SUPES.
THE ONLY ONE CAPABLE OF HELPING YOU.
MY GOD.
WHAT KIND OF SICK GAME IS THIS?
GAME?
I LIKE GAMES.
LET'S PLAY!

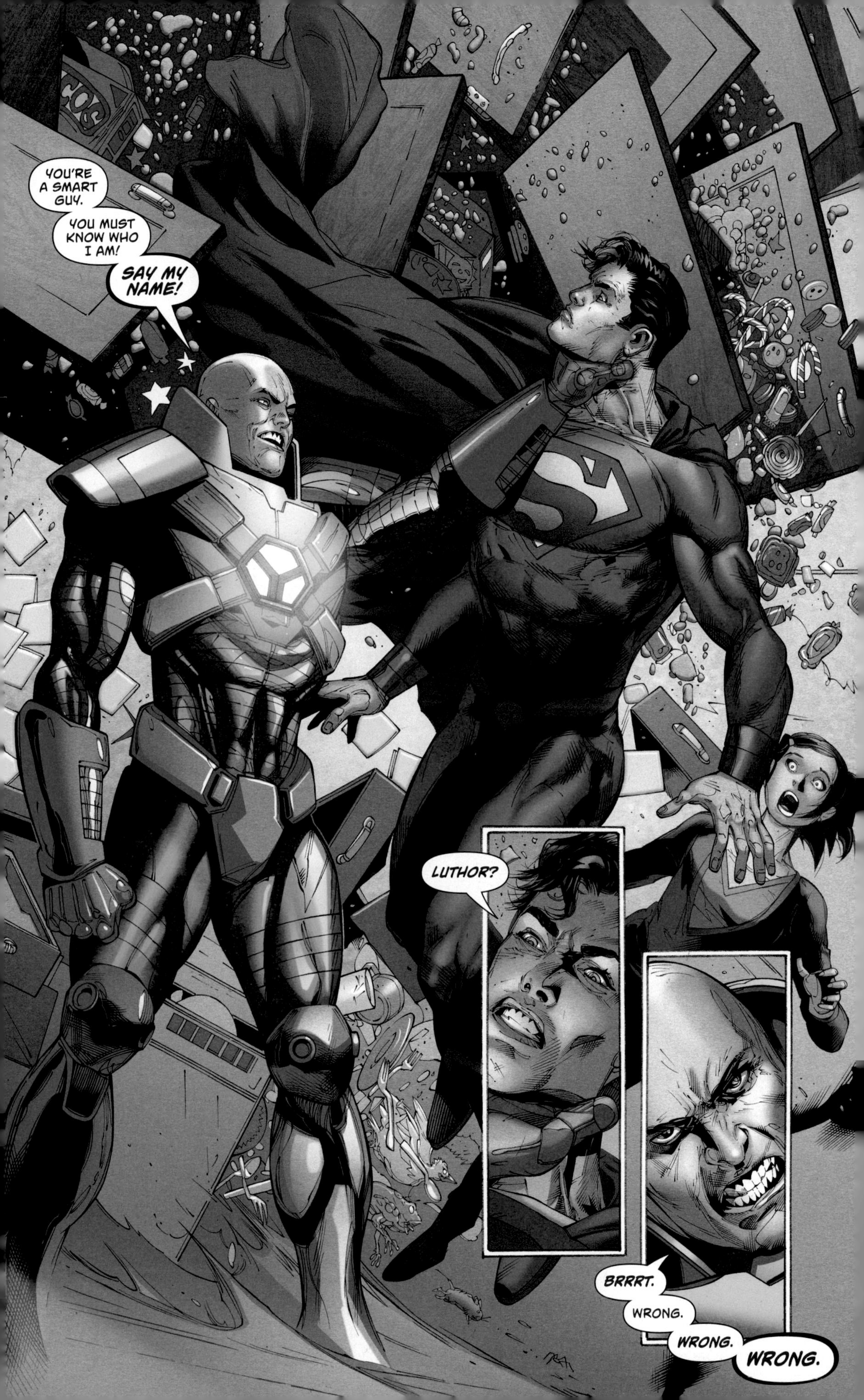
YOU'RE A SMART GUY.
YOU MUST KNOW WHO I AM!
SAY MY NAME!
LUTHOR?
BRRRT.
WRONG.
WRONG.
WRONG.

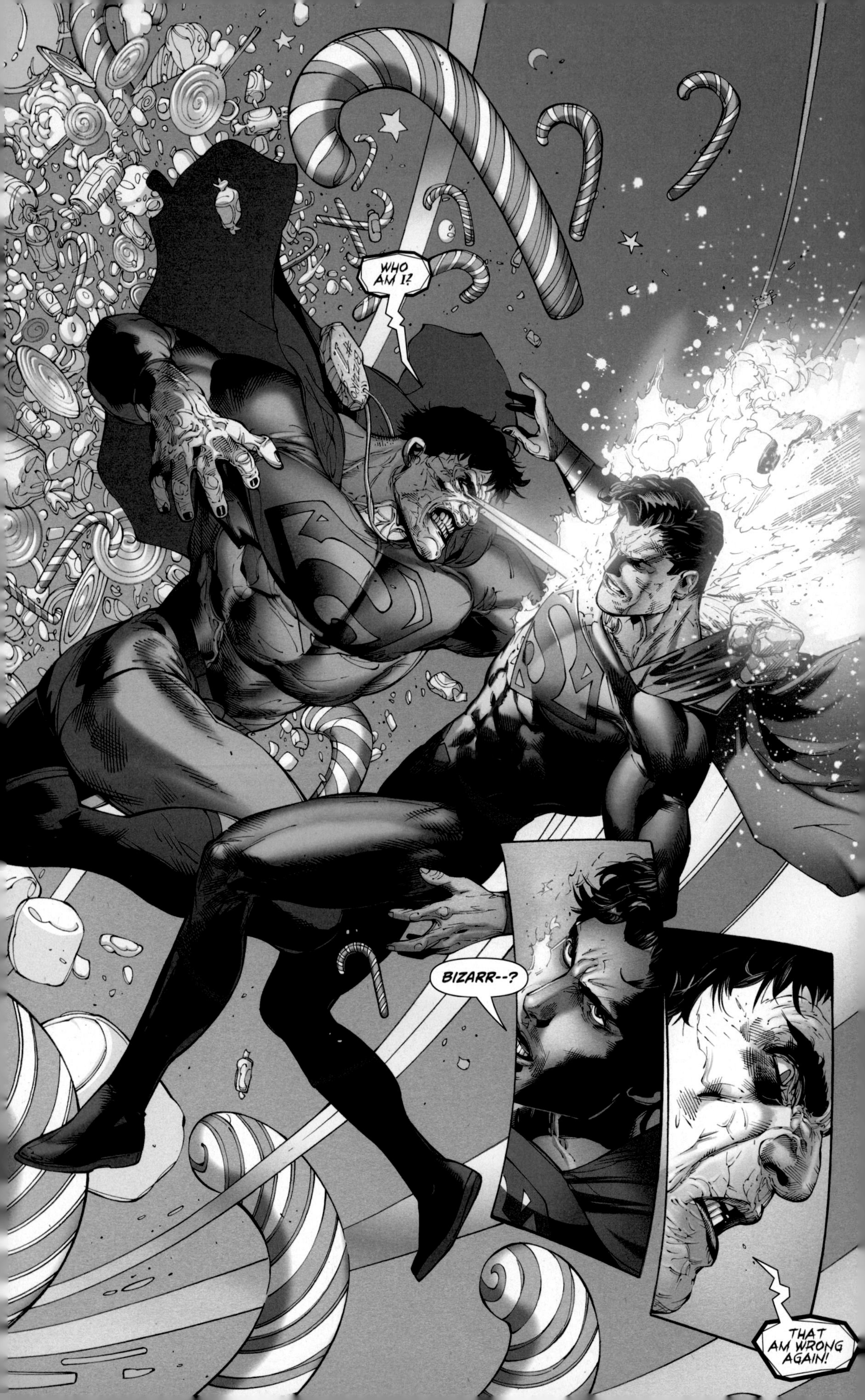
WHO AM I?
BIZARR--?
THAT AM WRONG AGAIN!

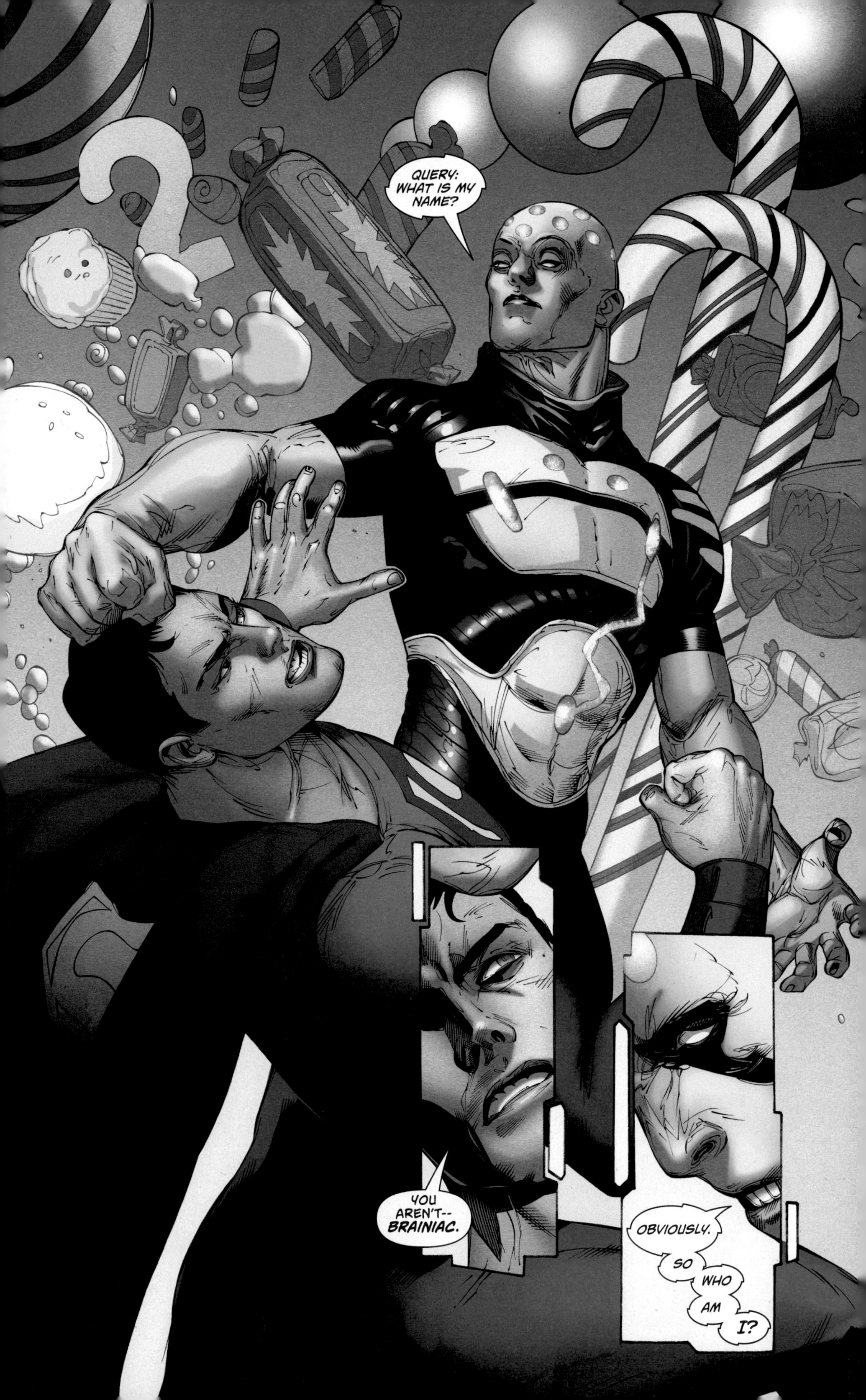
QUERY: WHAT IS MY NAME?
YOU AREN'T-- BRAINIAC.
OBVIOUSLY.
SO
WHO
AM
I?

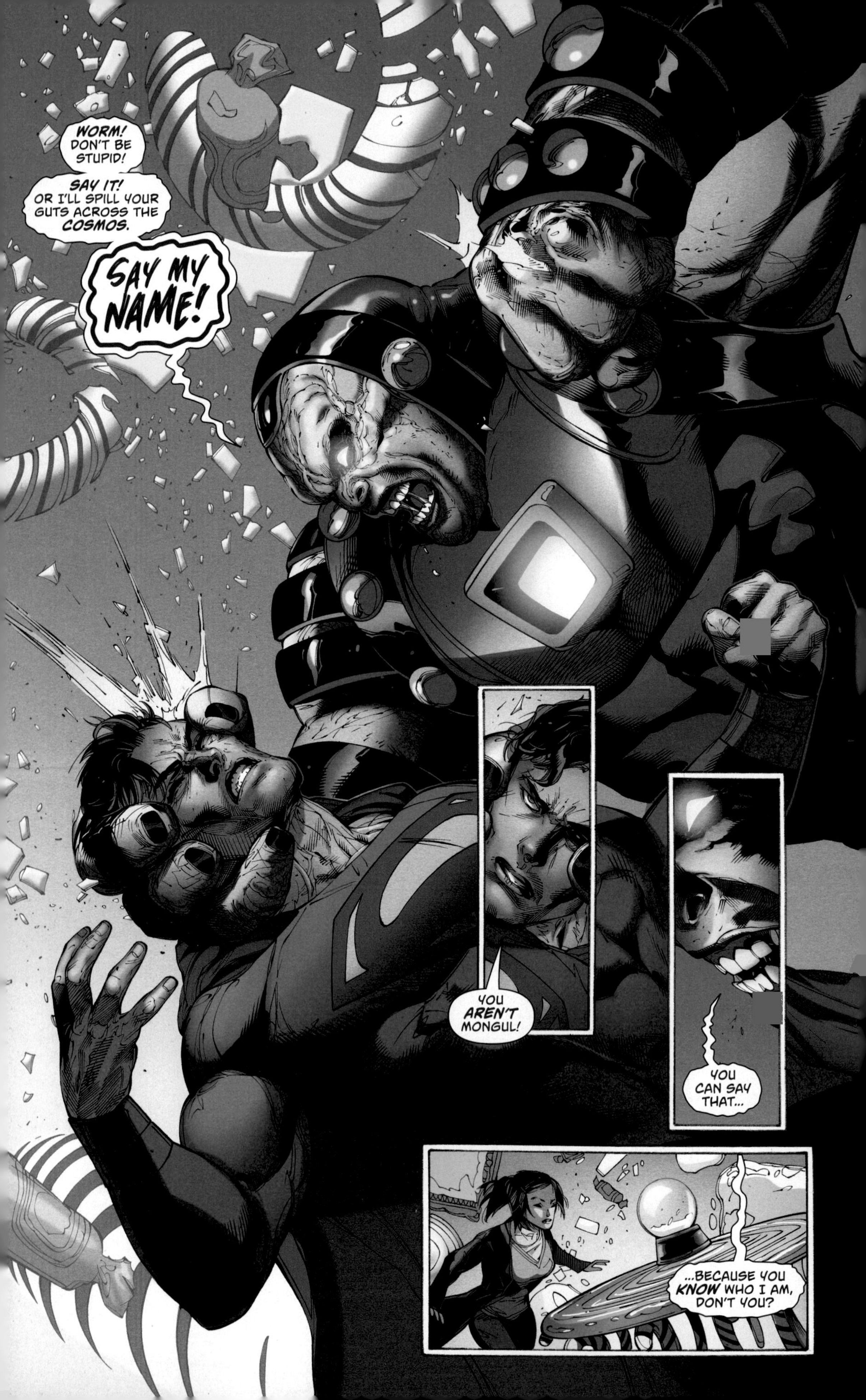
WORM! DON'T BE STUPID!
SAY IT! OR I'LL SPILL YOUR GUTS ACROSS THE COSMOS.
SAY MY NAME!
YOU AREN'T MONGUL!
YOU CAN SAY THAT...
...BECAUSE YOU KNOW WHO I AM, DON'T YOU?

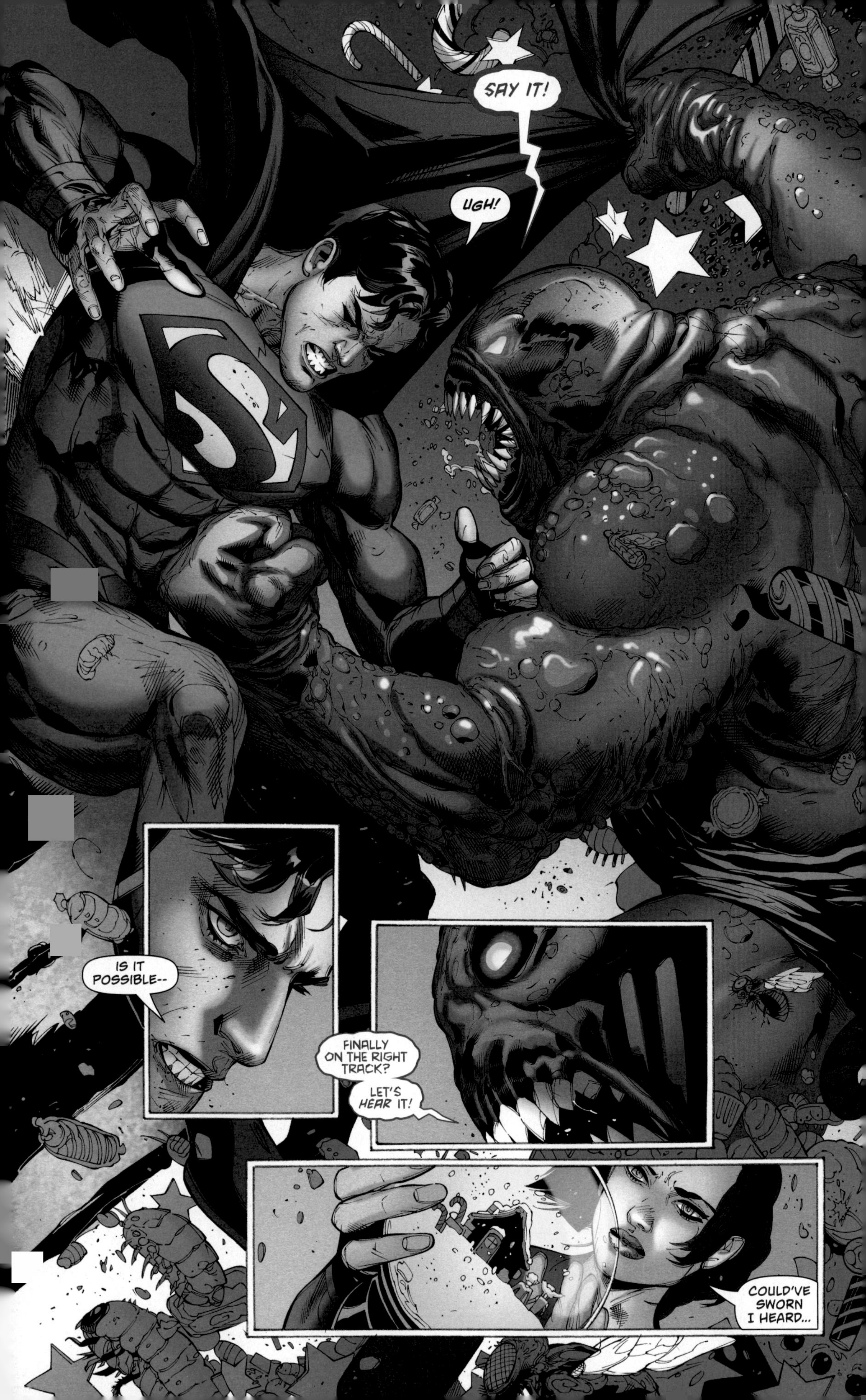
SAY IT!
UGH!
IS IT POSSIBLE--
FINALLY ON THE RIGHT TRACK?
LET'S HEAR IT!
COULD'VE SWORN I HEARD...

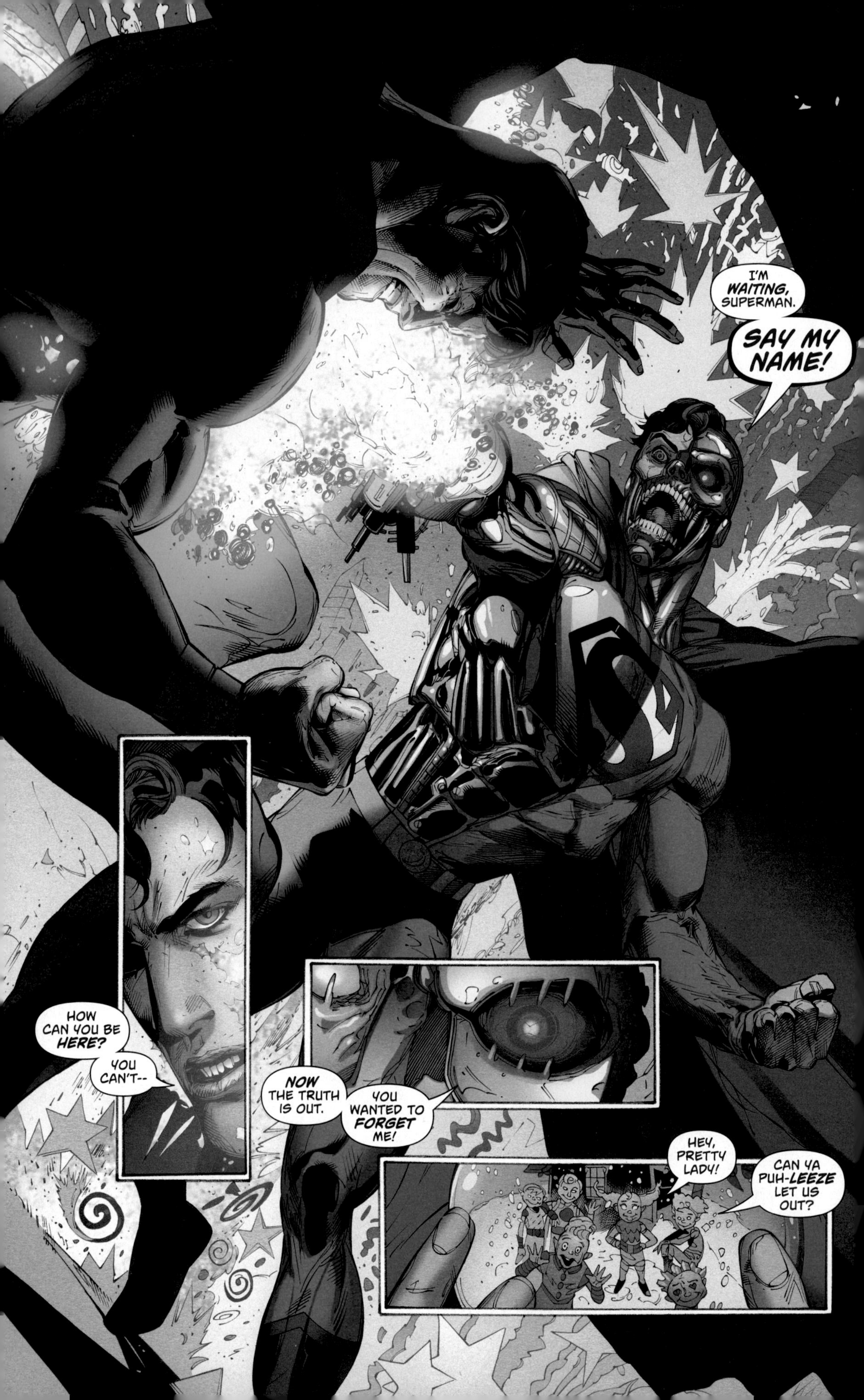
I'M *WAITING*, SUPERMAN.
SAY MY NAME!
HOW CAN YOU BE ***HERE?***
YOU CAN'T--
NOW THE TRUTH IS OUT.
YOU WANTED TO ***FORGET*** ME!
HEY, PRETTY LADY!
CAN YA PUH-***LEEZE*** LET US OUT?

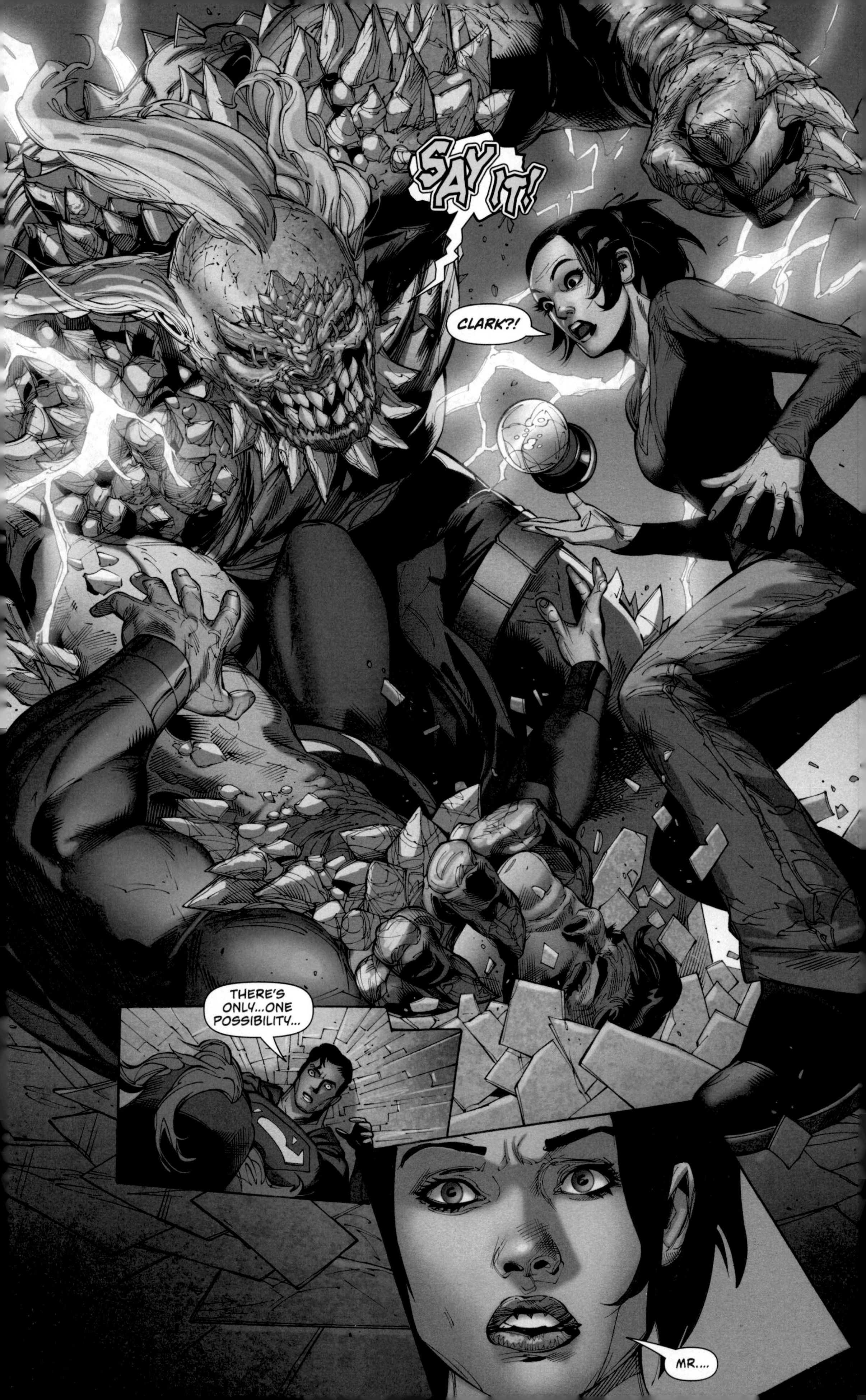
SAY IT!
CLARK?!
THERE'S ONLY...ONE POSSIBILITY...
MR....

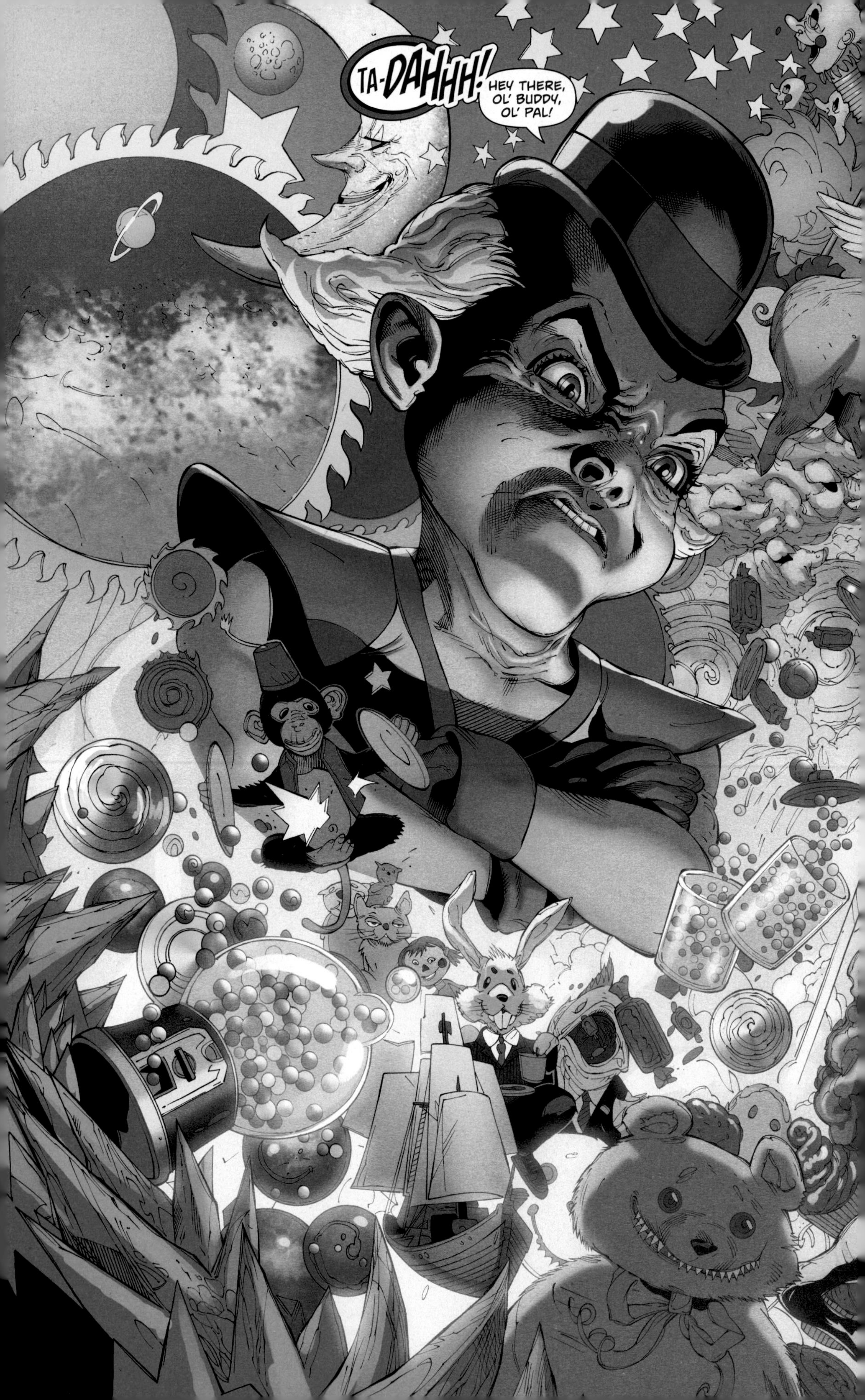
TA-DAHHH!
HEY THERE, OL' BUDDY, OL' PAL!

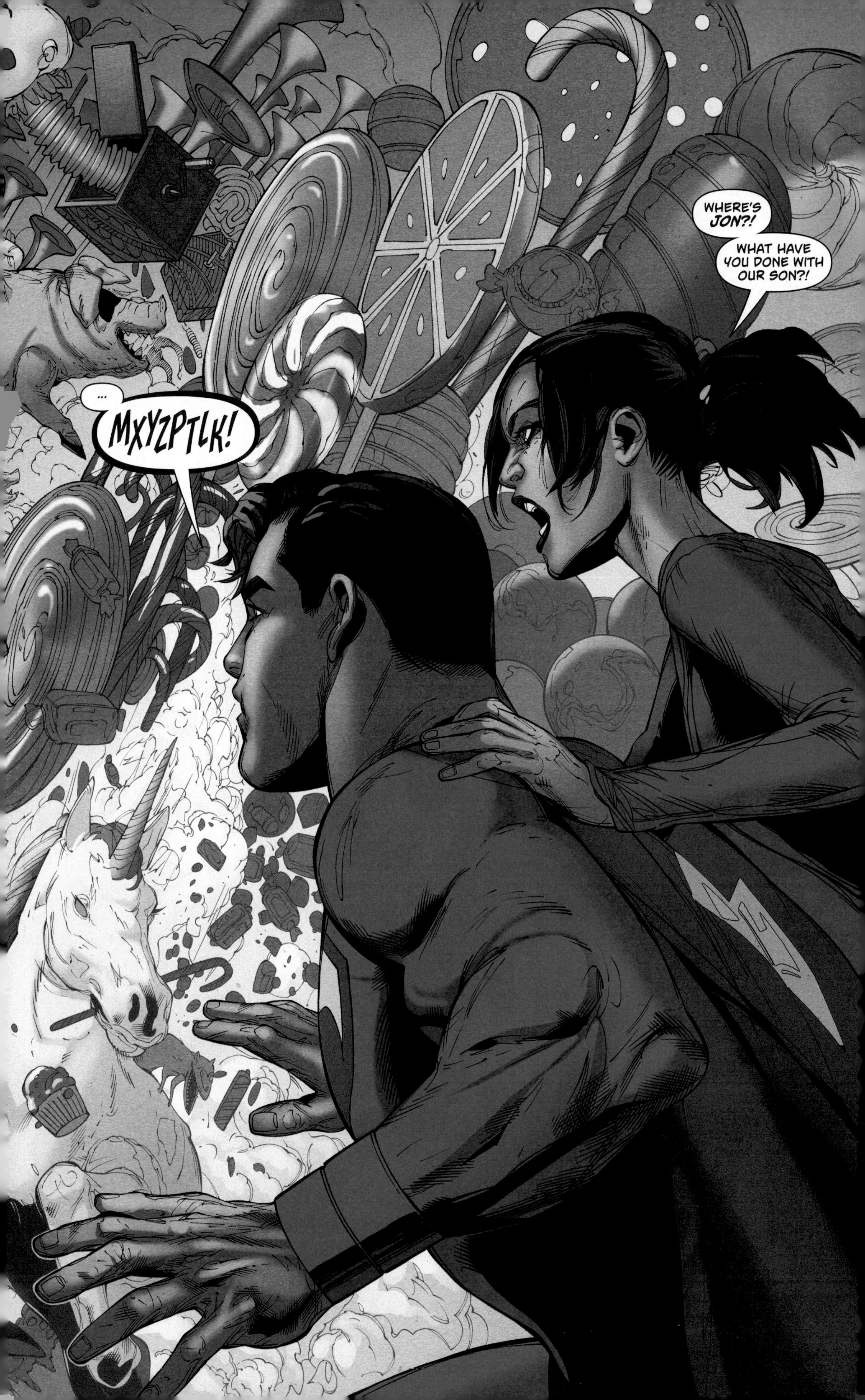
WHERE'S JON?!
WHAT HAVE YOU DONE WITH OUR SON?!
...
MXYZPTLK!

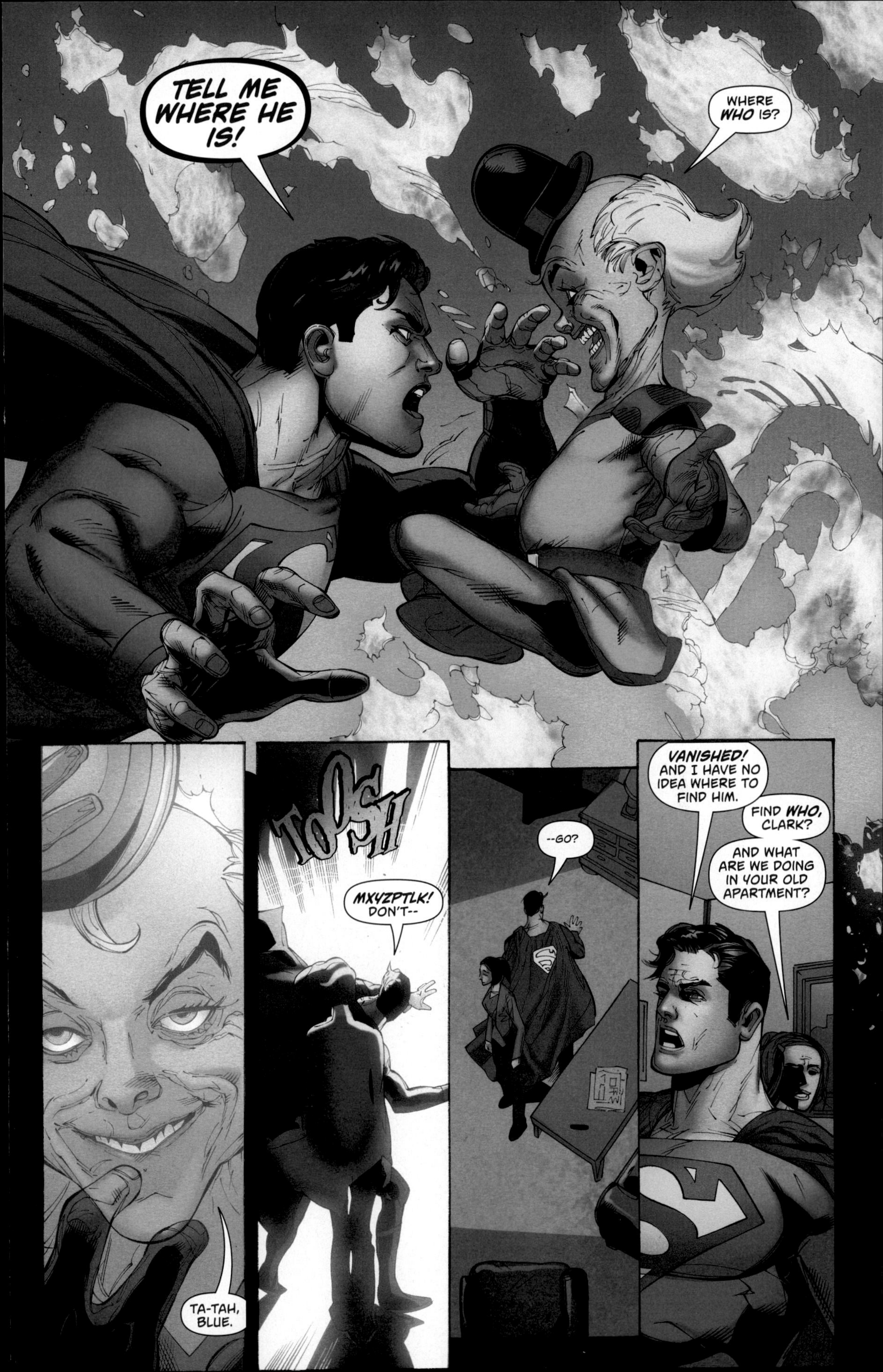

TELL ME WHERE HE IS!
WHERE WHO IS?
TA-TAH, BLUE.
TOOSH
MXYZPTLK! DON'T--
--GO?
VANISHED! AND I HAVE NO IDEA WHERE TO FIND HIM.
FIND WHO, CLARK?
AND WHAT ARE WE DOING IN YOUR OLD APARTMENT?

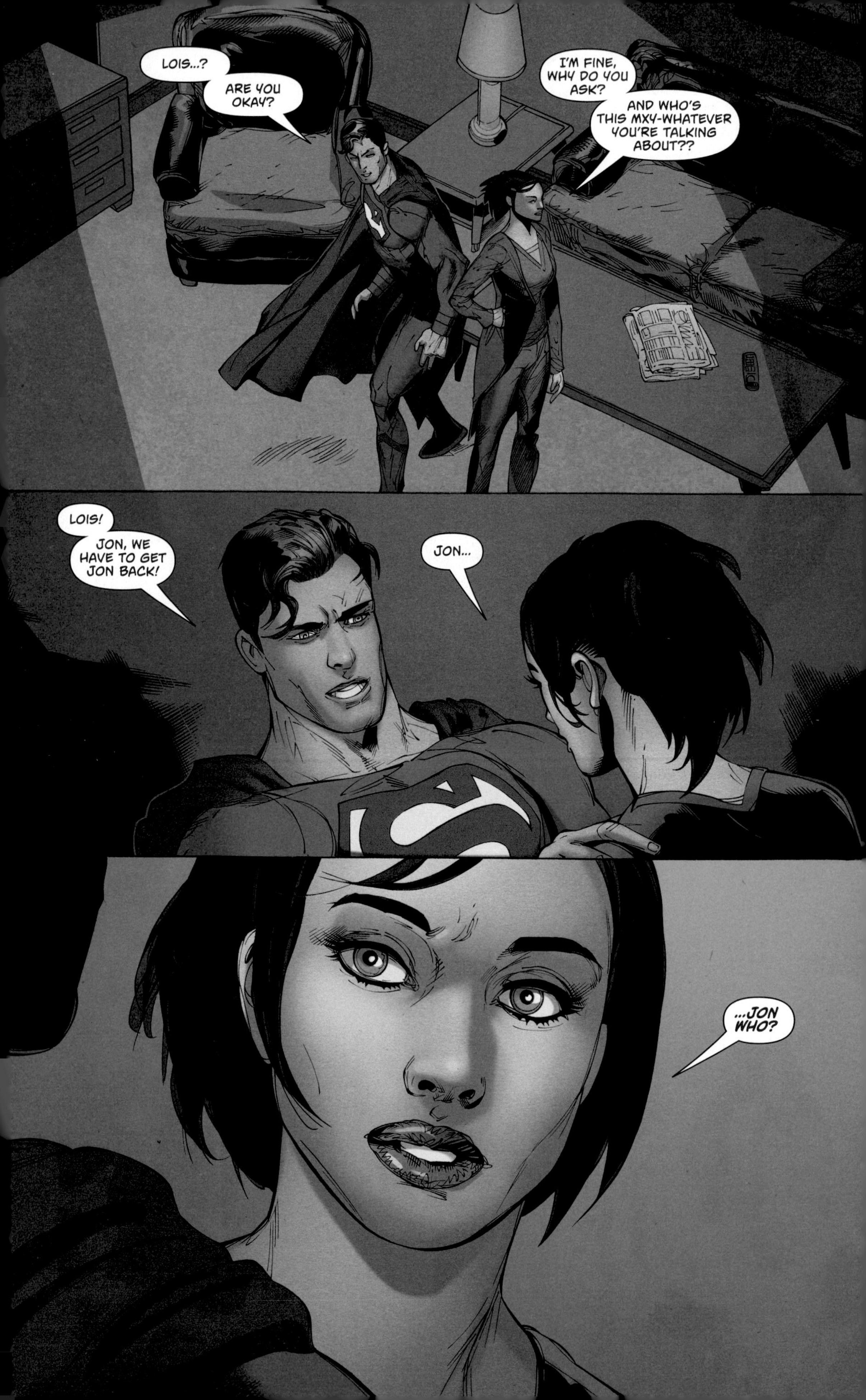
LOIS...?
ARE YOU OKAY?
I'M FINE, WHY DO YOU ASK?
AND WHO'S THIS MXY-WHATEVER YOU'RE TALKING ABOUT??
LOIS!
JON, WE HAVE TO GET JON BACK!
JON...
...JON WHO?

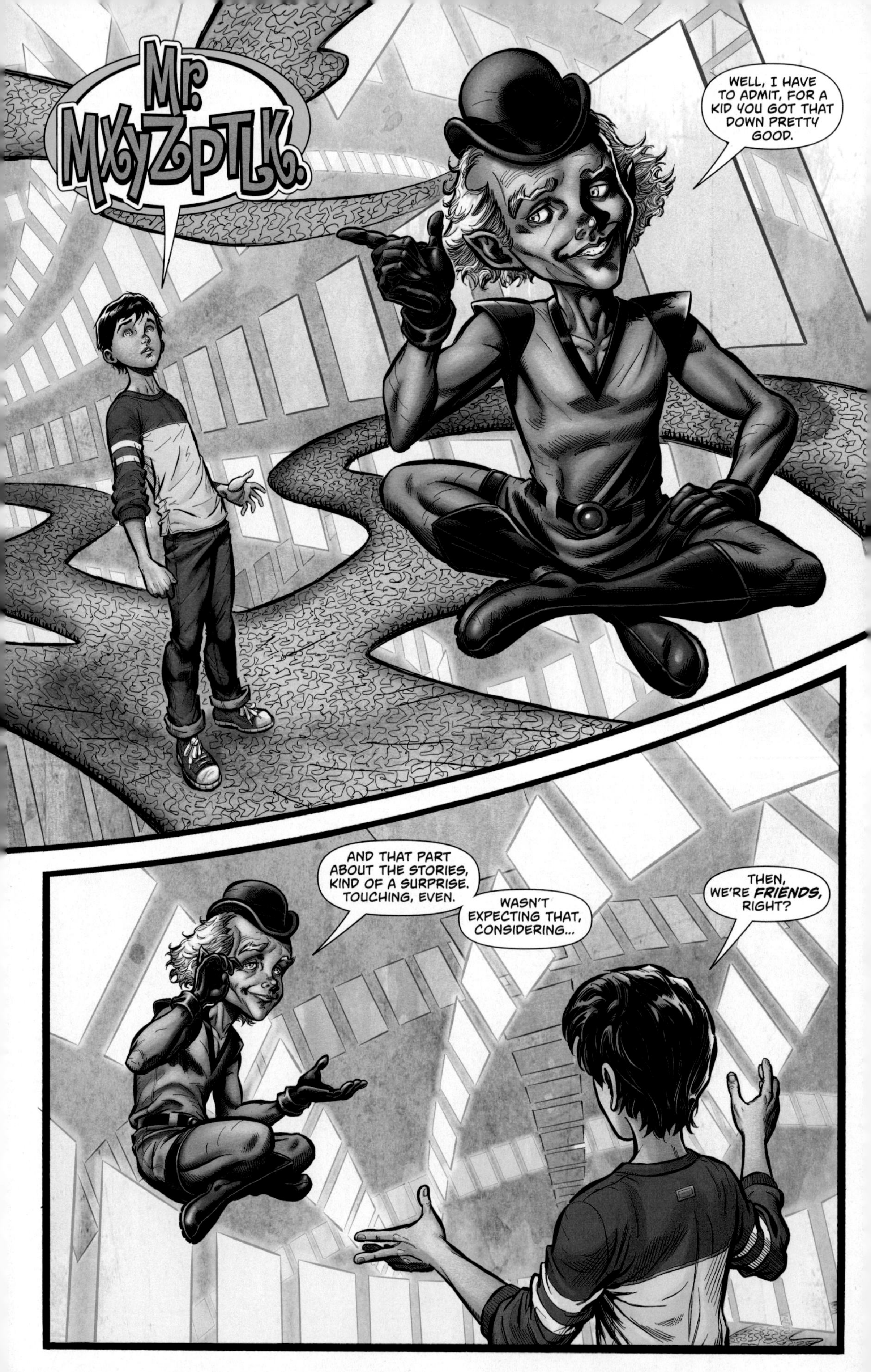
Mr. MXYZPTLK.
WELL, I HAVE TO ADMIT, FOR A KID YOU GOT THAT DOWN PRETTY GOOD.
AND THAT PART ABOUT THE STORIES, KIND OF A SURPRISE. TOUCHING, EVEN.
WASN'T EXPECTING THAT, CONSIDERING...
THEN, WE'RE FRIENDS, RIGHT?

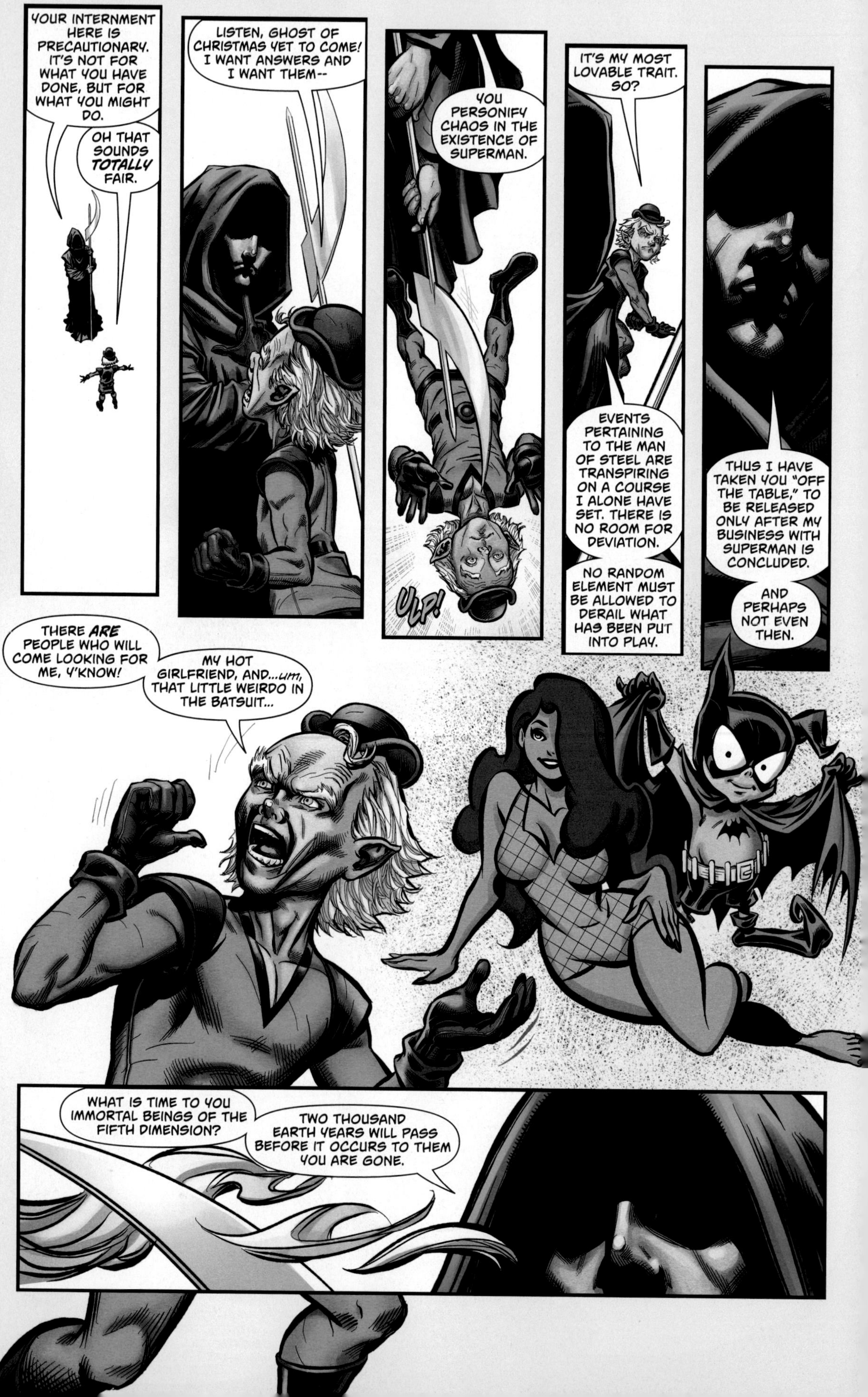
YOUR INTERNMENT HERE IS PRECAUTIONARY. IT'S NOT FOR WHAT YOU HAVE DONE, BUT FOR WHAT YOU MIGHT DO.
OH THAT SOUNDS TOTALLY FAIR.
LISTEN, GHOST OF CHRISTMAS YET TO COME! I WANT ANSWERS AND I WANT THEM--
YOU PERSONIFY CHAOS IN THE EXISTENCE OF SUPERMAN.
ULP!
IT'S MY MOST LOVABLE TRAIT. SO?
EVENTS PERTAINING TO THE MAN OF STEEL ARE TRANSPIRING ON A COURSE I ALONE HAVE SET. THERE IS NO ROOM FOR DEVIATION.
NO RANDOM ELEMENT MUST BE ALLOWED TO DERAIL WHAT HAS BEEN PUT INTO PLAY.
THUS I HAVE TAKEN YOU "OFF THE TABLE," TO BE RELEASED ONLY AFTER MY BUSINESS WITH SUPERMAN IS CONCLUDED.
AND PERHAPS NOT EVEN THEN.
THERE ARE PEOPLE WHO WILL COME LOOKING FOR ME, Y'KNOW!
MY HOT GIRLFRIEND, AND...um, THAT LITTLE WEIRDO IN THE BATSUIT...
WHAT IS TIME TO YOU IMMORTAL BEINGS OF THE FIFTH DIMENSION?
TWO THOUSAND EARTH YEARS WILL PASS BEFORE IT OCCURS TO THEM YOU ARE GONE.

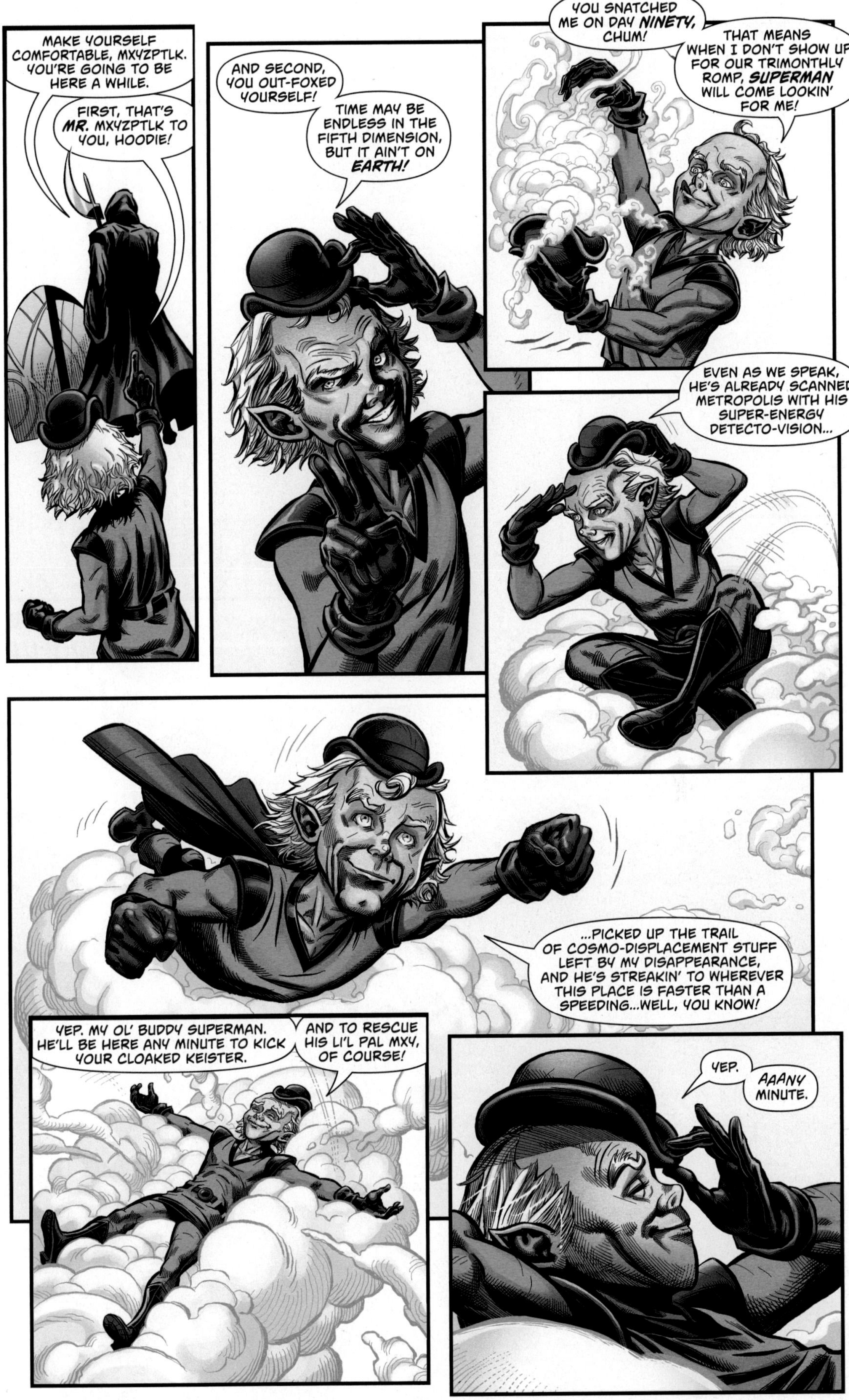
MAKE YOURSELF COMFORTABLE, MXYZPTLK. YOU'RE GOING TO BE HERE A WHILE.
FIRST, THAT'S MR. MXYZPTLK TO YOU, HOODIE!
AND SECOND, YOU OUT-FOXED YOURSELF!
TIME MAY BE ENDLESS IN THE FIFTH DIMENSION, BUT IT AIN'T ON EARTH!
YOU SNATCHED ME ON DAY NINETY, CHUM!
THAT MEANS WHEN I DON'T SHOW UP FOR OUR TRIMONTHLY ROMP, SUPERMAN WILL COME LOOKIN' FOR ME!
EVEN AS WE SPEAK, HE'S ALREADY SCANNED METROPOLIS WITH HIS SUPER-ENERGY DETECTO-VISION...
...PICKED UP THE TRAIL OF COSMO-DISPLACEMENT STUFF LEFT BY MY DISAPPEARANCE, AND HE'S STREAKIN' TO WHEREVER THIS PLACE IS FASTER THAN A SPEEDING...WELL, YOU KNOW!
YEP. MY OL' BUDDY SUPERMAN. HE'LL BE HERE ANY MINUTE TO KICK YOUR CLOAKED KEISTER.
AND TO RESCUE HIS LI'L PAL MXY, OF COURSE!
YEP.
AAANY MINUTE.

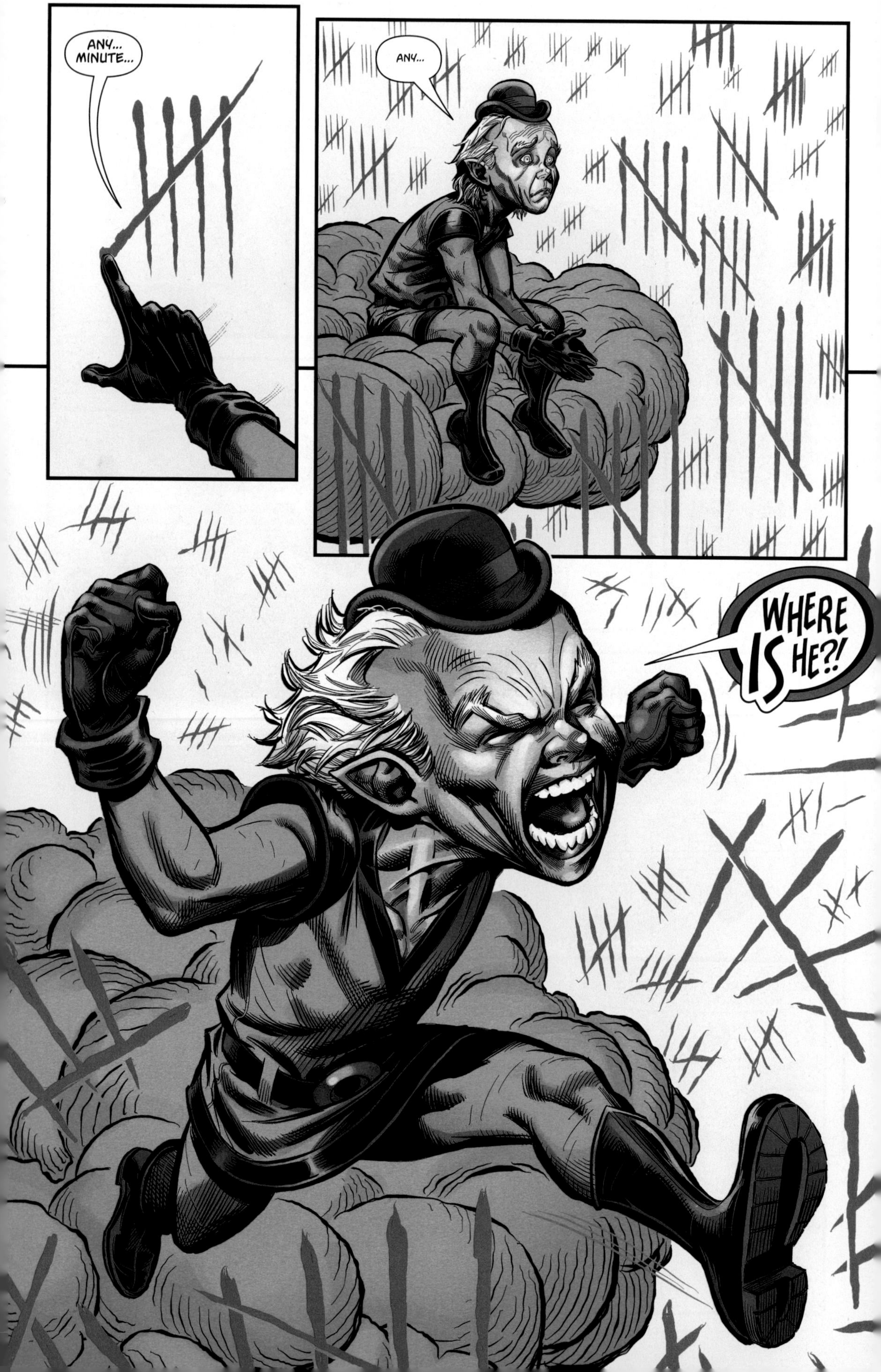
ANY... MINUTE...
ANY...
WHERE IS HE?!

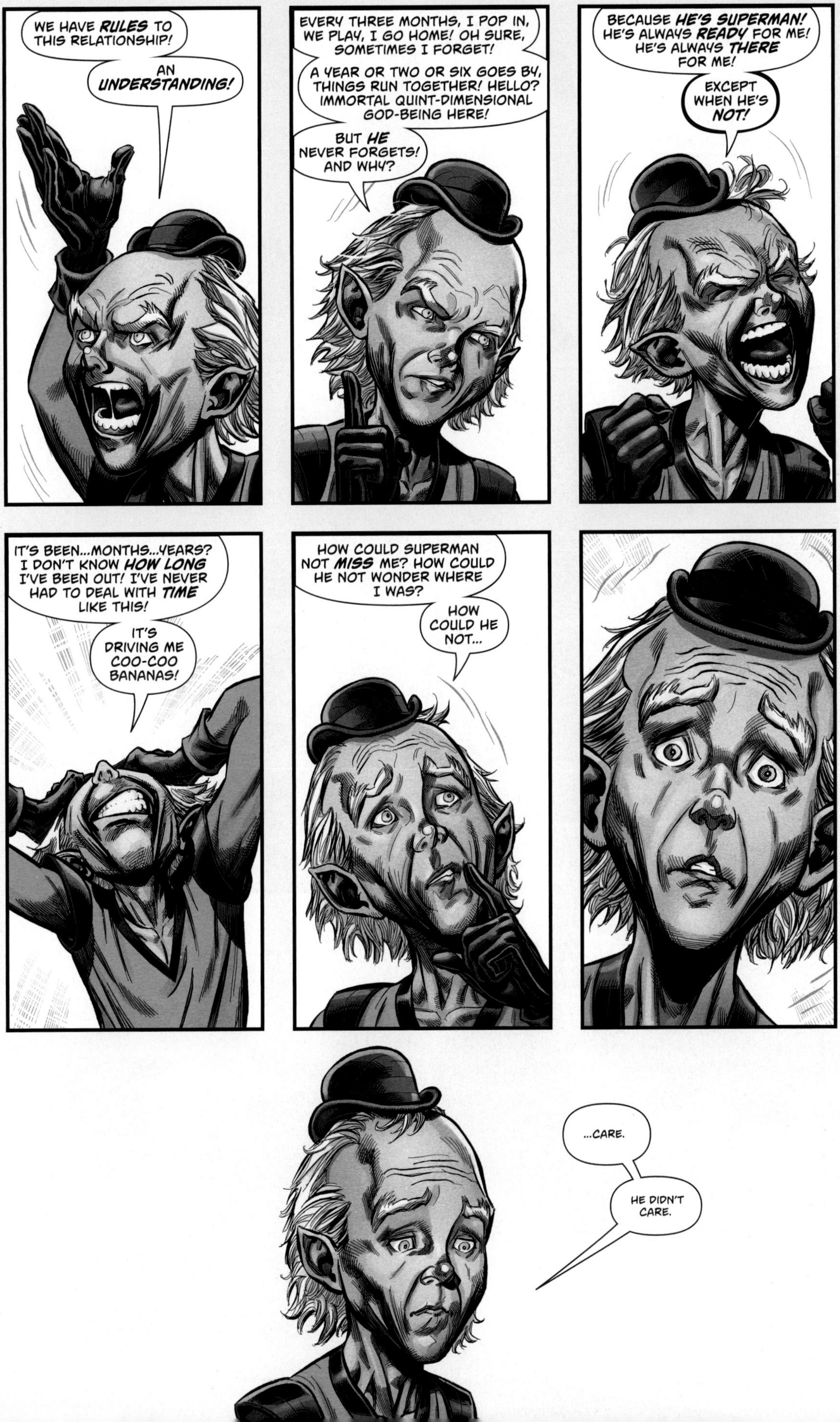
WE HAVE RULES TO THIS RELATIONSHIP!
AN UNDERSTANDING!
EVERY THREE MONTHS, I POP IN, WE PLAY, I GO HOME! OH SURE, SOMETIMES I FORGET!
A YEAR OR TWO OR SIX GOES BY, THINGS RUN TOGETHER! HELLO? IMMORTAL QUINT-DIMENSIONAL GOD-BEING HERE!
BUT HE NEVER FORGETS! AND WHY?
BECAUSE HE'S SUPERMAN! HE'S ALWAYS READY FOR ME! HE'S ALWAYS THERE FOR ME!
EXCEPT WHEN HE'S NOT!
IT'S BEEN...MONTHS...YEARS? I DON'T KNOW HOW LONG I'VE BEEN OUT! I'VE NEVER HAD TO DEAL WITH TIME LIKE THIS!
IT'S DRIVING ME COO-COO BANANAS!
HOW COULD SUPERMAN NOT MISS ME? HOW COULD HE NOT WONDER WHERE I WAS?
HOW COULD HE NOT...
...CARE.
HE DIDN'T CARE.

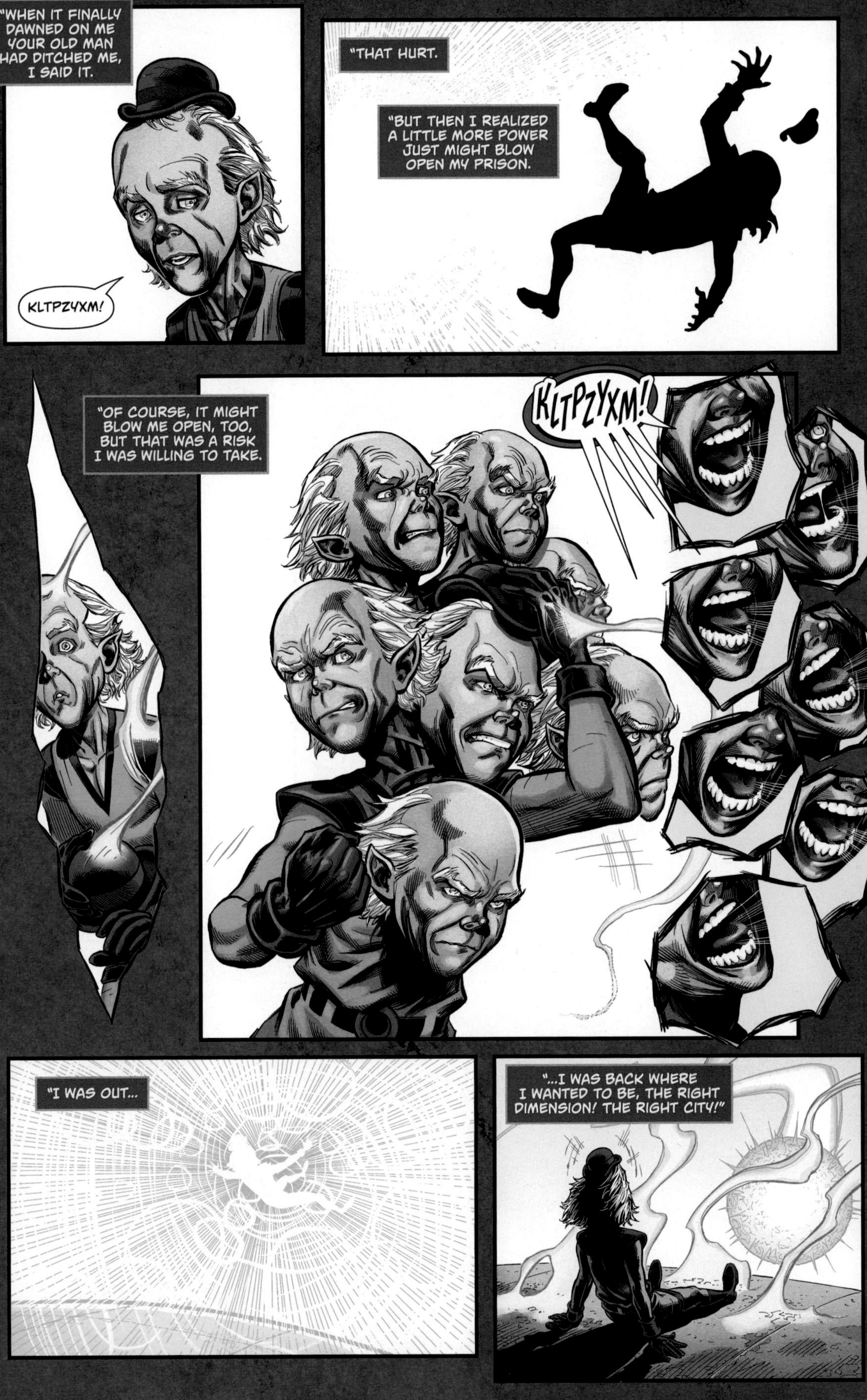
"WHEN IT FINALLY DAWNED ON ME YOUR OLD MAN HAD DITCHED ME, I SAID IT.
KLTPZYXM!
"THAT HURT.
"BUT THEN I REALIZED A LITTLE MORE POWER JUST MIGHT BLOW OPEN MY PRISON.
"OF COURSE, IT MIGHT BLOW ME OPEN, TOO, BUT THAT WAS A RISK I WAS WILLING TO TAKE.
KLTPZYXM!
"I WAS OUT...
"...I WAS BACK WHERE I WANTED TO BE, THE RIGHT DIMENSION! THE RIGHT CITY!"

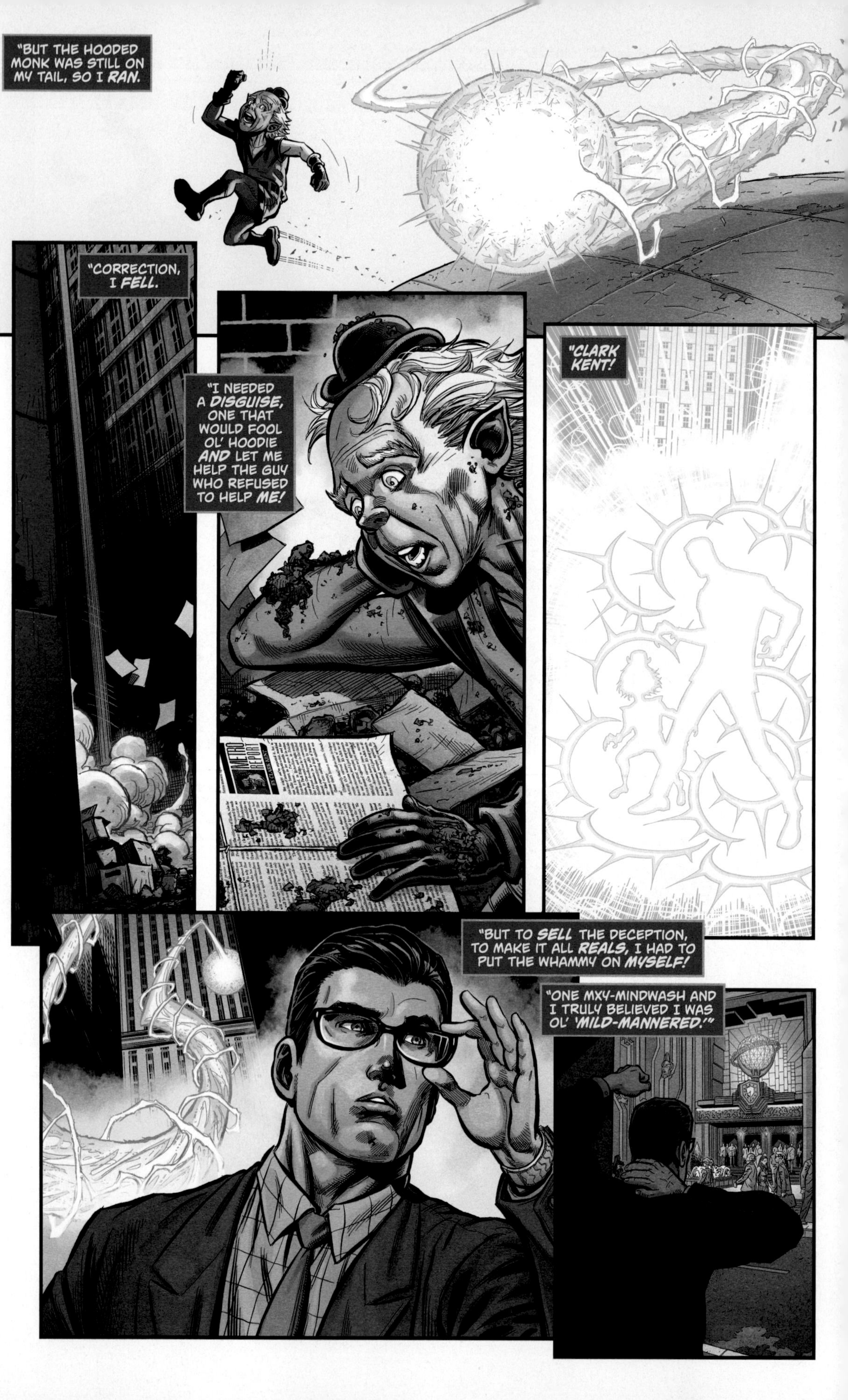
"BUT THE HOODED MONK WAS STILL ON MY TAIL, SO I RAN.
"CORRECTION, I FELL.
"I NEEDED A DISGUISE, ONE THAT WOULD FOOL OL' HOODIE AND LET ME HELP THE GUY WHO REFUSED TO HELP ME!
METRO REPORT
"CLARK KENT!
"BUT TO SELL THE DECEPTION, TO MAKE IT ALL REALS, I HAD TO PUT THE WHAMMY ON MYSELF!
"ONE MXY-MINDWASH AND I TRULY BELIEVED I WAS OL' 'MILD-MANNERED.'"

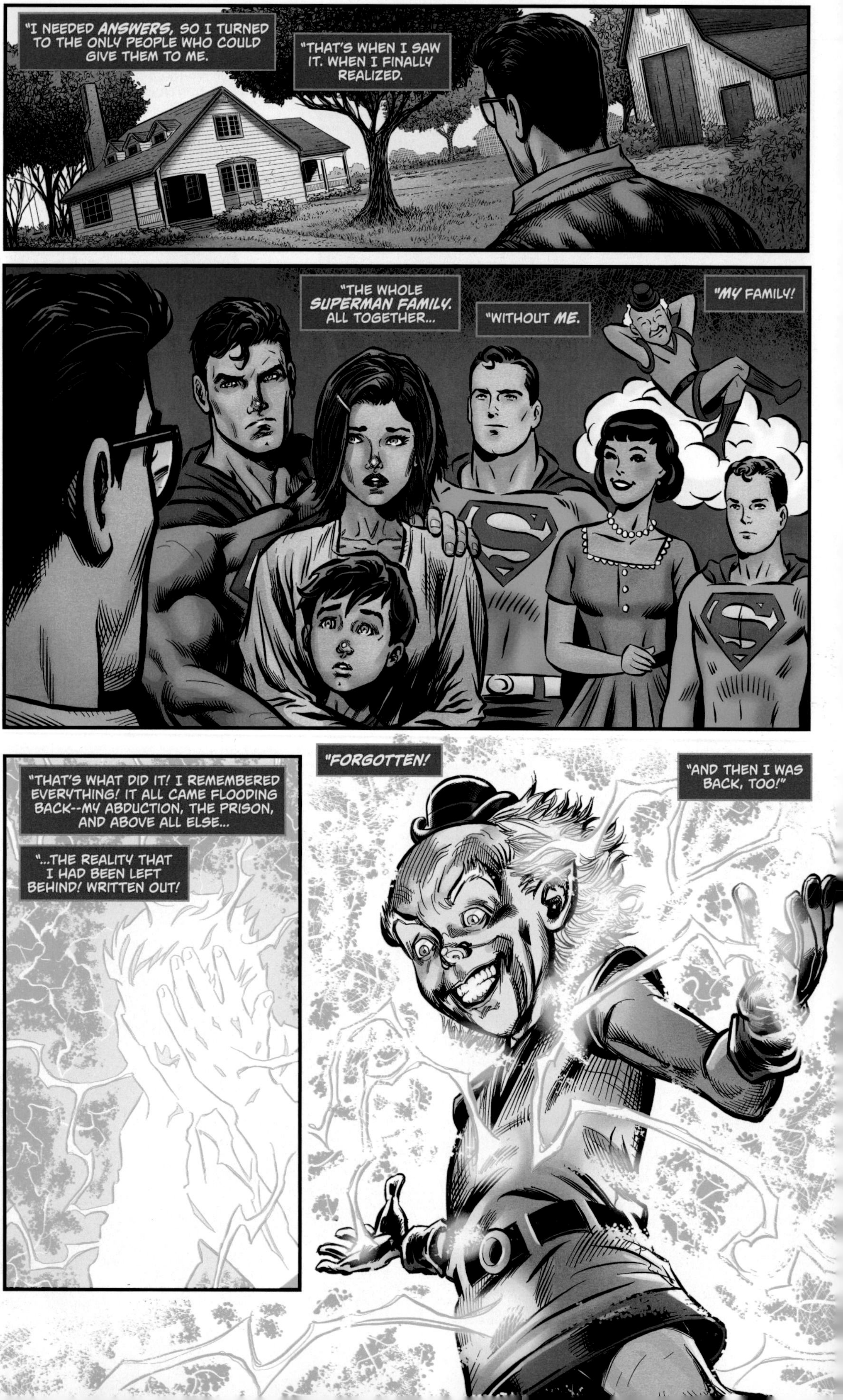
"I NEEDED *ANSWERS*, SO I TURNED TO THE ONLY PEOPLE WHO COULD GIVE THEM TO ME.
"THAT'S WHEN I SAW IT. WHEN I FINALLY REALIZED.
"THE WHOLE *SUPERMAN FAMILY*. ALL TOGETHER...
"WITHOUT *ME*.
"*MY* FAMILY!
"THAT'S WHAT DID IT! I REMEMBERED EVERYTHING! IT ALL CAME FLOODING BACK--MY ABDUCTION, THE PRISON, AND ABOVE ALL ELSE...
"...THE REALITY THAT I HAD BEEN LEFT BEHIND! WRITTEN OUT!
"*FORGOTTEN!*
"AND THEN I WAS BACK, TOO!"

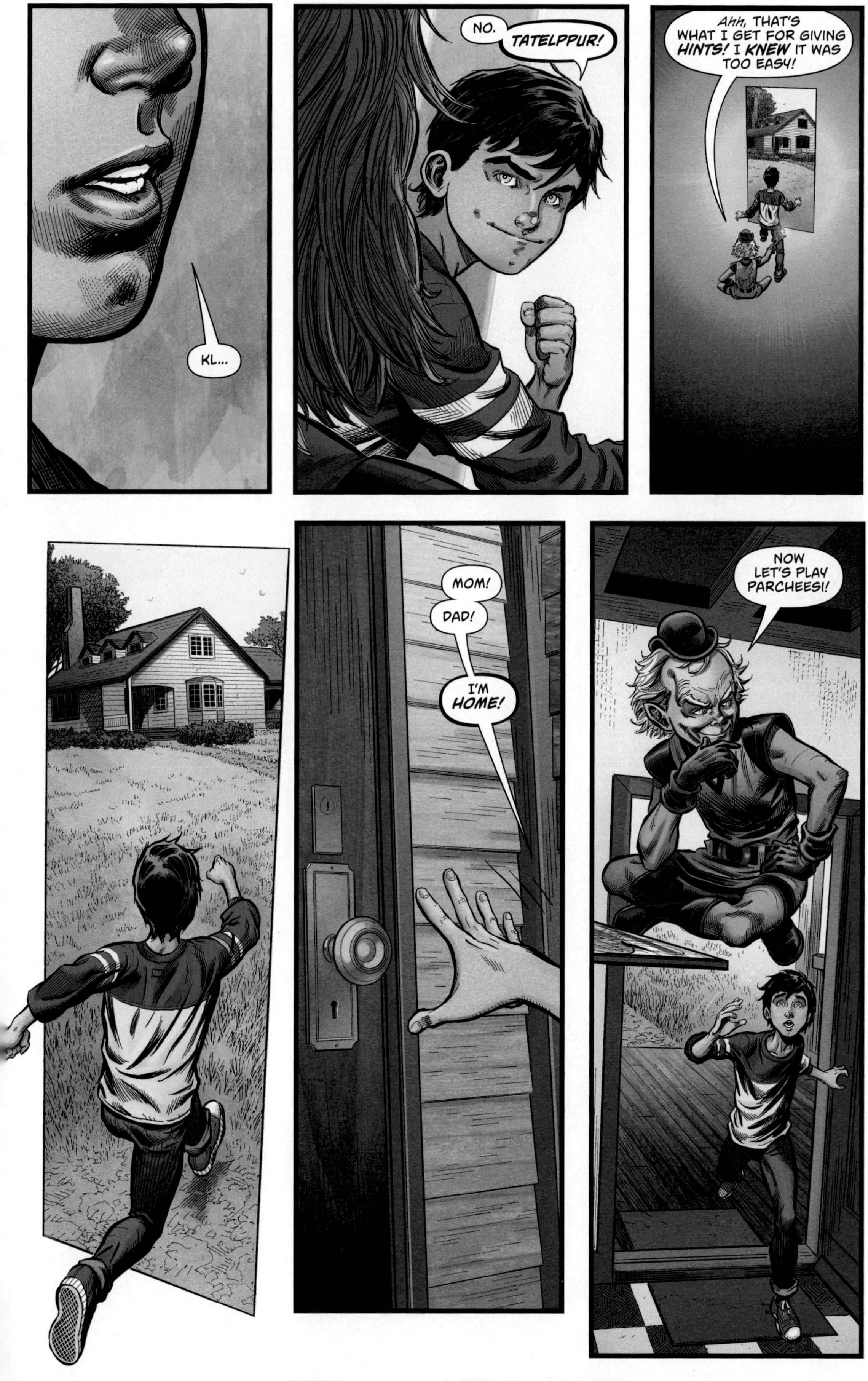
KL...
NO.
TATELPPUR!
Ahh, THAT'S WHAT I GET FOR GIVING HINTS! I KNEW IT WAS TOO EASY!
MOM!
DAD!
I'M HOME!
NOW LET'S PLAY PARCHEESI!

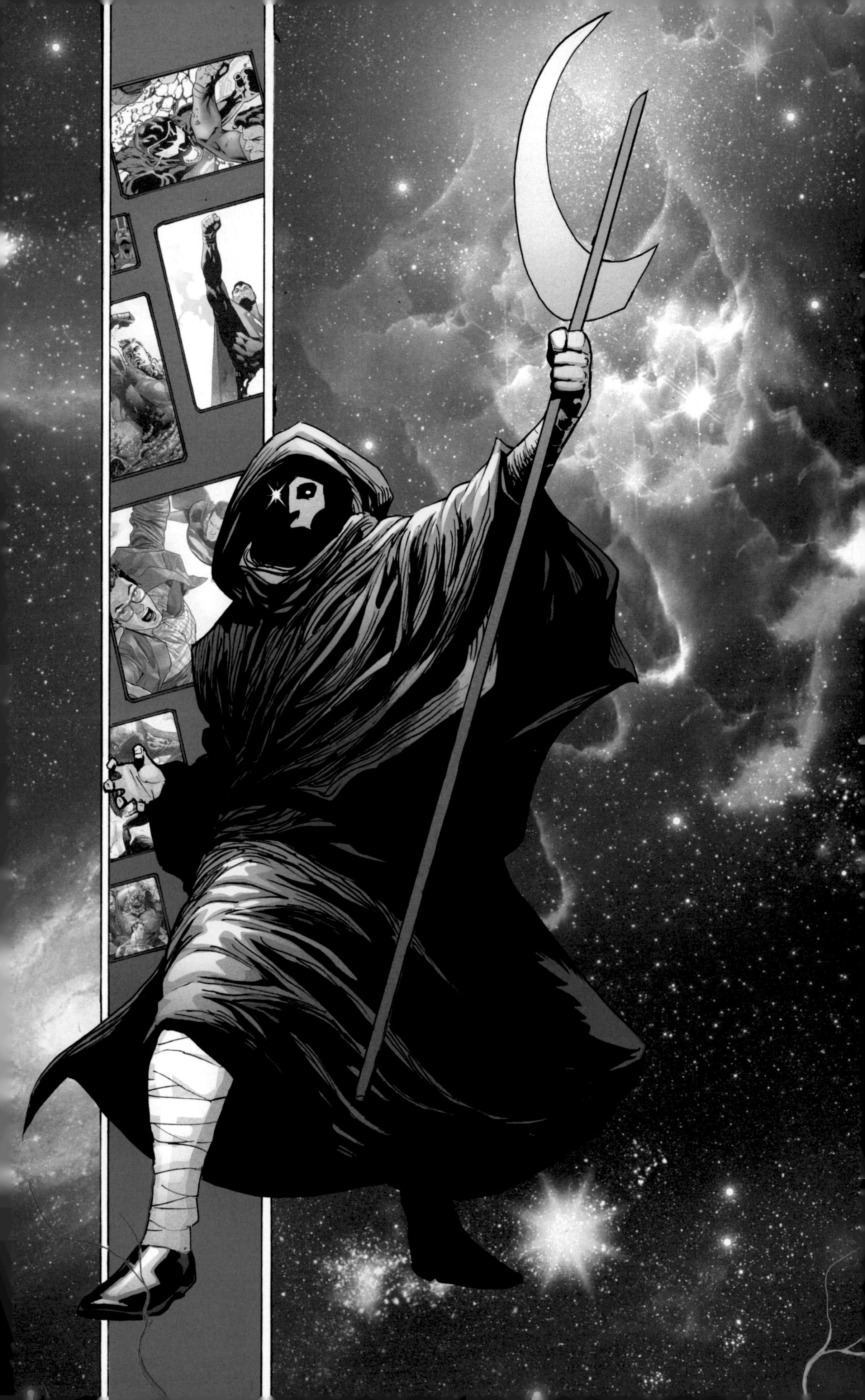

SUPERMAN: REBORN part three

PETER J. TOMASI & PATRICK GLEASON writer * PATRICK GLEASON penciller
MICK GRAY inker * JOHN KALISZ colorist
PATRICK GLEASON & JOHN KALISZ cover art

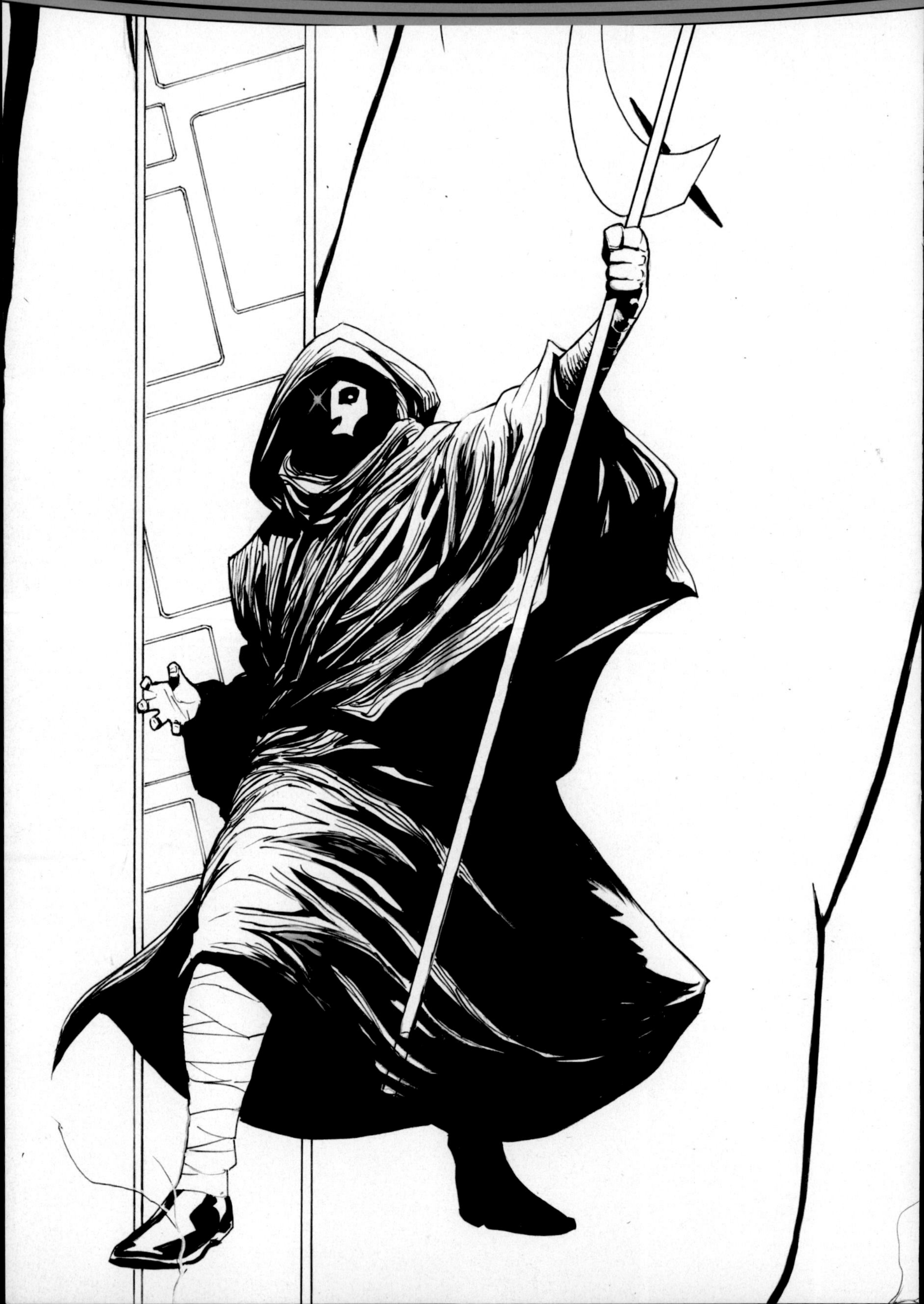

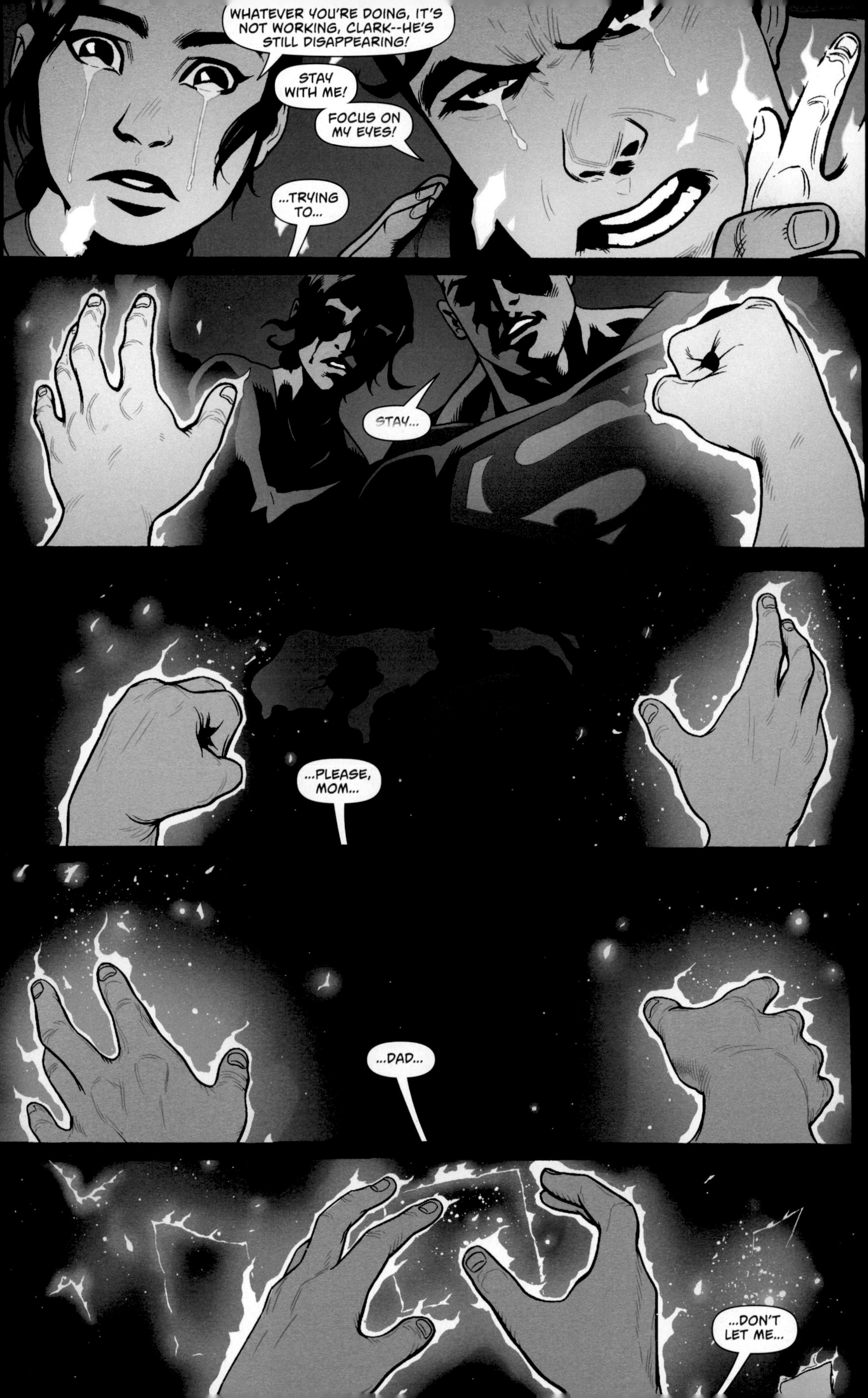
WHATEVER YOU'RE DOING, IT'S NOT WORKING, CLARK--HE'S STILL DISAPPEARING!
STAY WITH ME!
FOCUS ON MY EYES!
...TRYING TO...
STAY...
...PLEASE, MOM...
...DAD...
...DON'T LET ME...

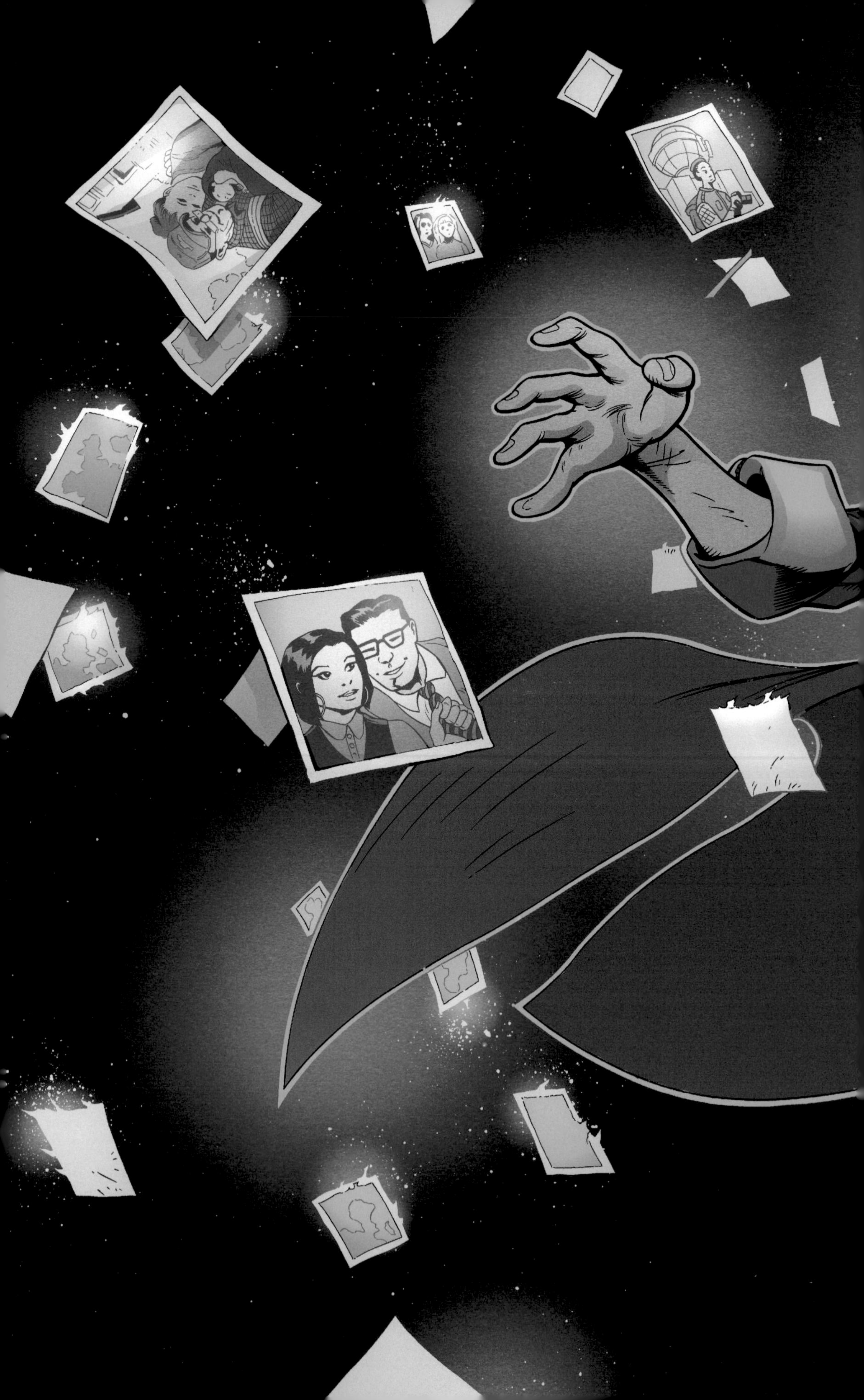

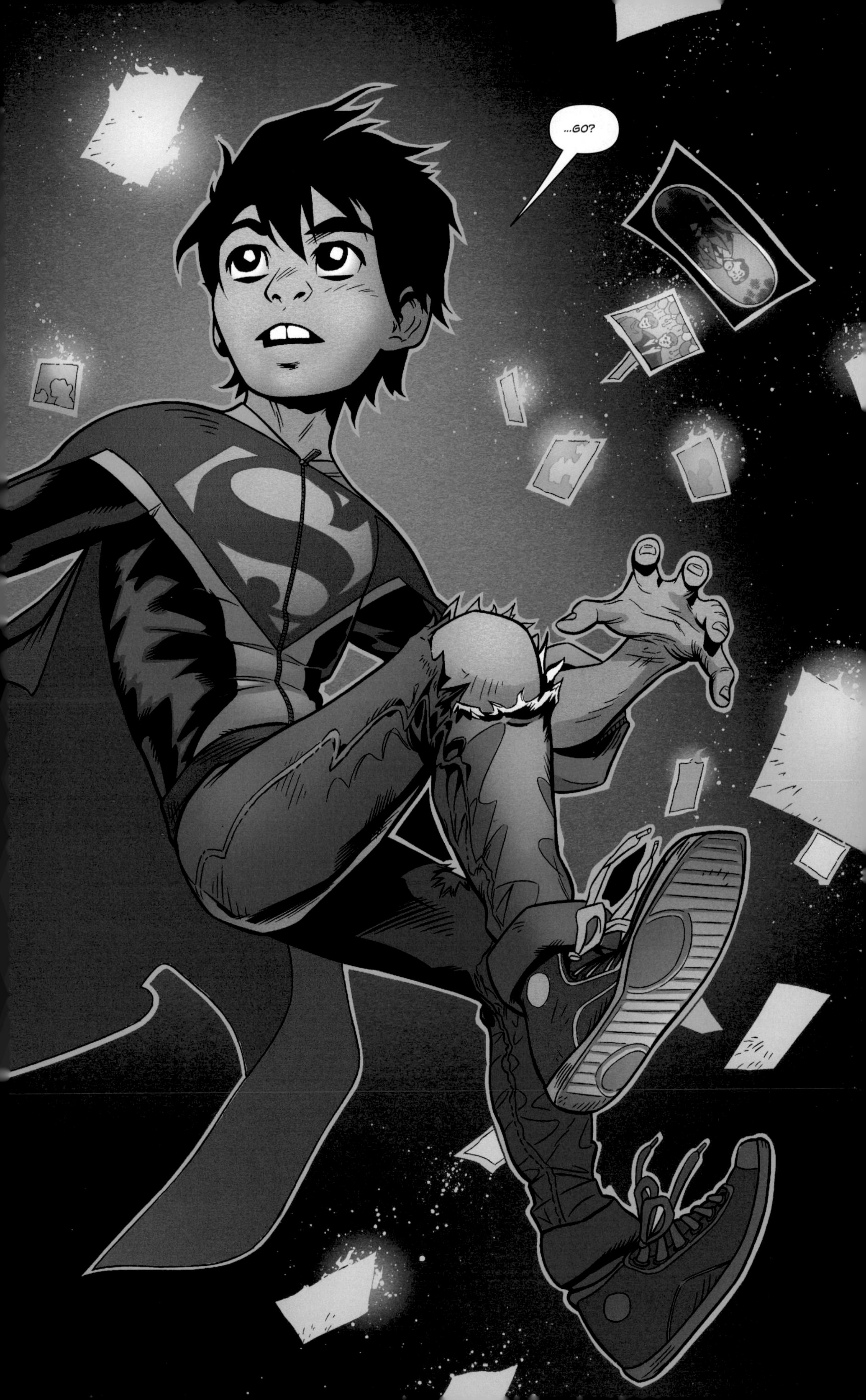
...GO?

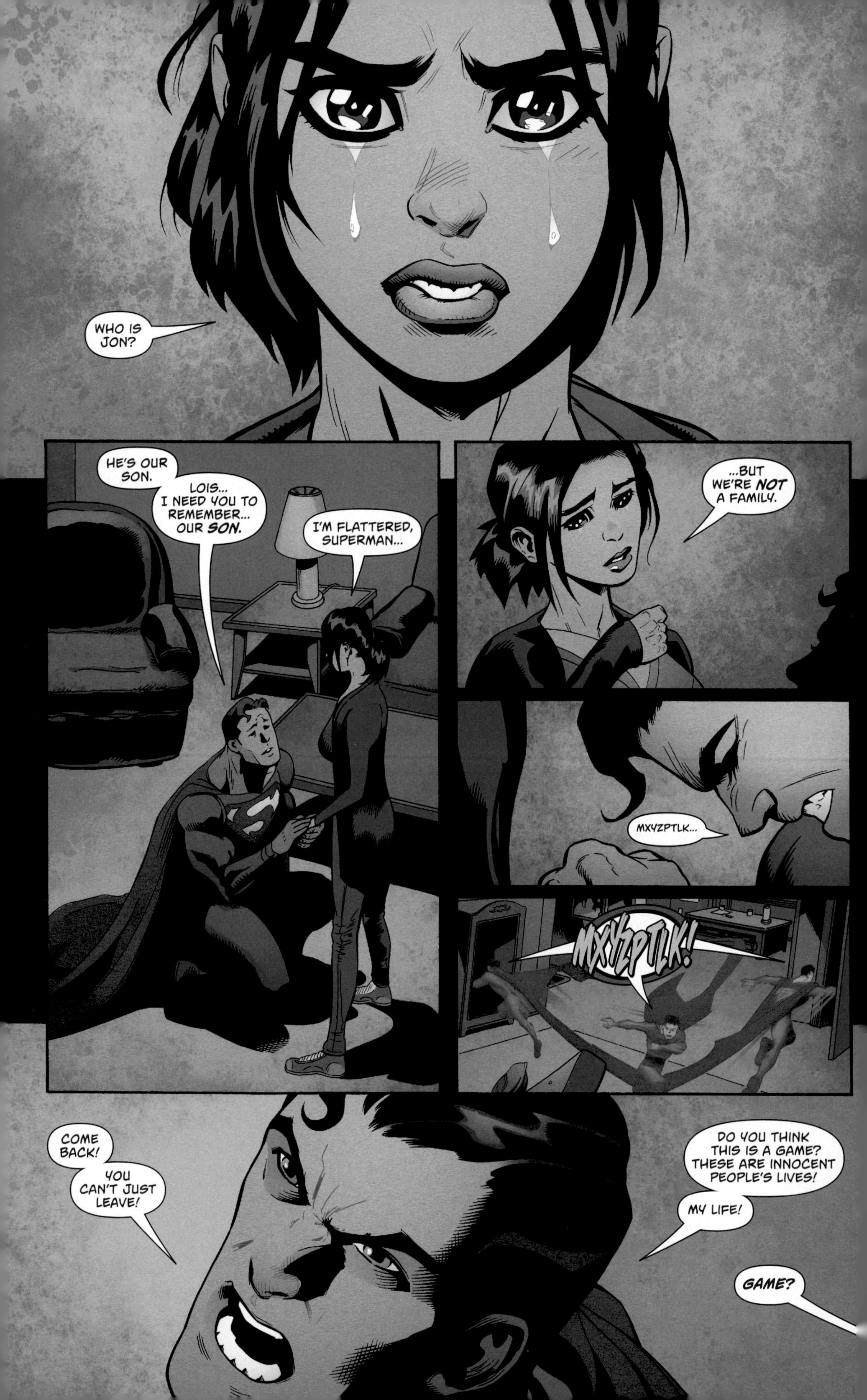
WHO IS JON?
HE'S OUR SON.
LOIS... I NEED YOU TO REMEMBER... OUR SON.
I'M FLATTERED, SUPERMAN...
...BUT WE'RE NOT A FAMILY.
MXYZPTLK...
MXYZPTLK!
COME BACK!
YOU CAN'T JUST LEAVE!
DO YOU THINK THIS IS A GAME? THESE ARE INNOCENT PEOPLE'S LIVES!
MY LIFE!
GAME?

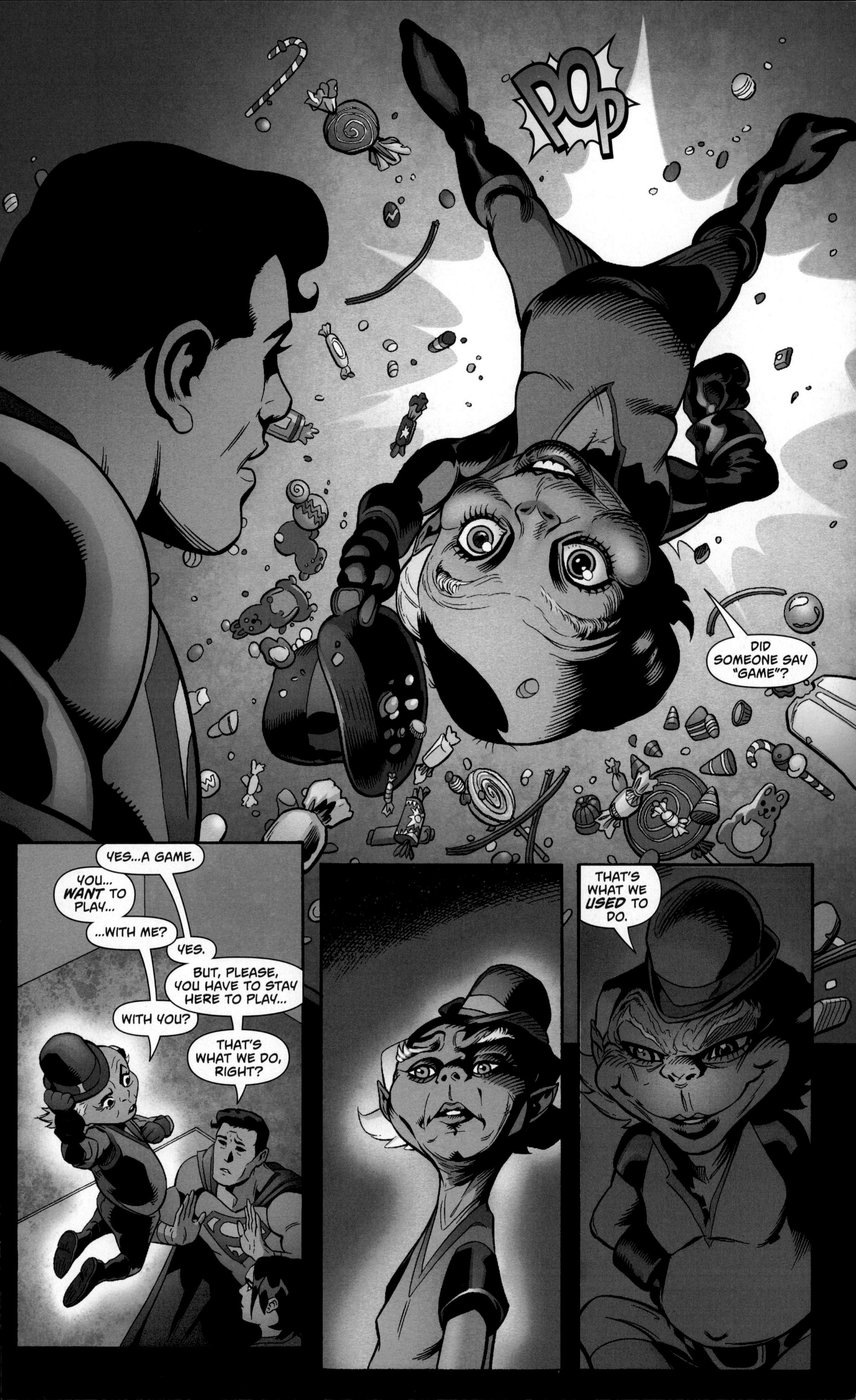
POP
DID SOMEONE SAY "GAME"?
YES...A GAME.
YOU... WANT TO PLAY...
...WITH ME?
YES.
BUT, PLEASE, YOU HAVE TO STAY HERE TO PLAY...
WITH YOU?
THAT'S WHAT WE DO, RIGHT?
THAT'S WHAT WE USED TO DO.

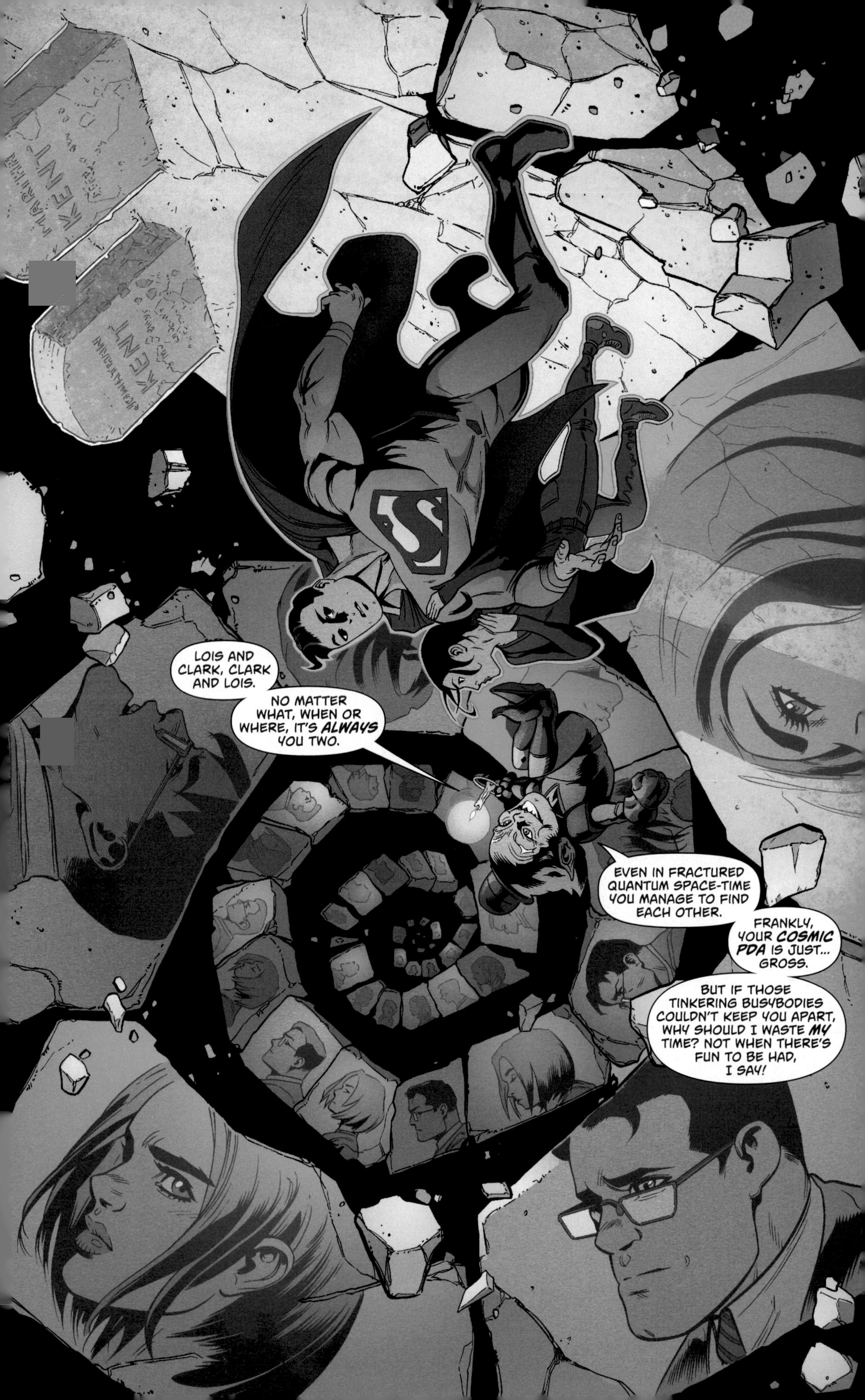

LOIS AND CLARK, CLARK AND LOIS.
NO MATTER WHAT, WHEN OR WHERE, IT'S ALWAYS YOU TWO.
EVEN IN FRACTURED QUANTUM SPACE-TIME YOU MANAGE TO FIND EACH OTHER.
FRANKLY, YOUR COSMIC PDA IS JUST... GROSS.
BUT IF THOSE TINKERING BUSYBODIES COULDN'T KEEP YOU APART, WHY SHOULD I WASTE MY TIME? NOT WHEN THERE'S FUN TO BE HAD, I SAY!

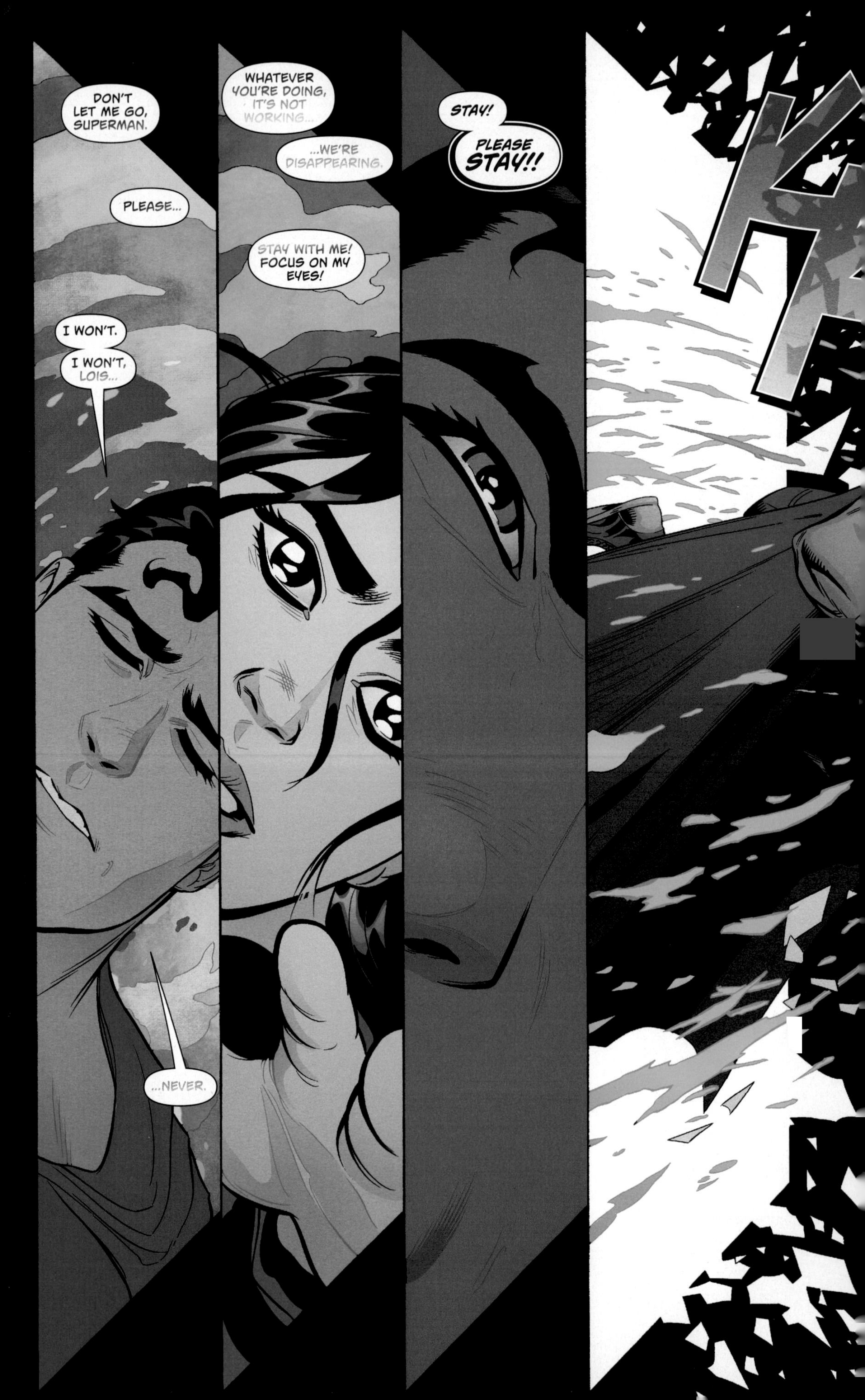
DON'T LET ME GO, SUPERMAN.
PLEASE...
I WON'T.
I WON'T, LOIS...
...NEVER.
WHATEVER YOU'RE DOING, IT'S NOT WORKING...
...WE'RE DISAPPEARING.
STAY WITH ME! FOCUS ON MY EYES!
STAY!
PLEASE STAY!!

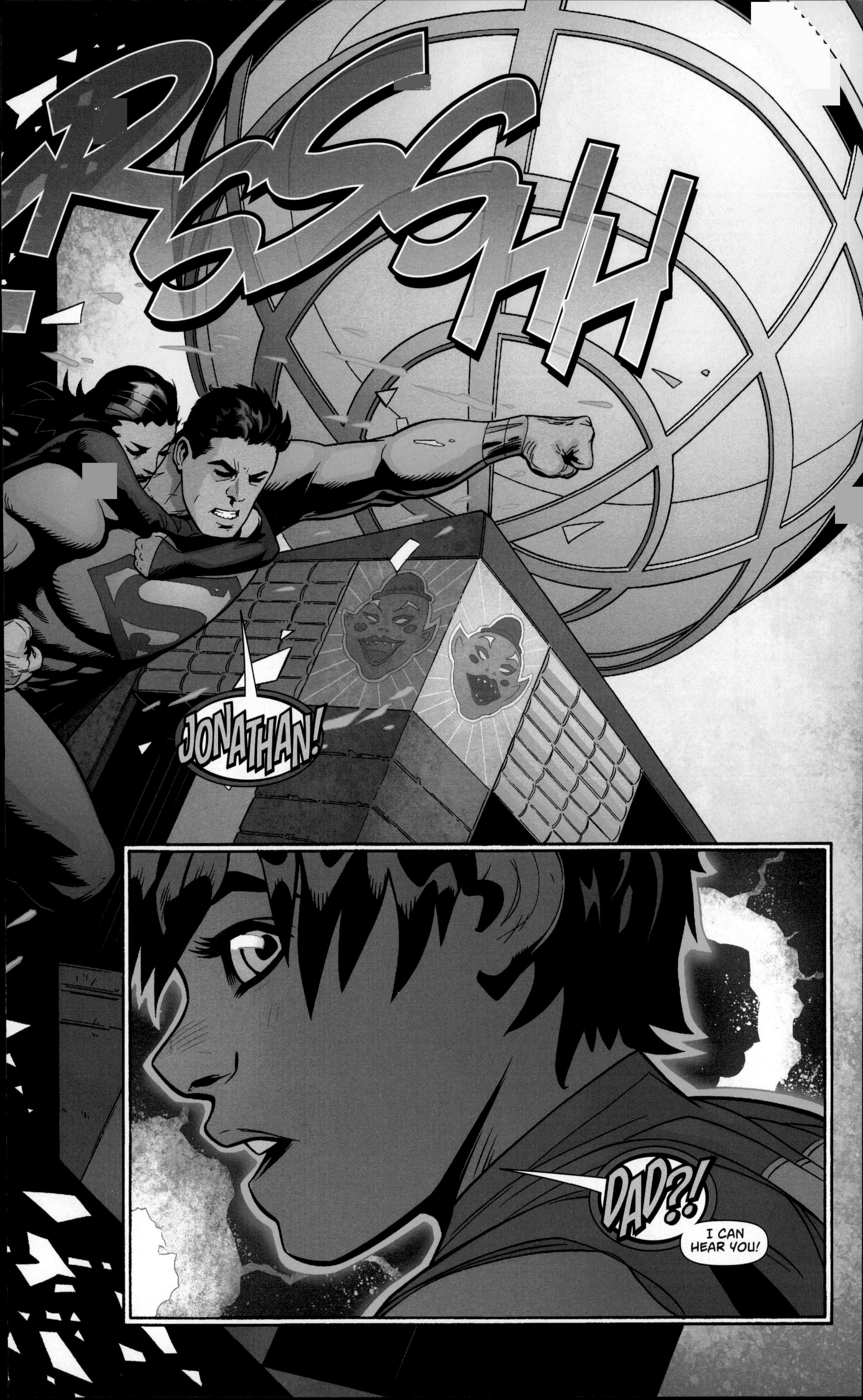
RSSHH
JONATHAN!
DAD?!
I CAN HEAR YOU!

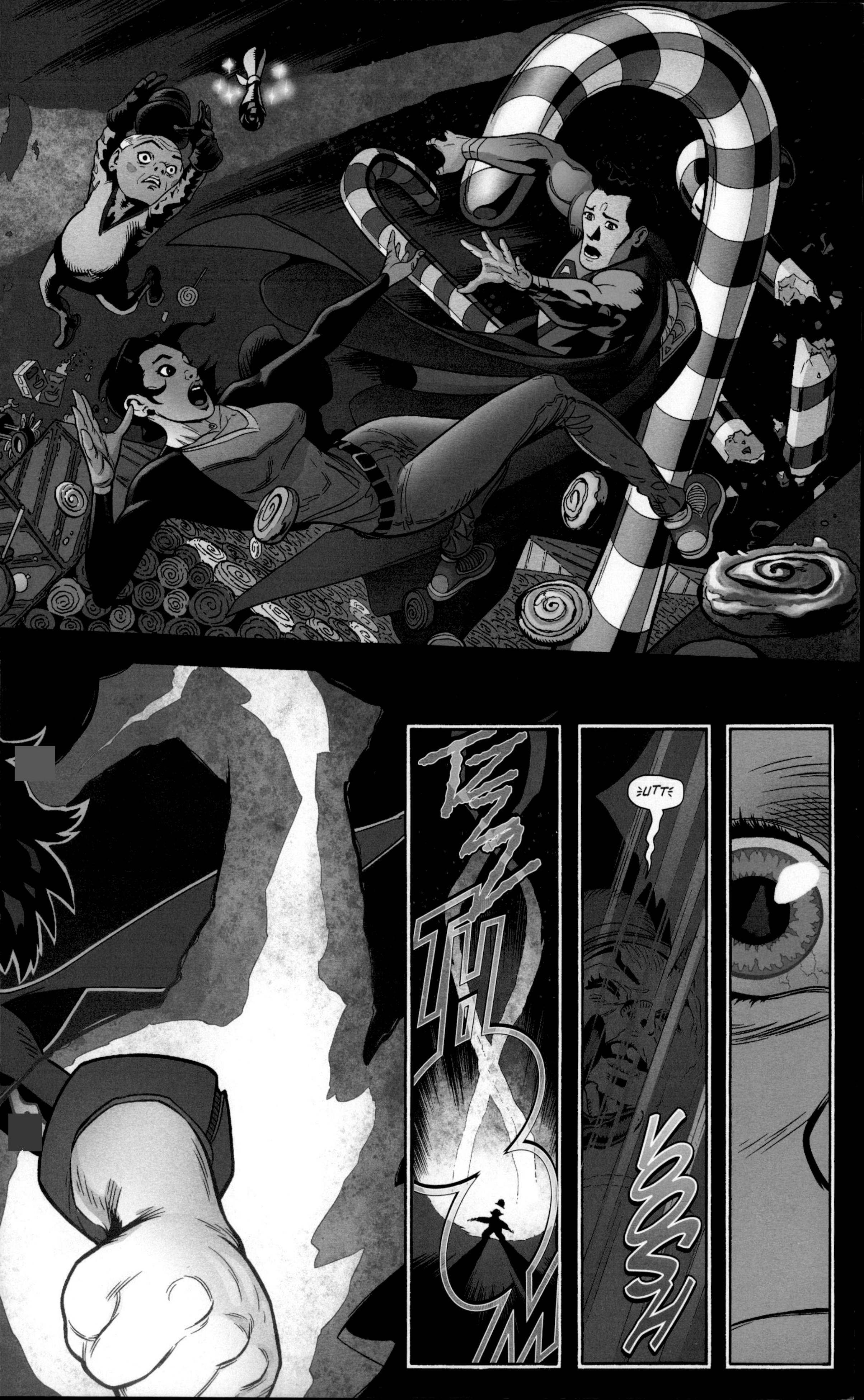
TZZTHOOM
UTT
VOOSH

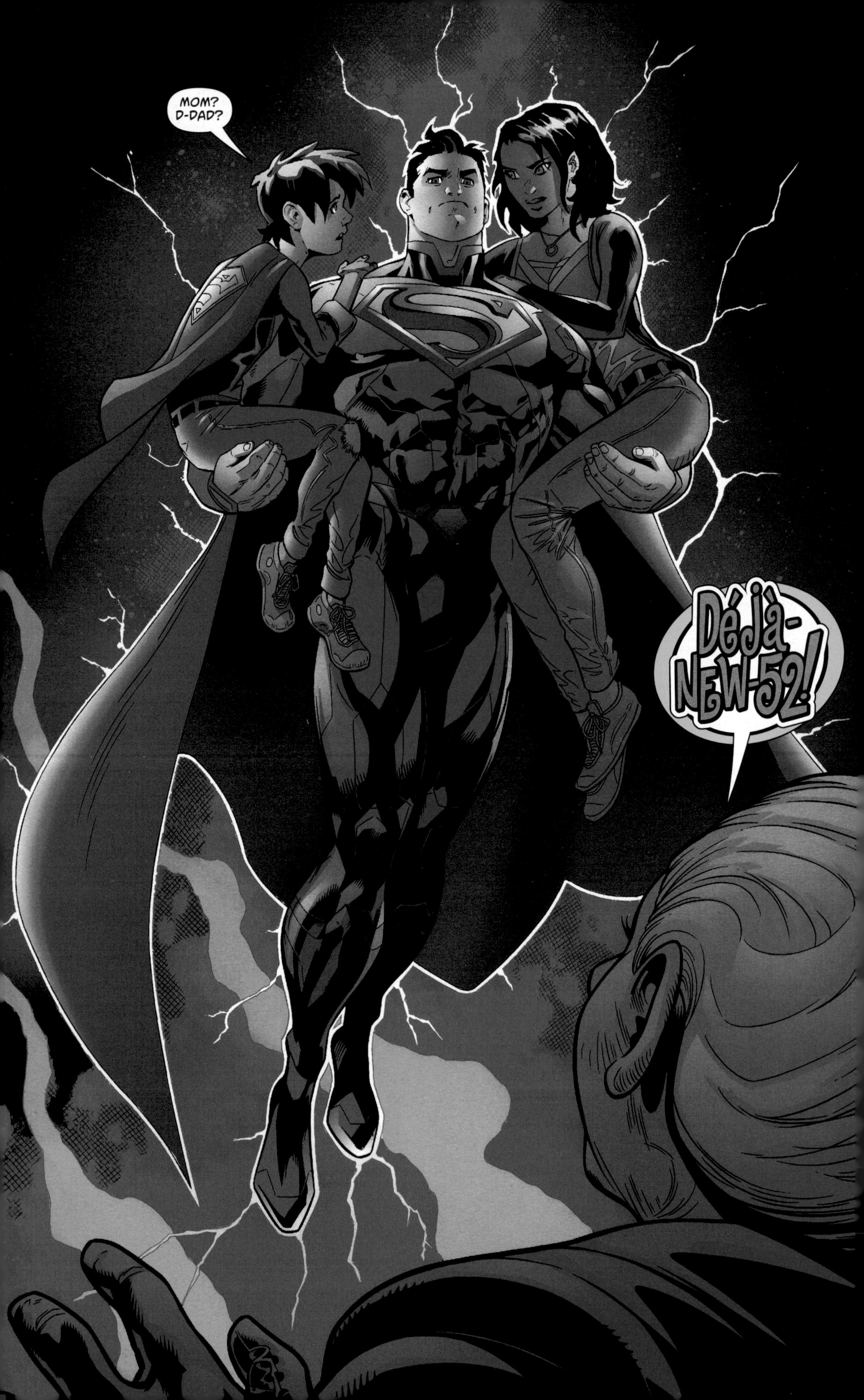
MOM? D-DAD?
DÉJÀ-NEW-52!

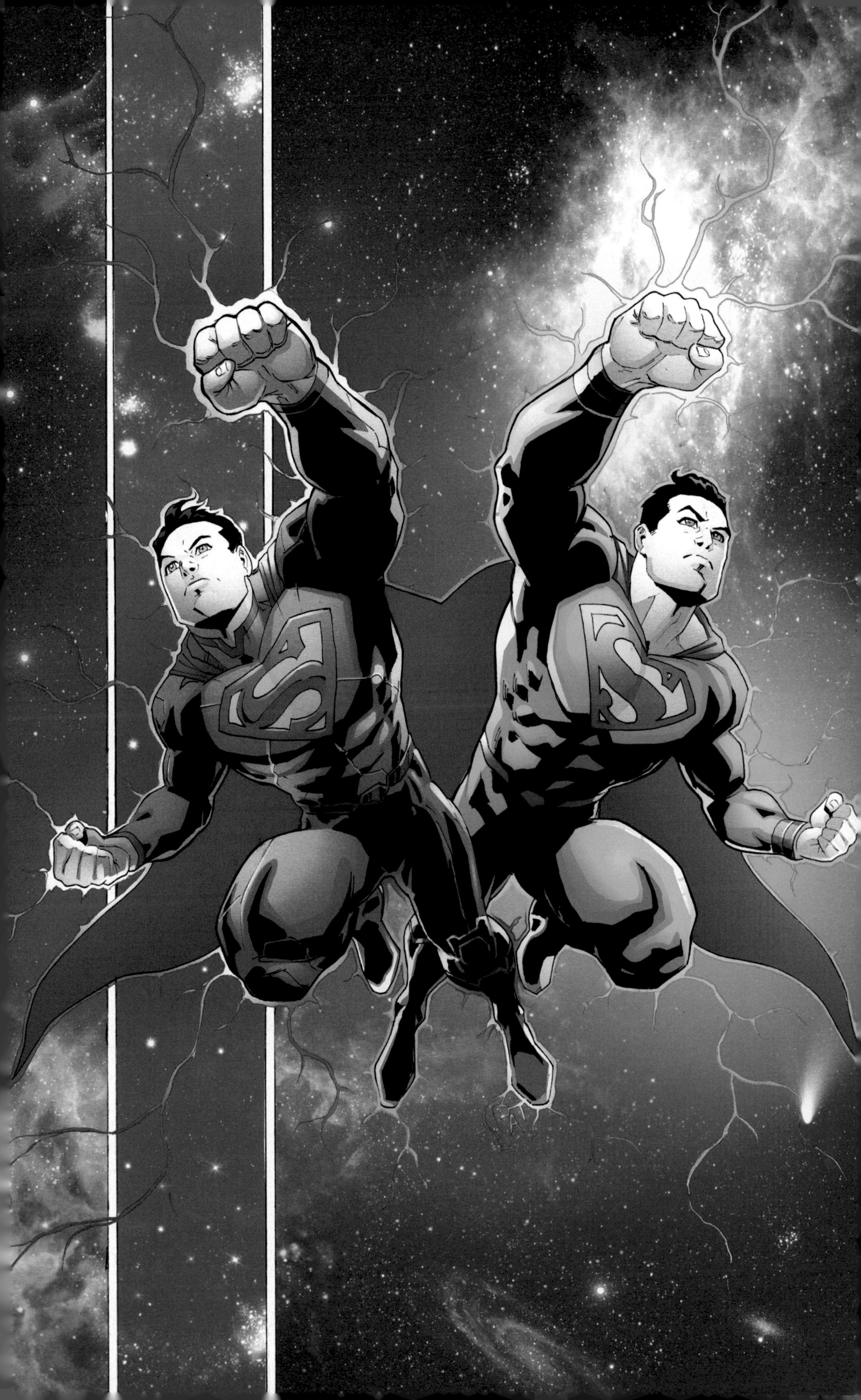

SUPERMAN: REBORN part four

DAN JURGENS writer * DOUG MAHNKE penciller

JAIME MENDOZA, CHRISTIAN ALAMY & TREVOR SCOTT inkers

WIL QUINTANA colorist * PATRICK GLEASON & JOHN KALISZ cover art

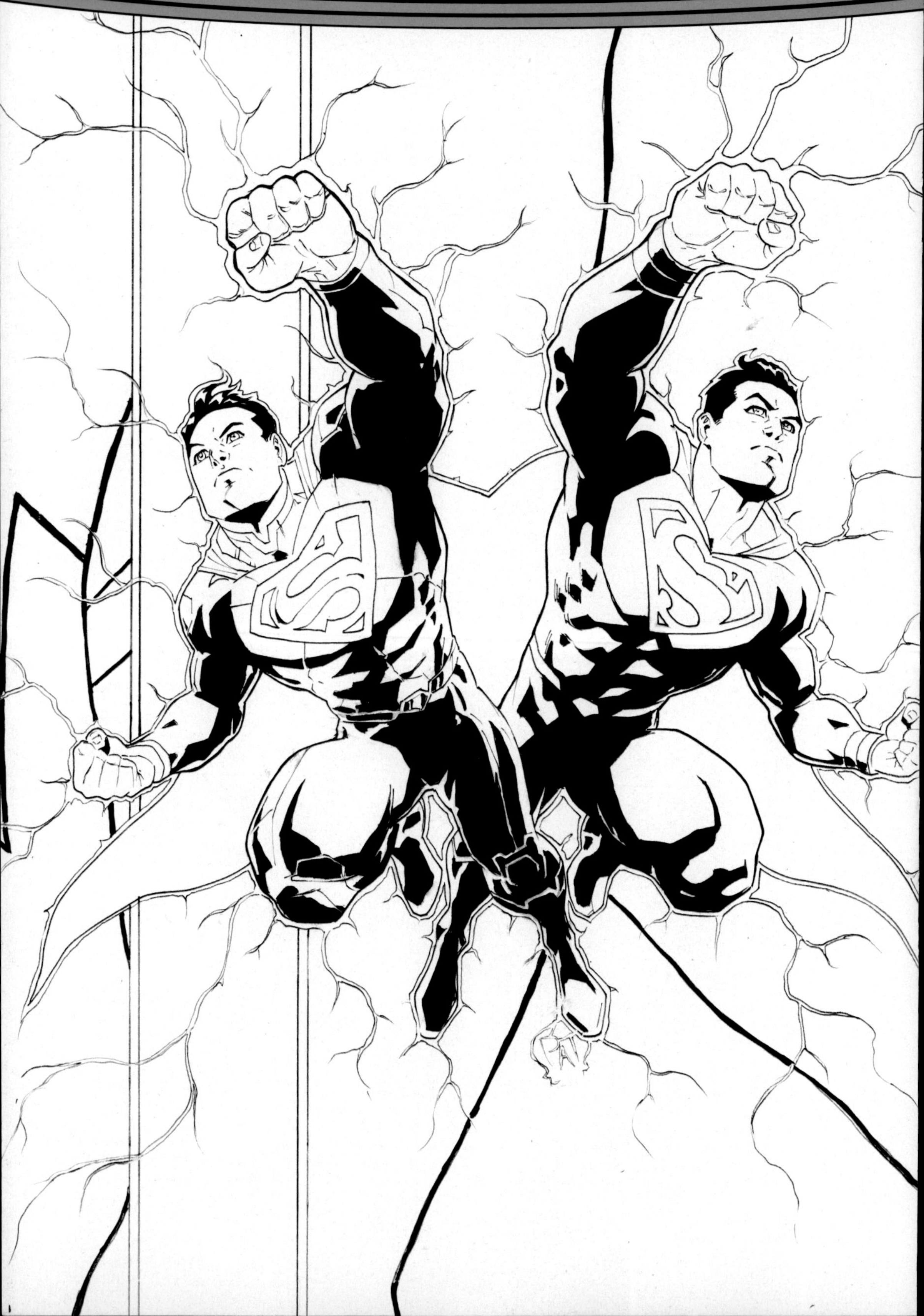

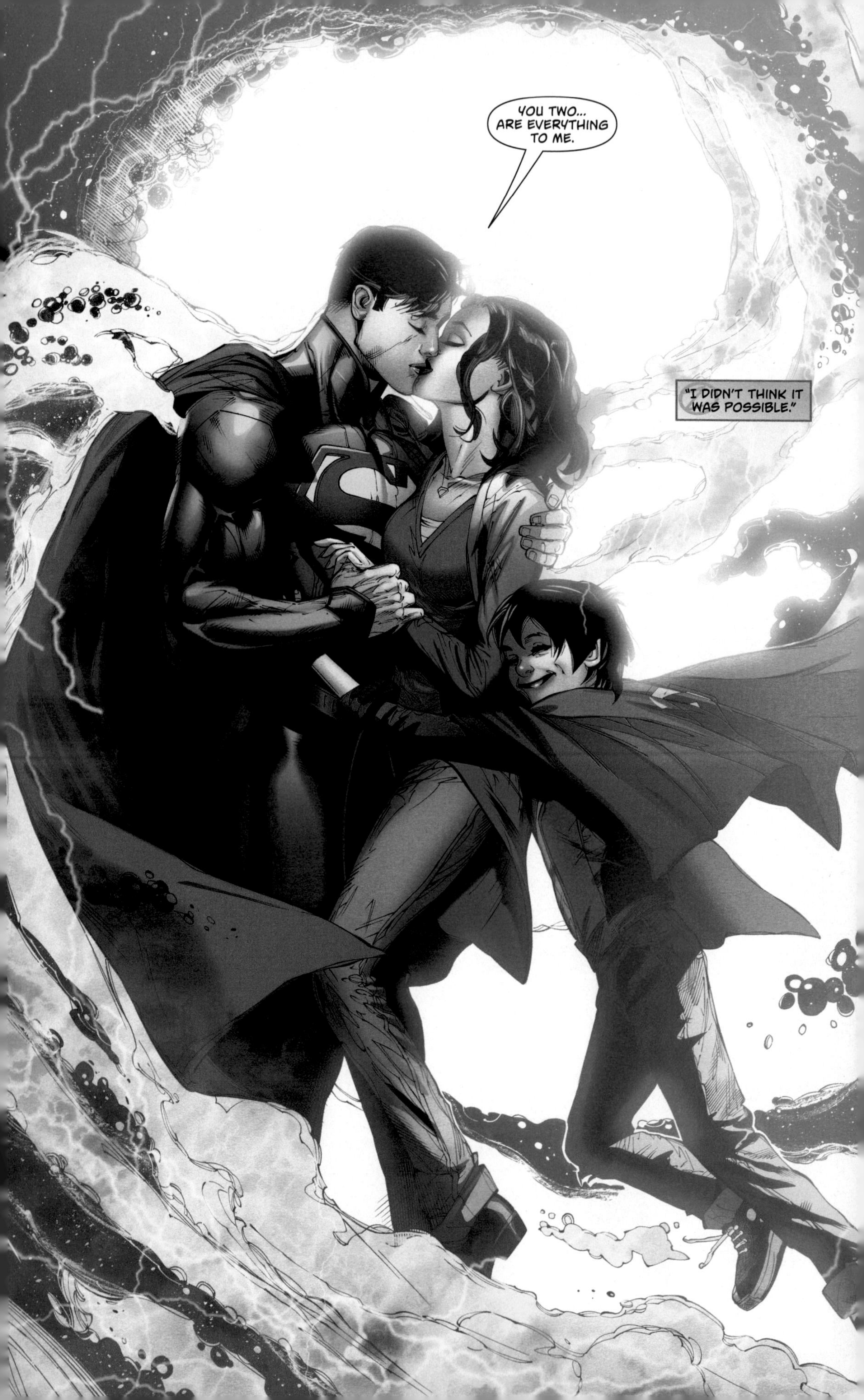
YOU TWO... ARE EVERYTHING TO ME.
"I DIDN'T THINK IT WAS POSSIBLE."

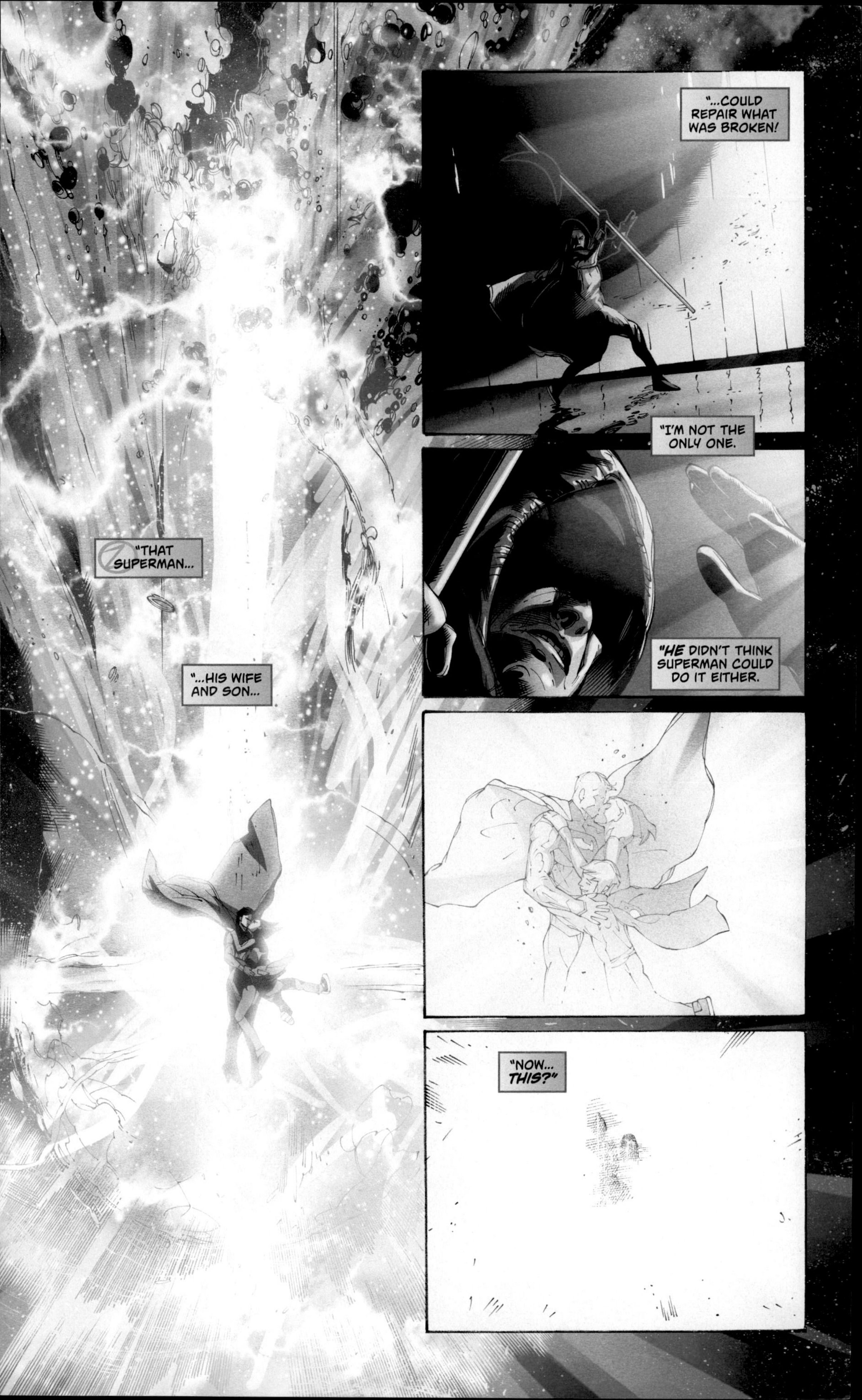
"...COULD REPAIR WHAT WAS BROKEN!
"I'M NOT THE ONLY ONE.
"HE DIDN'T THINK SUPERMAN COULD DO IT EITHER.
"THAT SUPERMAN...
"...HIS WIFE AND SON...
"NOW... THIS?"

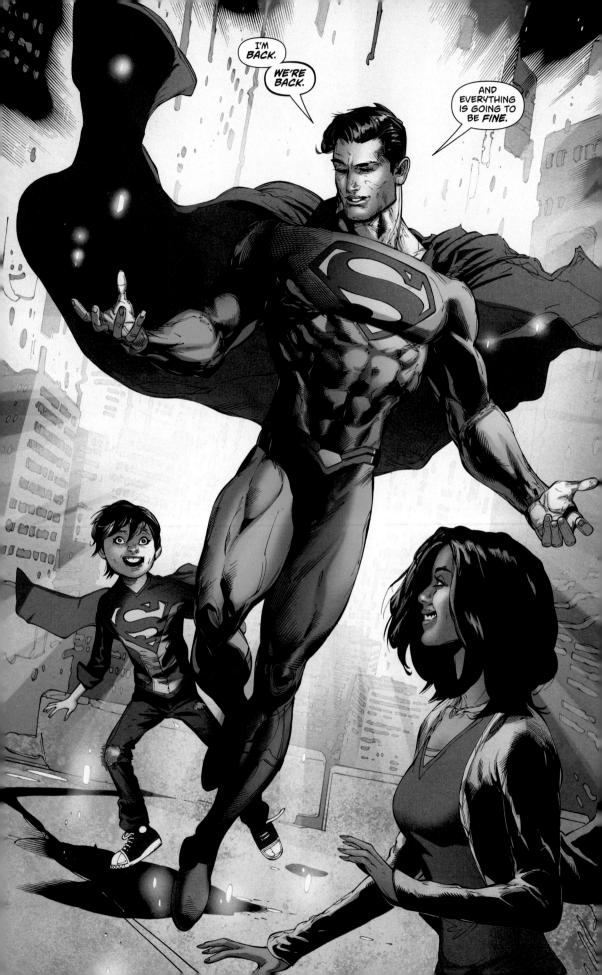

SUPERMAN REBORN

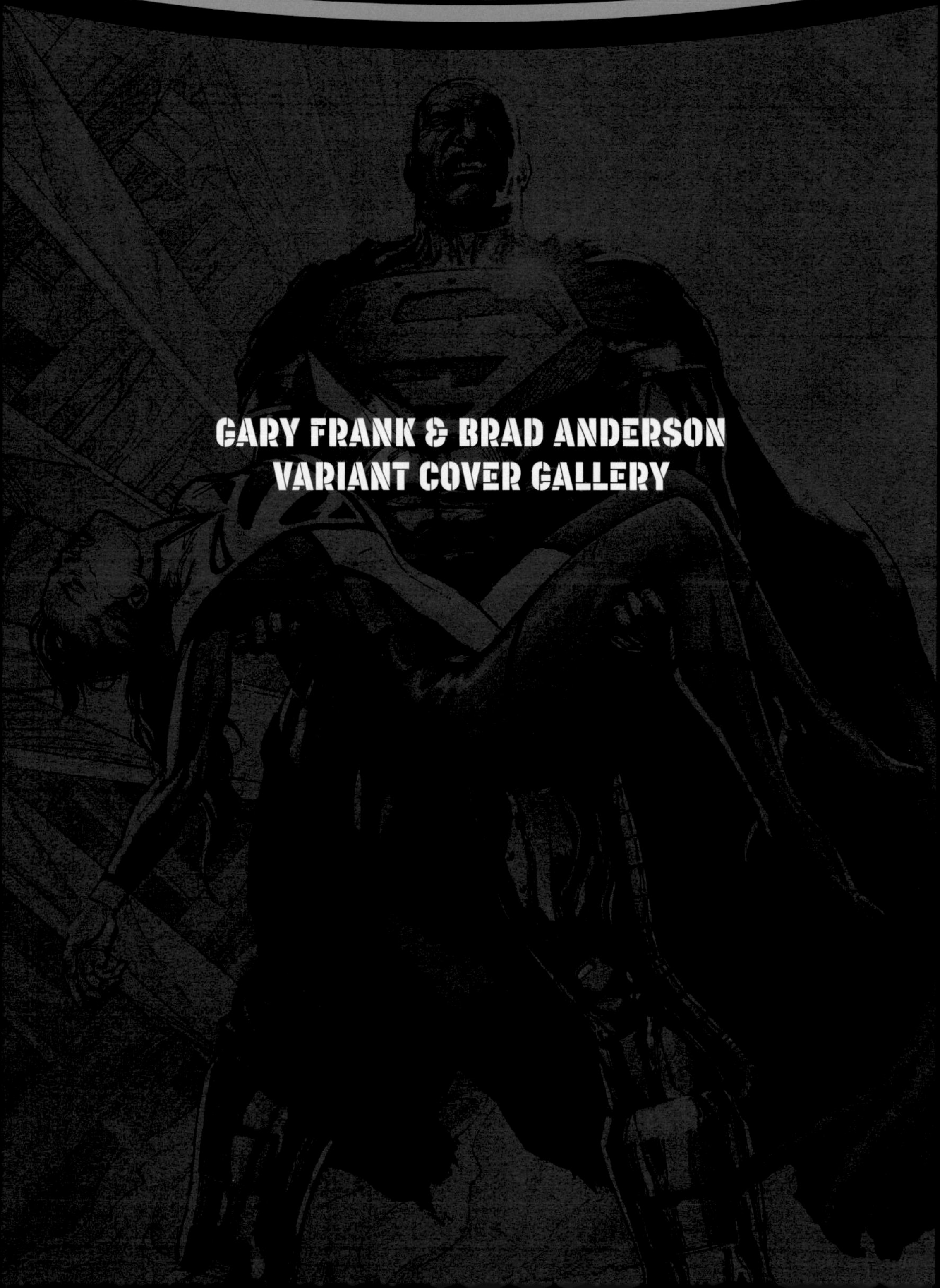

GARY FRANK & BRAD ANDERSON VARIANT COVER GALLERY

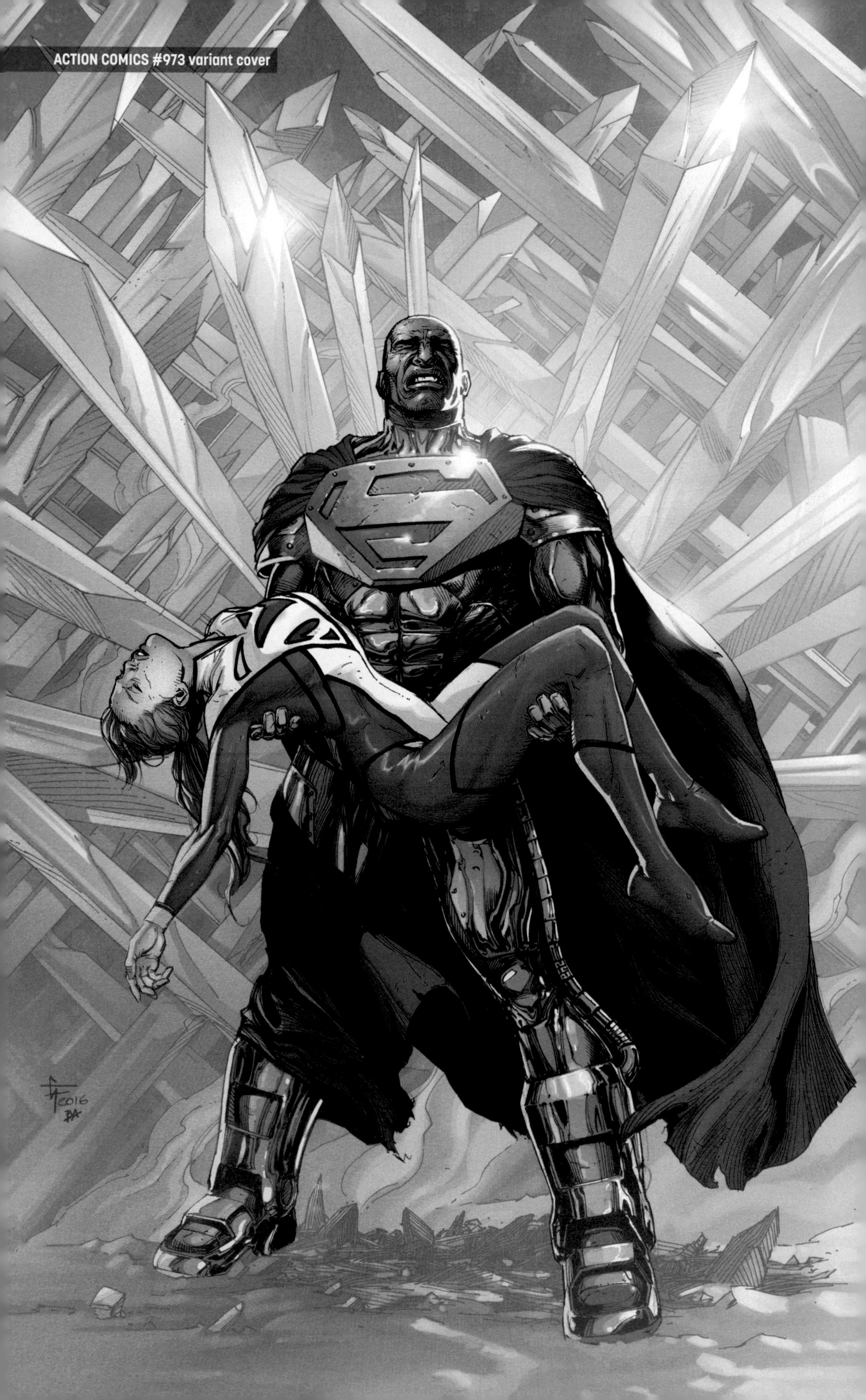

ACTION COMICS #973 variant cover

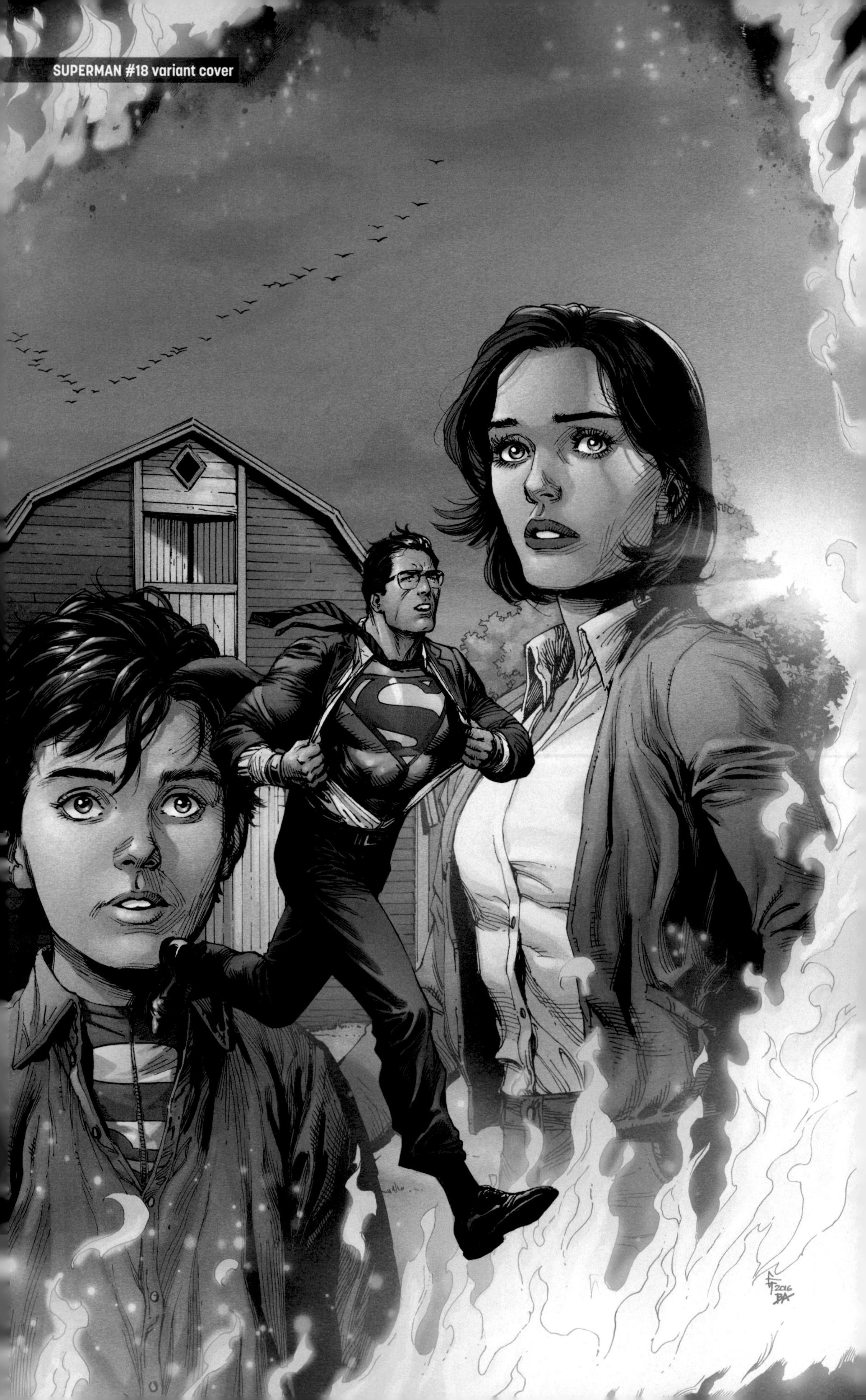
SUPERMAN #18 variant cover

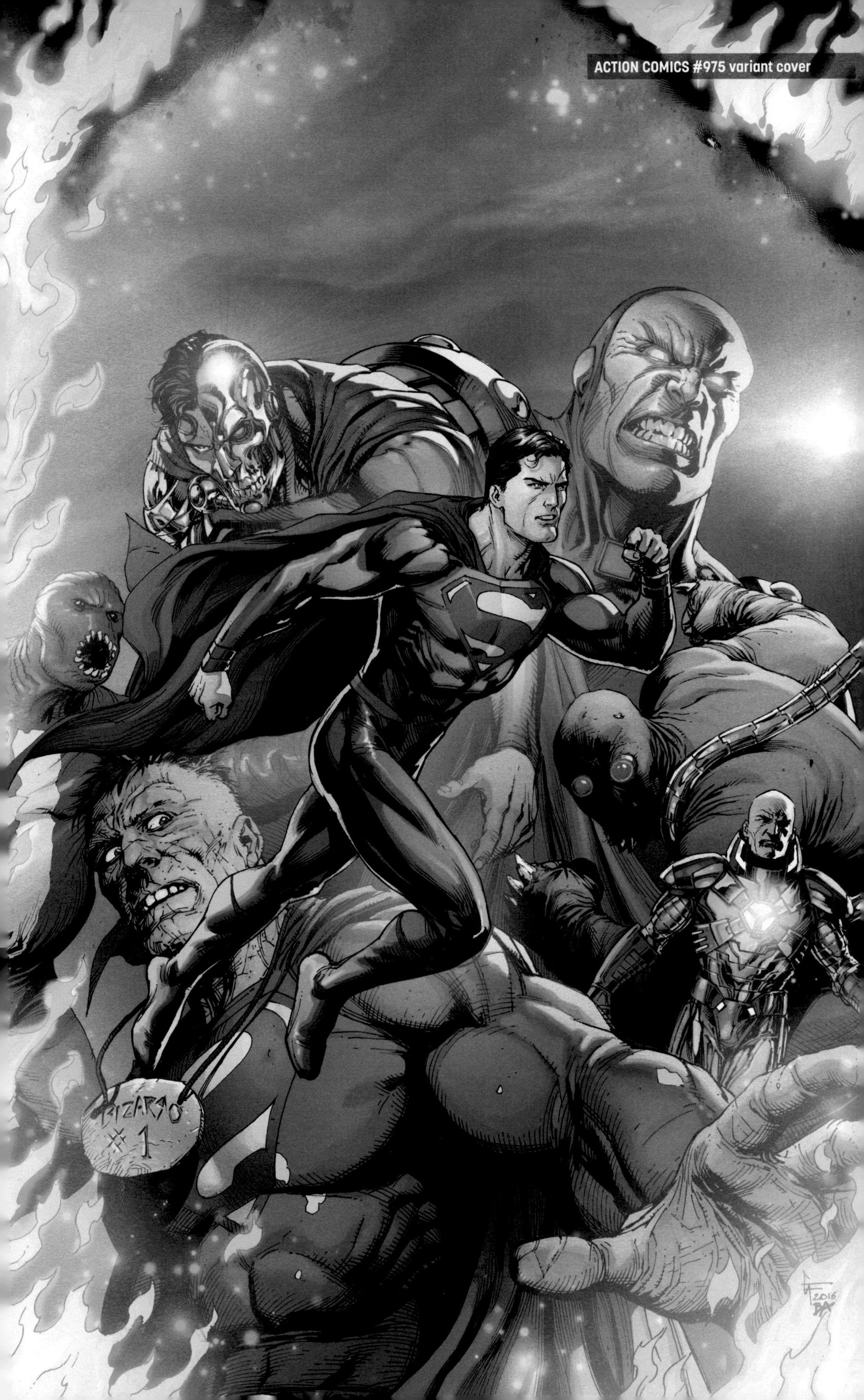

ACTION COMICS #975 variant cover

SUPERMAN #19 variant cover

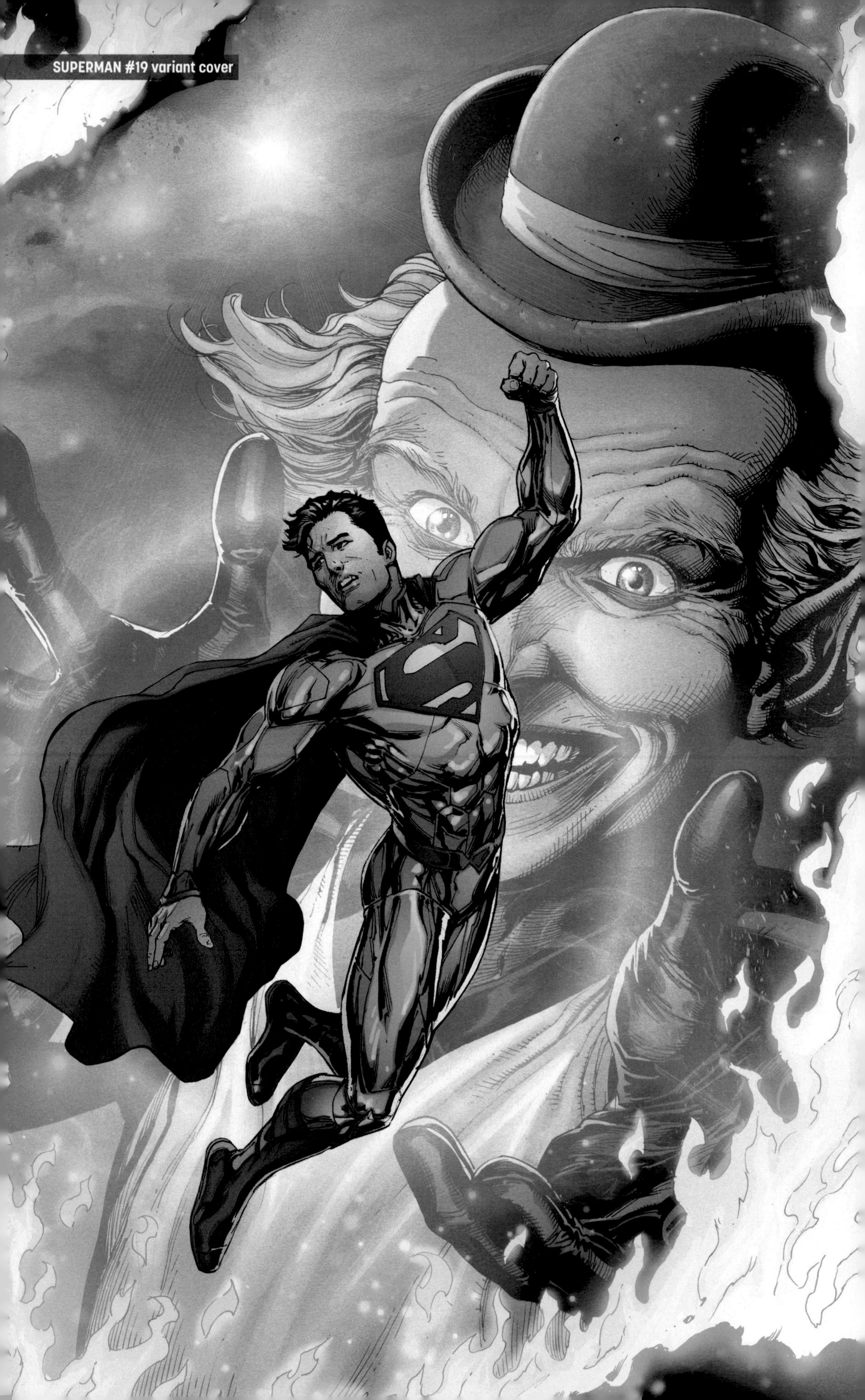

ACTION COMICS #976 variant cover

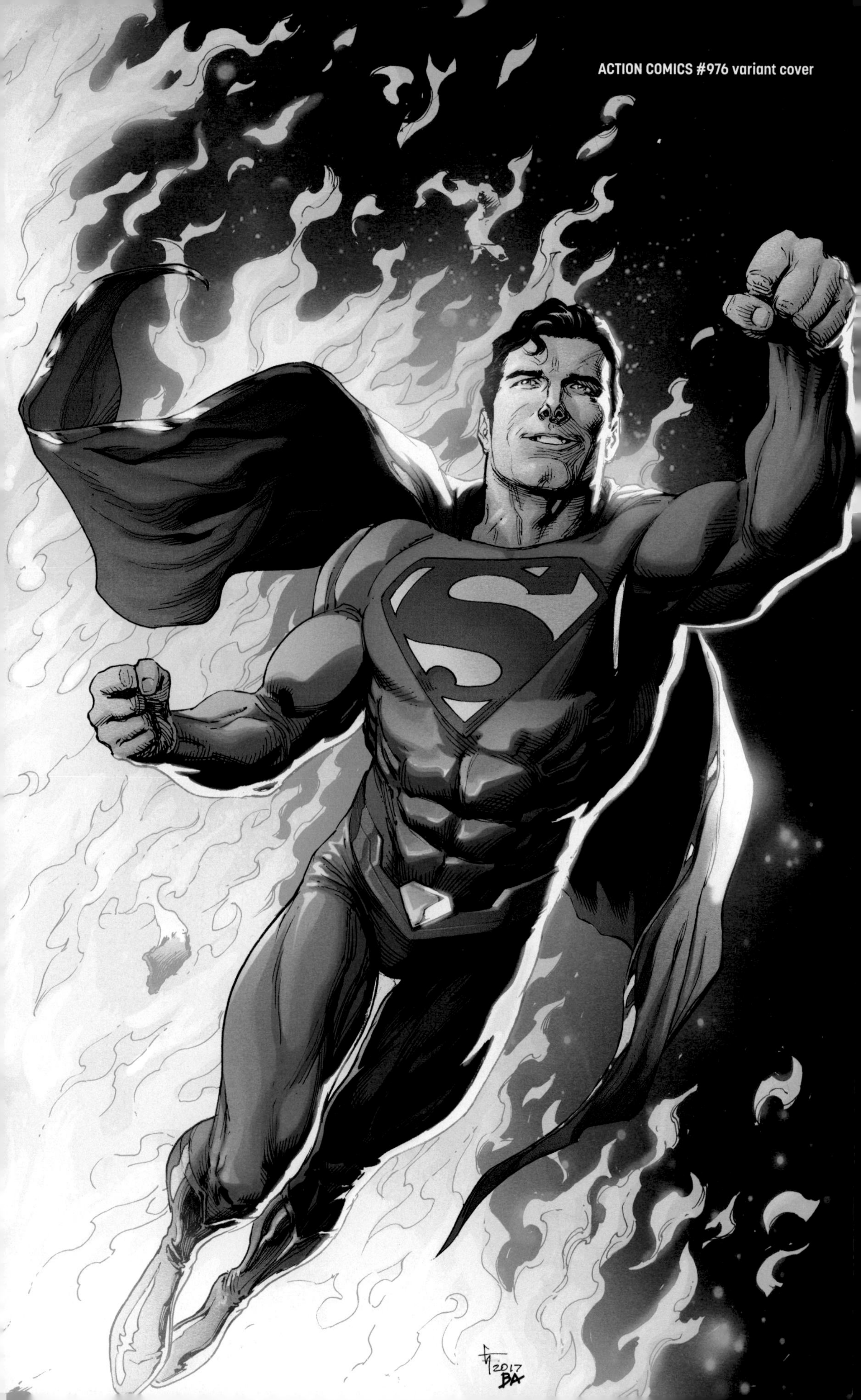

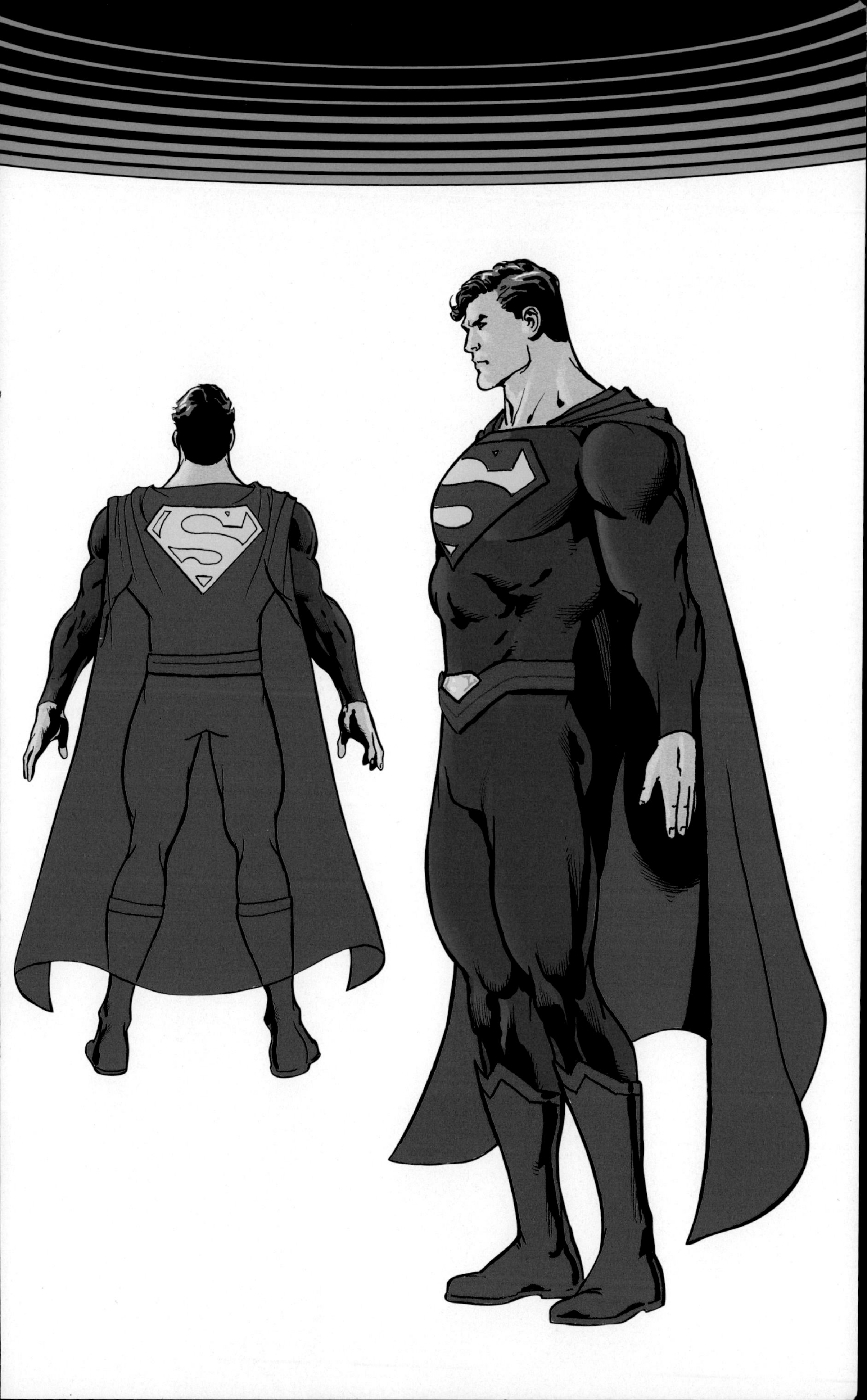

SUPERMAN REBORN CONNECTION SKETCH & COVERS BY PATRICK GLEASON

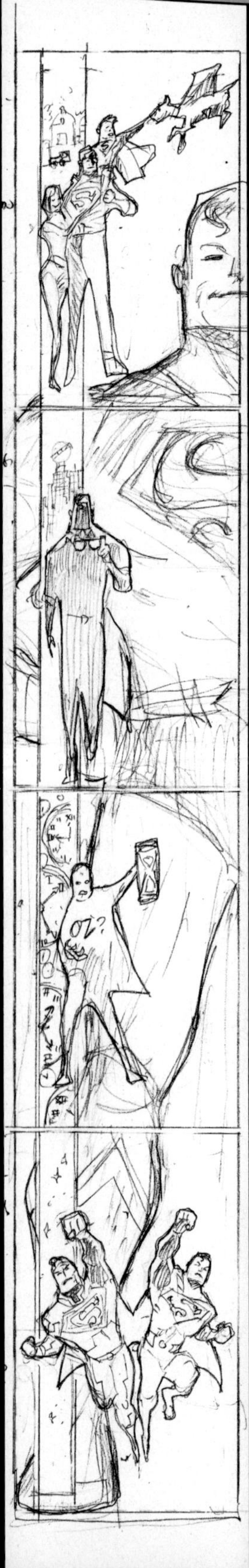

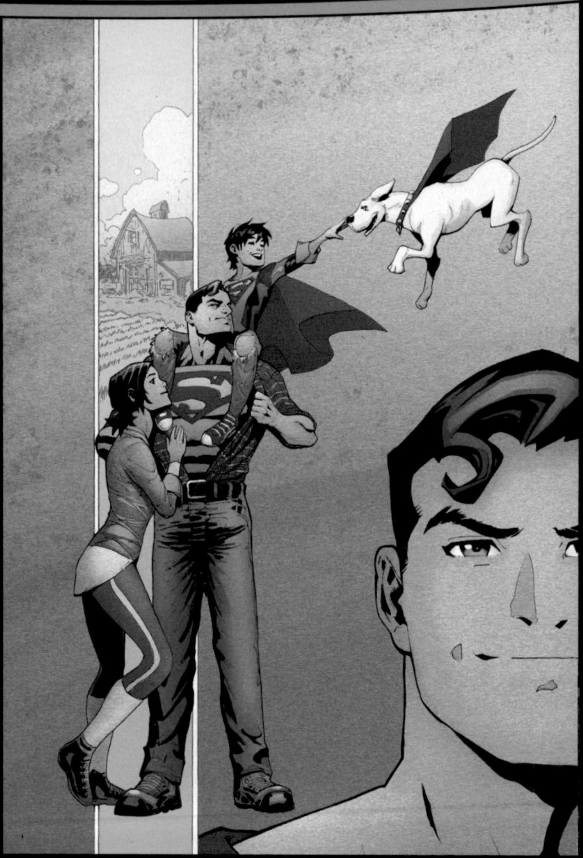

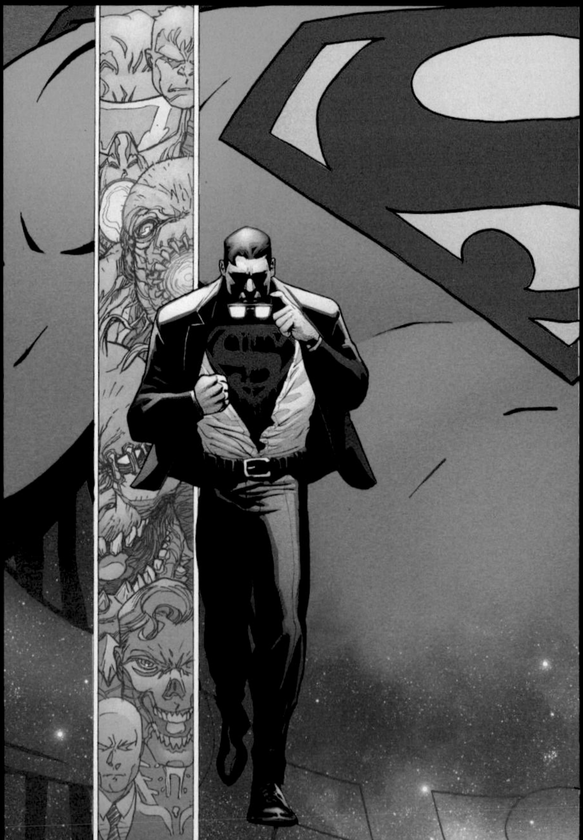

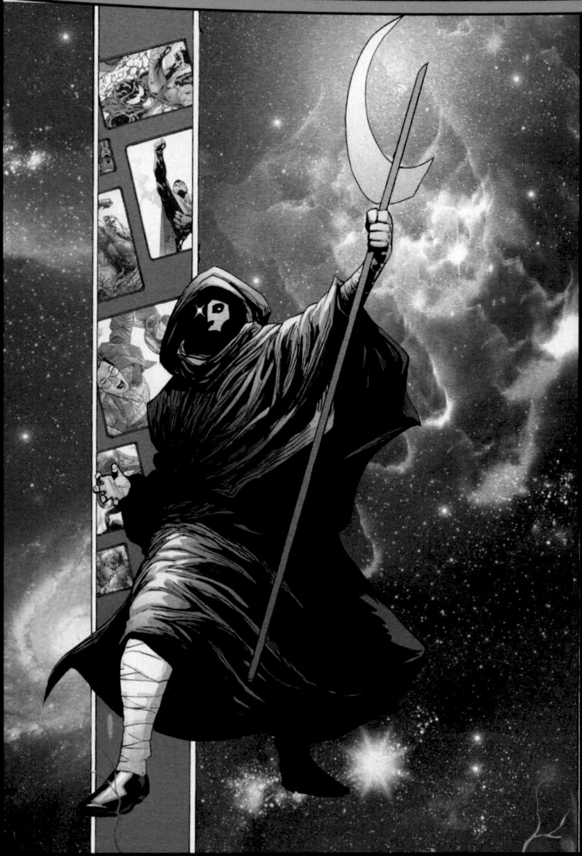

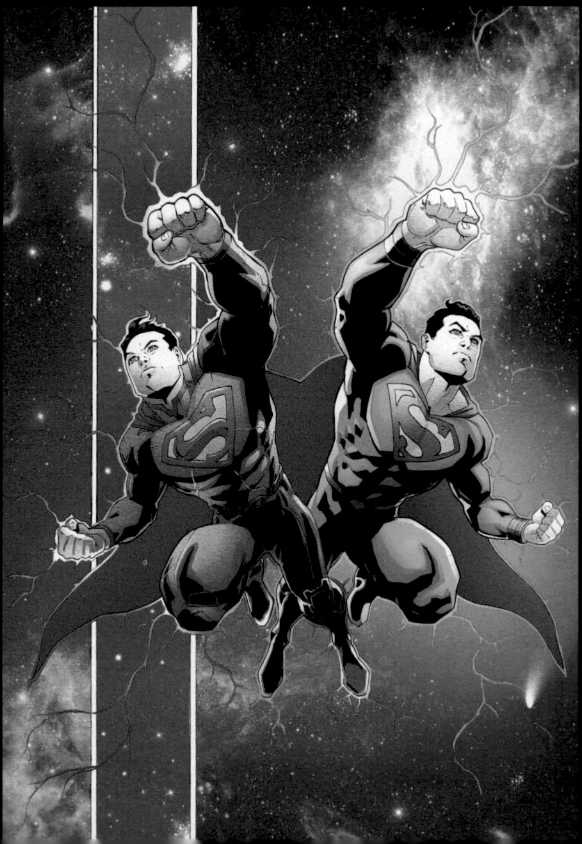

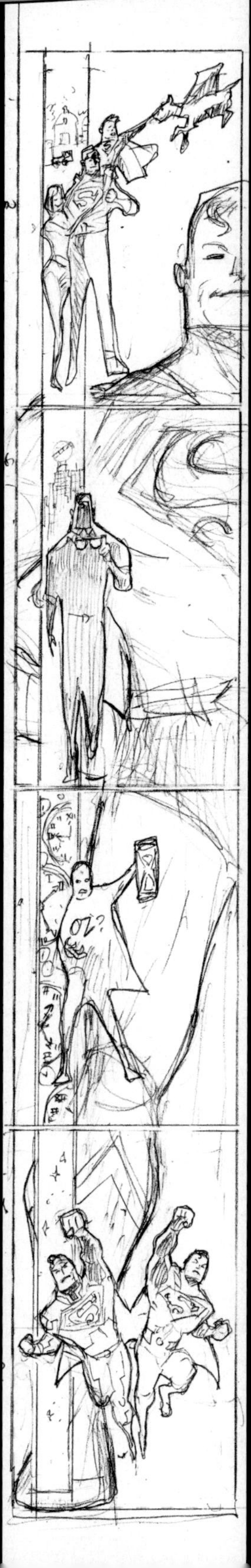
OZ?

UNUSED SUPERMAN COVER BY PATRICK GLEASON

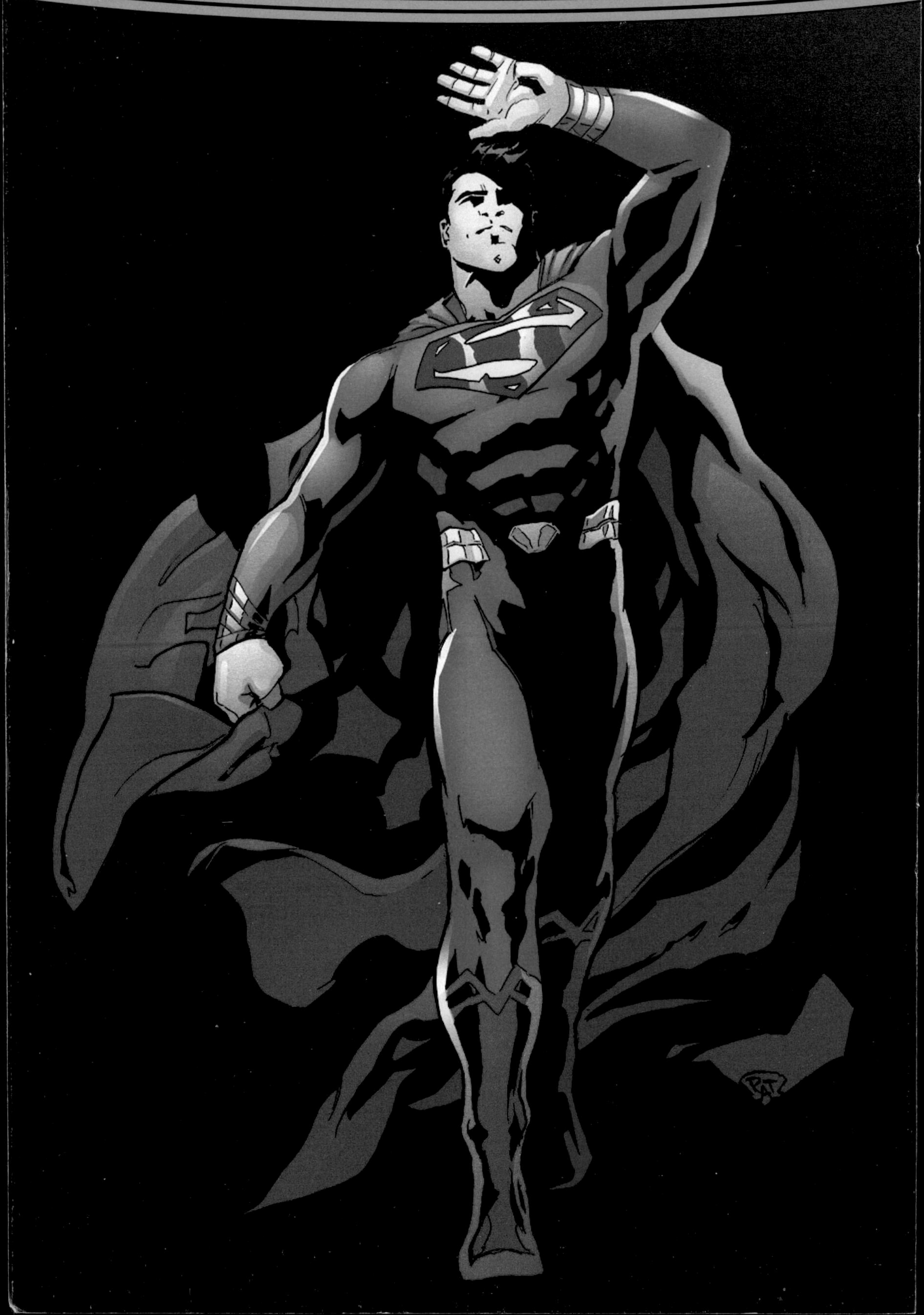